SECURE ELECTRONIC TRANSACTIONS
INTRODUCTION AND TECHNICAL REFERENCE

• • •

Secure Electronic Transactions
Introduction and Technical Reference

• • •

by
Larry Loeb

Artech House Publishers
Boston • London

658.472
L 825

Library of Congress Cataloging-in-Publication Data

Loeb, Lawrence H.
    Secure electronic transactions : introduction and technical reference / Lawrence H. Loeb.
      p. cm.
    Includes bibliographical references and index.
    ISBN 0-89006-992-1 (alk. paper)
    1. Electronic commerce—Security measures.   2. Business enterprises—Computer
networks—Security measures.   3. Internet (Computer network)—Security measures.
I. Title.
HF5548.32.L63   1998   98-2688
658.4'72—dc21   CIP

British Library Cataloguing in Publication Data

Loeb, Lawrence H.
  Secure electronic transactions : introduction and technical reference
  1. Electronic funds transfers—Security measures
  I. Title
  332.1'0285'58

  ISBN 0890069921

© 1998 ARTECH HOUSE, INC.
685 Canton Street
Norwood, MA 02062

All rights reserved. Printed and bound in the United States of America. No part of this book may be reproduced or utilized in any form or by any means, electronic or mechanical, including photocopying, recording, or by any information storage and retrieval system, without permission in writing from the publisher.

All terms mentioned in this book that are known to be trademarks or service marks have been appropriately capitalized. Artech House cannot attest to the accuracy of this information. Use of a term in this book should not be regarded as affecting the validity of any trademark or service mark.

International Standard Book Number: 0-89006-992-1

Library of Congress Catalog Card Number: 98-2688

10 9 8 7 6 5 4 3 2 1

To Gloria, who did, after all, loan me her desk.

CONTENTS

PREFACE

This book is both an introduction to and reference for the Secure Electronic Transaction (SET) protocol for the usage of payment cards over unsecured networks like the Internet. Developed in an effort first led by the MasterCard and Visa brands of payment cards, SET links together the cardholder, the merchant who is selling the cardholder something, and the financial institution acting as an intermediary in the transaction.

As we shall see, SET is a unique protocol that provides a way for customers to use their payment cards over the Internet securely and confidently. It is, in certain parts, not a simple system. This book will first guide you, a person with average technical knowledge, through the SET system as a process and then into the details.

If you are a manager trying to figure how SET will impact your business, you needn't follow all the technical details, but they will help you understand how SET does what it does. If you like reading business indicators to show you a market's potential, consider that Hewlett-Packard bought in 1997 the leading retail transaction's terminal provider Verifone for over a billion dollars just to enter the field. If you like tracking what the leading companies are doing, consider that Microsoft will supply a SET package to H-P/Verifone to handle their credit card transactions on the Internet. SET is going to be serious business in the future, and an understanding of the protocol can only deepen your business skills.

Hopefully, this book will give you the information you seek about SET, regardless of the technical depth you choose. SET has a story, and I'd like to tell it to you.

—Larry Loeb
North Haven, CT
December, 1997

ACKNOWLEDGMENTS

This book began life as an article in *Internet World*. That article would have never seen the light of day had it not been for Alan Meckler, who believed in what I could do. Thanks, Alan.

Alan Rose of Multiscience Press worked hard to both produce this book and find it safe harbor during the storm. I appreciate both.

The technical parts of the book draw heavily on the initial SET documentation created by Visa and MasterCard. To those writers who came up with this first draft documentation, my sincere thanks and appreciation.

Aram Perez, formerly of RSA and now Security Architect for Apple Computer, Douglas Burke, John Codd, and Peter Dapkus of Tenth Mountain were all tremendously helpful in reviewing drafts of the book and making excellent suggestions. I am indebted to all of you.

Chapter 1

• • •

ELECTRONIC COMMERCE

The degree to which some economists are misled by the fetishism attached to the world of commodities, or by the objective appearance of the social characteristics of labor, is shown, among other things, by the dull and tedious dispute over the part played by nature in the formation of exchange value . . . where did the illusions of the Monetary System come from? The adherents of the Monetary System did not see gold and silver as representing money as a social relation of production, but in the form of natural objects with peculiar social properties. And what of modern political economy, which looks down so disdainfully on the Monetary System? Does its fetishism become quite palpable when it deals with capital? How long since the disappearance of the Physiocratic illusion that ground rent grows out of the soil, not out of society?

—Karl Marx. *Capital*

Electronic commerce can mean many things, depending on your perspective. To some, it's digital cash created online by a digital bank and delivered through a digital wallet. To consumers, it may be ordering stuff over a web page and paying with a credit card. And to some, it's a retail channel unlike any other, just waiting for the next crop of digital middlemen to arrive and set up shops. E-commerce is probably wide and unstructured enough at this point in its development to be all these things to all these people at the same time. It's much like the old tale of the blind men attempting to describe an elephant only by what each of them could feel. Each came up with an accurate but partial report and drew a different conclusion about what the whole elephant was like.

We'll be looking in detail at a part of electronic commerce that uses branded payment cards (what we used to call credit cards back when they still gave you interest-free grace periods) as a way of paying a bill. The SET arena will be of major importance in commerce, but it's admittedly only part of what the overall landscape of future economic activity will turn out to be. Let's begin with a look at electronic commerce's beginnings and its current situation to develop a perspective to help us understand where SET will be of the most use.

A small disclaimer to begin with, however. In the most general sense, electronic commerce is what happens when goods and services are exchanged through some electronic mediator. This definition encompasses, for example, the Home Shopping Club on TV. It could even be stretched to include orders taken by telephone. However, the common usage of the term implies computer mediation of a transaction, not just some device that uses electricity. As the boundaries between computers and television grow smaller (especially with the advent of set-top boxes that connect a regular TV to the Internet through a modem or cable connection), this usage may change. But for now, when electronic commerce is discussed, we mean that computers are involved in the mix.

1.1 Electronic Data Interchange

The area of electronic commerce that developed first was Electronic Data Interchange (EDI). The Electronic Commerce World Institute's (www.ecworld.org) White Paper on Electronic Commerce defines EDI as "the application-to-application exchange of electronic data (in a structured, machine-readable format) across organizational boundaries, in such a way that no human intervention or interpretation is required."

Dawkins (1988) described two essential elements of EDI as:

♦ A standardized message that defines how data is to be represented. The format must be understood by both (or all) of the trading partners; and

♦ Software that interfaces the organization's in-house system(s) to the EDI communications system, as well as converting the messages to a standard format from that used by an in-house system and vice versa.

These requirements imply that for EDI to be widely used, parties must develop standards that facilitate EDI. In practice, these standards would probably evolve around vertical industries and their specific needs. Being able to file a medical claim for payment requires different information than what is needed to order an eyelet hook. Because of this, there have arisen many proprietary standards from various software manufacturers. (One researcher found 29 of them in 1991.)

The Tower of Babel effect threatens EDI. If X can "talk" to Y because they have agreed on data-exchange standards, and W can "talk" to Z with a different set of standards, how can X talk to Z? Such generalized communication can only come with widely accepted EDI standards. Governmental efforts may be necessary to unify interest groups around one standard.

In 1968, the US Transport Data Coordinating Committee (TDCC) was formed to coordinate developments for a unified set of EDI standards for transportation documents. (It was logical to start with transportation, since other goods and services depend so much on transportation.) It took the TDCC until 1975 to publish their first set of draft standards for air, motor, ocean and rail documents. The TDCC efforts were successful even though they took so long to be agreed upon because they gave birth to a unified standard set of EDI components. The TDCC effort inspired other industries to develop their own EDI "standards."

The American National Standards Institute (which is an official governmental body even though it gets its funding from the member organizations) was also alarmed by the proliferation. In 1979 ANSI empowered the Accredited Standards Committee to research and develop standards for business documents. This resulted in the ANSI X12 standards, which supplanted those created by the TDCC.

ANSI X12 is a generic kind of standard, where the specifics are decided by the member organizations. The development of ANSI X12 has been on an ad hoc basis by North American companies, and has ignored EDI developments in the rest of the world (which was emphatically not content to leave EDI in the hands of the North Americans) which developed the Electronic Data Interchange for Administration, Commerce, and Transport (EDIFACT) document translation standards. EDIFACT was designed to be the universal solution for all document translation activities worldwide. It has been accepted by the ISO and was published as ISO 9735 in 1987. In 1988, the UN agreed to maintain the EDIFACT standards, giving them the imprimatur of the world body. This has left North American companies that trade worldwide with the problem of supporting both the X12 and EDIFACT standards.

A similar situation was faced by traders in the United Kingdom. Until recently, TRADACOMS was the most widely used standard in the UK. TRADACOMS was developed by users through the Article Number Association (ANA), but it never achieved accreditation status from the British Standards Institute. A proposal has been made to harmonize TRADACOMS and UN/EDIFACT by the ANA and SITPRO (the British Simplification of Trade Procedures Board) working together. As a result, the UK Trade Message Convention has been formed, based on the UN Trade Data Interchange standards.

The Electronic Commerce World Institute defines an EDI standard in Chapter 7 of its EDI Roadmap:

> Generally, an EDI standard consists of several separate entities:
>
> - A syntax—the set of rules controlling the structure of a message (i.e., a grammar);
> - A directory of message types (i.e., invoice, order);
> - A directory of sections;
> - A directory of words.
>
> An EDI message can be broken into several components:
>
> - Syntax—the set of rules controlling the structure of a message (i.e., a grammar);
> - Standardized Codes—the representation of plain language which simplifies the task of processing the data transmitted;
> - Data Elements—the smallest indivisible piece of data which is equivalent to words in the spoken language;
> - Segments—a set or group of related data elements (i.e., name, address);
> - Messages—a set or group of segments in the order specified by the standard. Each message represents a specific transaction (i.e., an invoice).

This definition involves a number of concepts that characterize all electronic commerce and not just business-specific documents. It sums up the need for a standard to define and provide for all the actions that can be expected in normal transaction use. Ideally, a standard would also provide for exception handling in a rational manner so that any errors are handled gracefully.

It is interesting to note that the transport method of a message is nowhere included in the ECWC definition of an EDI standard. Indeed, it seems foolish to standardize only one method of data transport when electronic communication has shown itself to be so diverse. That is, a true standard would be completely transportable among differing transport protocols. But in practice, most commercial EDI is transferred these days over data networks that support the X.400 series of standards.

The X.400 standard evolved as EDI users, forced to use translation schemes that were hardwired into proprietary networks, cast about to find alternate data transport methods. Indeed, it is obvious that the network services available to EDI will greatly affect the functional situation. It may be that the two parties in the EDI transaction exchange messages only at certain times and handle the transaction in a batch mode (where many transactions are handled at one fixed time). The batch mode, which uses different network resources than if the transactions are sent to be processed when they are initiated (real time), may not be suited for all businesses that wish to benefit from EDI. Therefore, additional services to support nonbatch EDI were written up as an EDI specific X.435 component of the X.400 standard. X.435 defines additional services, such as delivery and nondelivery of notification, time-stamping, multidestination delivery, grade of delivery selection, deferred delivery, hold-for-delivery, and full interworking. These background network services that EDI requires for data handling support the EDI model by organizing the data used in EDI into useful chunks; however, they are far too low-level to be part of the actual EDI transaction.

In practice, ANSI X12 is the most widely used EDI standard in the world simply because there are so many North American EDI users. More complex than EDIFACT, X12 standards generally require each element to have a very specific name. (Other naming conventions are also different. For example, an EDI document in ANSI X12 terminology is known as a "transaction set" whereas in EDIFACT terminology it is known as a "message.") This explicit naming convention is probably why the X12 standards have 700 segments while EDIFACT has only 80. EDIFACT segments allow for generic or multi-use through a qualifier that is transmitted during use. That allows for a lower data element count (300) than X12 (1100), and only one beginning segment (called a header) compared with the 60 of X12. EDIFACT does lead X12 in composite types (a group of data that gives meaning to other data), which illustrates what any engineer knows—that the tradeoffs in the design process end up showing in the result. X12 is explicit, while EDIFACT handles diversity not by enumerating it, but by compositing data elements. Each approach has its advantages and disadvantages and leads to a different result.

EDI standards may vary in Europe (and in the rest of the world, for that matter) from country to country even though they all may be called EDIFACT. Local language implementations may have imposed variations that coalesce into a country-specific version of a standard. The UK version of EDIFACT differs from the German, for example.

1.2 FINANCIAL EDI

◆ ◆

Electronic commerce for the financial universe has made possible a bank's Automated Teller Machines, as well as that little Point Of Sale (POS) terminal next to the cashier that lets you pay the bill not with a check, but with a swipe of the same card you would use at the ATM. Until recently, the financial EDI industry has been concentrated on Automated Clearing Houses and similar financial industry "back room" functions, such as international electronic funds transfers.

The ECWC also published a white paper that lists the benefits of Financial EDI (FEDI):

From a payee perspective:

- A reduction in the number of personnel involved with processing paperwork;
    — Reduced manual invoice validation and reconciliation;
    — A reduction in error rates;
- Improved cash or funds management and cash forecasting;
    — Guaranteed settlement on the due date (i.e., the excuse "the cheque is in the mail" no longer applies);
- A reduction in stationery usage;
- A reduction in bank transaction fees;
    — Reduced uncertainties in the payment cycle;
- Improved employee morale as employees are freed from mundane tasks;
- Increased reporting capabilities such as real time access to balance information, cash position, transaction history, problem accounts etc.

The white paper then goes on to consider benefits to the payer:

- A reduction in the number of personnel involved with processing paperwork;
- Reduced manual invoice validation and reconciliation;
- A reduction in error rates;

- Improved cash or funds management and cash forecasting;

- Guaranteed settlement on the due date;

- Improved trading partner relationships;

- Increased reporting capabilities such as real time access to balance information, cash position, transaction history, problem accounts etc.;

    — A reduction in the number of banks with which companies conduct business as well as the number of bank accounts a company operates; (Many large organizations operate many bank accounts with numerous banks. Implementing financial EDI allows an organization to simplify its banking operations.)

    — The reduction or elimination of cheque processing;

    — A reduction in postage;

- A reduction in stationery usage

Of course, these kinds of benefits motivate the introduction of any EDI system, not just a financial one. However, even more than in other EDI situations, the extent to which financial EDI benefits are realized will depend on the degree to which EDI can be integrated into existing systems. An ideal financial EDI system should be able to interface with the Accounts Payable or the Accounts Receivable systems, as well as to integrate payment data with report generators.

An organization may fear that EDI will lead to the loss of the "float," the time that the funds backing a check remain on deposit (and potentially pay interest) until needed for payment. But it may be that the increased precision of the payment process can offset any perceived float losses. For instance, if a company can be assured that payment will reconcile on a certain day with FEDI, the reduced uncertainty may allow it to better manage the amount of liquid cash assets it maintains and put the cash to more productive uses until it is needed. Instead of having to estimate when the cash will be present, a company will know the reconciliation time and thus be able to keep its cash working for it until that time comes. The increased precision of FEDI may also allow for better control of payments that will be made to that company by others using FEDI, so that intake of funds may be done in a rapid and efficient manner.

Wright (1991) characterized electronic payments as having two components—the value component (e.g., pay ABC Co. $100) and the remittance data (e.g., this pays invoice #898 and #1235). The value component can be bundled in a transfer from one business to another and cover any number of remittance instantiations. If the remittance data does not accompany the value component, the payee must match up the two, which is a major inefficiency in the financial system. Some analysts think that the reconciliation function will have to be performed by the payee, for a number of reasons. It may be that the business has separate treasury and account-receivable organizations, or that the usual method of data transfer (i.e., a bank's network) may not be able to transmit the remittance data at the same time. While value data can be tagged with a remittance data tracer number to automate reconciliation, the payee is still responsible for the reconciliation.

It has been the trend over the last few years for bank networks to upgrade their services and hardware to provide for better transport of remittance data, a task that was left to the niche value-added networks in the past. However, it would be a mistake to think that the value data and the remittance data must be linked together in lockstep for FEDI to be workable.

FEDI hasn't been helped by the fact that the many fund-transfer systems found around the world are mostly incompatible with each other. The British interbank check-clearing system CHAPS (Clearing House for Automated Payment Systems) uses a completely different set of standards than those used by the Society for Worldwide Interbank Financial Telecommunications (SWIFT). The British standard was copied by the Australian interbank cheque-clearing scheme, BITS (Banks Internal Transfer System), and so it is also incompatible with SWIFT.

SWIFT commenced operating in 1973 as a non-profit cooperative society organized under Belgian law. It was the world's first major FEDI scheme, and ended up controlling a substantial part of the global payment-related transactions of banks. It now links over 4,000 banks in 105 countries. The ECWC estimates that in 1993, 457 million messages were generated with an estimated $2.5 trillion being transferred every day by SWIFT. Of the daily 2 million messages, 75% relate to payment transactions in the form of settlement instructions, cover messages, or statement entries and related items. The other 25% relate to messages that support customer activities (e.g., foreign exchange) and securities. SWIFT requires a specialized interface device as well as its own software.

The U.S. and Asian interbank check-clearing schemes use different standards from both of those discussed above. Payment messages use a specific ANSI transaction set called the ANSI 820 transaction (defined in ANSI X12.4 and called the Payment Order/Remittance Advice) to transmit payment and remittance data simultaneously.

The other ANSI X12 financial transaction is the ANSI 810, which is equivalent to an invoice. Implementation guides contain specific information about each data element that can be included in a given transmission set. This standard is flexible enough to allow modification for a specific company's needs. The FEDI documents can also serve as the common document for any two trading partners exchanging information via EDI. The standards even allow a company to write an interface for other applications, for example, to receive remittance details into its account receivable system.

"Electronic Commerce and the NII," a white paper produced by the Commerce Department, notes that "the Clearinghouse for Interbank Payment Systems coordinates daily bank-to-bank

transactions worth nearly $2 trillion while the nation's network of
more than 75,000 Automated Teller Machines (ATMs) handles
more than 6 billion transactions per year." FEDI's importance will
continue to increase as the world banking system adopts
interoperating standards.

1.3 JEPI

JEPI (CommerceNet-W3C Joint Electronic Payments Initiative) is
a multi-industry project to develop a standard mechanism for
browsers, servers, and payment middleware to negotiate among
payment methods and protocols across the Web. Although it is
Web-centric, it can be thought of as an FEDI standards
development project. JEPI has stated that it will make its end
products SET-compliant where indicated.

Examples of payment instruments JEPI will address include credit
cards, debit cards, electronic cash, and checks. The payment
protocols under investigation by JEPI, which include SET, will
define the message format and flow required to complete a
payment transaction. Payment transport encompasses the
message-transmission mechanism: S-HTTP (Secure HyperText
Transport Protocol), SSL (Secure Sockets Layer), SMTP (Simple
Mail Transfer Protocol), and TCP/IP (Transmission Control
Protocol/Internet protocol) are all categorized as transport
technologies that can be used for payment purposes.

The JEPI steering committee provides overall direction for the
project. The members are CommerceNet, Financial Services
Technology Consortium, Open Software Foundation, and the
W3C (World Wide Web Consortium).

In addition to the steering committee, eight companies make up
the JEPI core team. These companies, which have committed

substantial human and/or financial resources to the project, are CUC International, CyberCash, GC Tech, IBM, Microsoft, Open Market, VENDAMALL, and the Xerox Corporation. Additional design assistance for the JEPI suite is being provided by Digital Equipment Corp. and VeriFone.

The JEPI Outer Team includes the following companies, which are participating in a review capacity: Bellcore, BT, Citibank, Deloitte and Touche Consulting, First Virtual Holdings, France Telecom, Marshall Industries, NACHA, NetBill (Carnegie Mellon University), Netscape, NTT Software Laboratories, Nokia, Novell, Oracle, Sligos, Tandem, Information Sciences Institute, and Zenith Data Systems.

Since JEPI has stated that its goals will coincide with those of SET, JEPI may prove to be an important coalition of the companies that will eventually advance the SET protocols. As of this writing, JEPI has not defined the area of electronic financial negotiation in the way that some had hoped, which has, for example, forced Japanese SET participants to add to their transactions (during the wakeup phase) a way of determining additional business information about the upcoming SET transaction. There may be modifications made in the future to the transport part of the SET protocol as JEPI efforts come to fruition.

1.4 DIGITAL CASH/DIGICASH

In 1983, David Chaum had an idea. Aware of the public key/ private key cryptography that Diffie and Hellman had developed in 1976 (see Chapter 2), Chaum connected the new cryptography concepts with the idea of electronic commerce and came up with the idea of "digital money." His first version of this idea resembled an electronic bank check, since of course the first version of almost anything new tends to resemble the older thing it is replacing. (Garages were first built far away from houses like stables.)

Early in the United States economic development, each financial institution issued its own money—a piece of paper that said that the bank had so much gold or silver on deposit and physically present at the bank. If you wanted to reduce the abstraction and walk into that bank and trade the paper for metal (the "real" money), you could do so. Now banks issue small pieces of magnetically and optically encoded paper that have personal signatures on them. Other small pieces of paper (called cash and supposedly produced by the government) are treated with reverence by any one possessing them and are exchangeable for goods and services. These pieces of paper are treated as money by people because they believe in the paper totems. The paper is a physical realization of that abstraction called "money."

Everyone who is party to the processing of a paper check has to leave their mark on it as an audit trail. Banks stamp their stamps and lines all over a check. By examining these markings, we can even determine who did what and when they did it. And so it is with the digital check that Chaum invented.

He realized that digitally signing a block of data binds the signer to that data. If the signer is a bank or financial institution, some level of financial bonding is also implied.

Let's say that the essential elements of a check are a bank's name, the checking account's number, the name of the owner of that account (payer), the amount of the check, and the destination (payee). Let's process ("sign") that block of data with the account owner's private key (a data structure we will define in detail in Chapter 2 that has useful cryptological properties) to produce a result $E1(\text{check})$. To prove that the payee cashed the check, the payee could sign his or her own digital signature, ($E2$), by applying a private key to the check to obtain payment. The resultant $E2(E1(\text{check}))$ could be further signed by the payee's bank (E3) and by the payer's bank (E4) when presented for payment. At the end of the full transaction, the E4(E3(E2(E1(check)))) verifies that each party has processed the check and in what order. Nesting the signatures provides an audit trail that could not be easily forged

There are other criteria that any digital money system must adhere to. Let's consider the digital check described above. What will stop that check from being presented multiple times by someone making a copy of it? If the signed message just looks like some letters and numbers in ASCII, anyone could simply copy and paste this data into messages with different headers on them and present them for payment. The simplest answer to this problem is to serialize the e-checks when they are created. The electronic bank receiving the check must then verify that this serial number has not been presented for payment at this account number, which implies, of course, that the records of every e-check ever presented for an account must be kept ad infinitum.

Security of such a simple digital check can be enhanced by a number of techniques. For example, both the recipient (or destination) of the check and the serial number of that check could be encoded with the public key (see Chapter 2) of the recipient. It would also be possible to use some shared secret key. If the encoding is done with the recipient's public key, the recipient can unlock his or her name by decoding the check with a private key and thus obtain the serial number. (This is the big secret we're holding out until you get to Chapter 2.) This is a step above the simple check, but still does not address other limitations.

For example, the bank that actually pays the check would be able to connect the transaction between the presenter of the check (payee) and the originator of the check (payer). This sort of transaction becomes totally non-anonymous, which is not a characteristic of cash. If a payee gives a dollar to someone and then that someone uses it to pay something else, the third party has no idea where that dollar came from. A simple serialized digital transaction lacks the anonymity of cash.

In "An Introduction to e-cash" (1994) Chaum describes an e-cash system that depends on "blinded" signatures to protect payer/payee information:

> In the simple withdrawal, the bank created unique blank digital coins, validated them with its special digital stamp, and supplied them to Alice (who has an account with the bank). This would normally allow the bank at least in principle to recognize the particular coins when they are later accepted in a payment. And this would tell the bank exactly which payments were made by Alice.
>
> By using "blind" signatures, the bank can be prevented from recognizing the coins as having come from a particular account. The blinding operation is a special kind of encryption designed so that it can only be removed by the party who placed it there. It can be reversed using the public key digital signature process, and can thus be removed without disturbing the signature.
>
> Instead of the bank creating a blank coin, Alice's computer creates the coin itself at random. Then it hides the coin in a special digital envelope and sends it off to the bank. The bank withdraws one dollar from Alice's account and makes its special "worth-one-dollar" digital validation like an embossed stamp on the envelope before returning it to Alice's computer.
>
> Like an emboss, the blind signature mechanism lets the validating signature be applied through the envelope. When Alice's computer removes the envelope, it has obtained a coin of its own choice, validated by the bank's stamp. When she spends the coin, the bank must honor it and accept it as a valid payment because of the stamp. But because the bank is unable to recognize the coin, since it was hidden in the envelope when it was stamped, the bank cannot tell who made the payment. The bank which signed can verify that it must have made the signature, but it cannot link it back to a particular object or owner.

Although this kind of blinded signature makes e-cash more anonymous, it does not address another practical question, such as who shall administer the payment gateways and networks necessary to allow various e-banks to settle accounts among themselves and other administrators, an infrastructure problem that has stymied many innovative systems.

Chaum went on to found DigiCash, N.V., in the Netherlands to address these business questions in the real world. Thus far, it has used the traveler's check as a model, a "bearer's instrument" that uses discrete chunks of currency. DigiCash provides a digital wallet to carry its tokens, and merchants give change in newly minted currency or credit, so one attribute of cash (divisibility into smaller units) is sidestepped by having the e-bank mint new tokens when needed. The transaction is also a finalized transaction in that it is self-reconciled (from the bank's viewpoint) when it is presented for payment. One transfer goes to one account based on one serial number. That's it, since of course there is no provision for repudiation of a transaction with a "bearer's instrument." When that serial number is presented and accepted by the bank, it is removed from the list and can't be re-spent, just like a traveler's check.

In many ways, SET has characteristics that are the opposite of those usually associated with digital money. Digital money by itself can cause a transaction to occur (especially the "bearer's instrument" kind). SET requires a functional meeting (or at least an exchange of messages) of all the interested parties before a transaction can occur. A SET transaction must be authorized by all the parties concerned in order to complete, while merchants in the digital money realm may change the resultant value of a digital cash token. SET merchants cannot directly touch cardholder information, which is available only to the Issuer (and by extension the Payment Gateway), while digital money merchants can derive transaction/recipient information.

1.5 CYBERCASH

◆ ◆

William Melton is a name not well-known outside the technical community, but one of his ideas probably touches your life every day. He founded Verifone, the company that H-P bought for over $1 billion. Their little blue-gray machines with the one-line luminescent display, printer, and swipe cardreader on the side are used by many retail establishments in everyday payment card transactions for verification of the card.

Melton went on to found CyberCash with Daniel Lynch. CyberCash, which has positioned itself as a hybrid between the banking and the Internet community, hopes to be a gateway company that uses the Internet as a message transport. CyberCash customers interface with a CyberCash server, which in turn communicates with the banking system's Automated Clearing House (ACH) to actually effect transactions. Their architecture is flexible enough to handle payment cards as well as cash and debits.

The innovation that CyberCash brought was keeping the customer's financial data away from the merchant during the transaction. This is a leap in functional security because it adds a fence around the financial data without adding the computational overhead of a blinded signature. In fact, CyberCash tries to keep the amount of information it knows about a transaction to a minimum. It doesn't maintain a record of the merchandise bought, only of the amount of the transaction. (Merchants could still generate this correlation if they wanted to, however.) It also doesn't keep a copy of the customer's encryption key in its records, so that the key could not possibly be turned over to anyone else.

Making a payment card purchase with CyberCash generates an invoice that is sent to the customer for verification and payment method selection. When the customer gets the invoice (say, through e-mail), he or she checks it for correctness. The payment card information is appended to the order and then encrypted by the CyberCash software. The encrypted financial data and the unencrypted order information are then sent to a merchant. The merchant then appends some unique identifier to the message (which may vary depending on the transaction status), encrypts the entire block, and sends it to CyberCash. CyberCash then reformats the information in a manner acceptable to the ACH (performing the Value Added Networking functions). The ACH then processes the transaction as a regular payment card transaction in the mainstream banking system. For cash transactions, CyberCash has a working agreement with the Wells Fargo Bank of California to hold money in escrow. This account is debited by CyberCash for each cash transaction, and a service fee charged.

As a system, CyberCash has much to recommend it. It attempts to address security issues through its own methods of enforcing security. It interfaces simply (from the user's standpoint) with the existing banking network. And it is up and running now. The main disadvantage of the system is that everything must be done using CyberCash's special tools and software.

1.6 PAYMENT CARD COMMERCE ONLINE: THE BEGINNINGS

Payment cards are another hybrid system of commerce. They are grounded in the physical world of currency and checks, though the tallying and authentication is done electronically. A bill is presented by the payment card's issuer and paid by the cardholder through conventional banking means.

There are several participants in any payment card transaction:

♦ The first is the *cardholder,* who uses a payment card that has been issued by an Issuer. The cardholder shops for something, decides to buy it, and is ready to pay using a payment card.

♦ The *issuer* is the financial institution that established the account used and actually issues the payment card to the cardholder.

♦ The *merchant* offers services or goods for sale, and has a relationship with an acquirer.

♦ An *acquirer* is an institution that has a financial relationship with the merchant for the processing of payment card authorizations and can make payments for card transactions to the merchant.

♦ The *payment gateway* is operated by an acquirer and processes payment card authorizations and payments. Third parties may operate some of the devices under the authority of the Issuer and the acquirer. For the discussions that follow, we ignore the third party and assign their actions to the enabling financial institution.

To complete a transaction, each participant must be able to trust its partner in the transaction. The cardholder trusts the merchant to take payment via the card and deliver the goods, while the acquirer trusts the merchants by virtue of having a pre-established financial account with them. The cardholder also indirectly trusts the system that the acquirer participates in by paying his or her card account upon demand.

From the merchant's point of view, payment card transactions are classified as "card present" and "card not present." Card-present transactions are those where the cardholder is physically present and hands the card to the merchant. Since the merchant can see the cardholder and the actual payment card, there is a higher level of confidence that no fraud is being performed. Card-not-present transactions are those in which the cardholder orders goods from a merchant by mail or by telephone. (These are referred to as MOTO transactions.) Since the merchant cannot see the person or the actual card, there is a lower degree of confidence that fraud is not being committed. Both types of transactions are described in the following paragraphs.

First, let's look at how a payment card might be handled currently. A simple card transaction begins when someone physically gives his or her card to a cashier to pay for something and the cashier "swipes" the card through a reader/dedicated data machine that is either built into the cash register or bolted onto its side by a vendor like Verifone. The dedicated processor then sends the data from the magnetic strip on the card down an ordinary dialup telephone line and connects via the dialup line to another computer, which is usually connected to a secured financial network.

It's important to remember that in this example the card transaction actually begins by an action of the merchant; that is, it starts with the merchant presenting card information to an acquirer. The computer system called by the merchant belongs either to an acquirer or to some acquirer-designated financial system or clearing house and it can authenticate the card account number and the charge amount along with the merchant who placed the call. All this communicating and authenticating happens before the cashier's register can print out the register receipt.

Because of the reliability and high automation of such a setup, it costs less for the acquirer and the payment gateway to process these automated "card present" transactions than paper charge slips. The fee that a card's financial acquirer imposes on a merchant for an automated "card present" transaction is usually less than on other card-use situations. This leads savvy businesses to invest in the hardware for automated transaction, since they believe that they will make it up in the lowered fee imposed doing card business.

A nonautomated card transaction requires a merchant to imprint the card information on a slip of paper, telephone the acquirer to obtain authorization for the transaction, and then deposit the charge slips with a financial institution to obtain payment. Because of the higher cost levied by the acquirer and gateway, it is not preferred by most merchants and remains only as a backup or low-volume method.

Sometimes, however, a cardholder will want to use a card (and thus generate transaction fees for the acquirer) to guarantee payment but cannot present the card itself—when shopping from a catalog, for example, or ordering flowers over the phone. The Mail Order/Telephone Order (MOTO) transaction has been designed by card issuers to handle the card-not-present situation. In a nonautomated MOTO card transaction, like the nonautomated "card present" transaction, someone has to write the cardholder's order down onto a special transaction form, and then call the acquirer for approval. Only then can the transaction go forward. The record of this transaction (and approval) have to be gathered together with other similar paper records and bundled off to the bank for deposit. At the bank, a teller has to manually separate these envelopes from other deposits and either send them off for further processing or proof them there.

When merchants started taking orders by computer they were first handled in the MOTO fashion, but without the paper. The first of the big electronic retail centers was created on one of the first big online computer conferencing systems, CompuServe. CompuServe created an "online shopping mall" in combination with an outside organization that actually ran the place. They processed and filled the orders for merchandise that were generated. (The organization, called CUC International, is still around and is currently involved with others in the

WorldWideWeb Consortium's JEPI effort.) People would "enter" the mall by typing its name into the CompuServe system prompt: "GO MALL." CompuServe would then link to the shopping area and execute the interface program. Once there, consumers could read verbose descriptions of items offered for sale from which they could order and then pay for with their payment card. CUC would use its own networks to process the order and get it to the issuer for authorization. (This was facilitated by the fact that CompuServe was owned by H. & R. Block, a major financial network owner.) In many ways, this mall was a wired catalog.

1.6.1 Early Web Security: S-HTTP and SSL

The pioneers of commerce on the World Wide Web thought they had a different problem than efficiency about payment card orders. They were not concerned with the issuer's back-office efficiencies in the slightest. Because the Internet is a notoriously insecure network, the commerce server designers realized that people wouldn't want to use their credit card numbers to place orders on the Net. If it is possible for persons unknown to monitor financial transactions, the information sent from one place to another could form the basis of automated fraud using the payment card information.

The anticipated problem of automated fraud led the early server designers to a cryptographic-based solution. Instead of transmitting information from a customer's browser as "plain" (or unencrypted and hence easily readable by others) text during an order or other "secured" session, the information sent to the merchant's server would be encrypted. Any "listeners" on the network that intercepted the data packets would see only unintelligible data if the encryption was effective. The "one-time" secret key encryption seemed robust enough to assure packet confidentiality.

This "end-to-end" security model is different from yet
complementary to that used in SET, which is designed to
implement only one form of electronic commerce, not the whole
of it. The commerce pioneers were concerned with their own
client-to-server communications and not the security of the
ordering/fulfillment system from beginning to end. If they
processed an order in a secure manner, it was up to others
dealing with the other parts of the full end-to-end system to make
their own parts of the system secure.

SET (as we will see later) uses encryption as part of a message
process that is centered around the implementation of a
transaction. The S-HTTP and SSL methods that the pioneer
secure server makers developed took this concept deeper—in
SSL's case, to the data transport level. Both methods encrypt the
messages that pass through them, once the client browser and
server agree on how they will understand each other (usually by a
one-time secret key). Everything that occurs between client and
server gets encrypted, not just financial transaction data, which is
a totally different (and much more global) kind of security than
that provided by SET.

S-HTTP, an extension of HTTP developed by Rescorla and
Shiffman (1994), allows messages to be encrypted, signed, or
authenticated. Any combination of these operators is also
allowed, for nine different transmission modes that are selectable
at the beginning of the HTTP negotiation between client and
server. Each party states a preference either explicitly (by
embedding certain HTML commands in the page) or implicitly.
That is, by not embedding the request, one side indicates that it is
not configured for an S-HTTP session.

S-HTTP currently supports the PKCS-7 and PEM standards
developed by RSA, Inc., as well as Zimmerman's PGP
implementation. The SHTTP-Privacy-Domains HTML statement
specifies which of these is to be used for the page or session.

Certificates in S-HTTP (and in other security systems) are constructs that describe who is guaranteeing a particular key, which is usually implied by the choice of privacy domain. However, the S-HTTP protocol allows users to choose which certificate types are acceptable. Choices can be made at the beginning of a session for specific key-exchange algorithms, signature algorithms, what hash method will be used for the message digest, and how the symmetric (secret key) content will be encoded by use of the proper HTML commands. The HTML commands are of the form:

```
SHTTP-[identifier]:[orig|recv]-
[optional|required|refused]=[identifier data]
```

SSL (Secure Sockets Layer) was developed by Netscape to be a lower level encoding than SHTTP. Designed to be a transparent layer to both client and server, it sits just on TCP/IP in the data transport hierarchy and encrypts all TCP/IP traffic passing through one network connection ("socket"). SSL first has the client and server agree on a cipher and a key for the session, and may then (optionally) authenticate the client.

The message-transfer sequence in SSL is fairly straightforward:

♦ The client first issues the CLIENT-HELLO message, which contains the ciphers that the client understands, a challenge that is made up of random data, and a session number that may be present from a previous session that was interrupted.

♦ The server responds with the SERVER-HELLO message. If a session is being reestablished, new keys are selected. If this is a new session, then the server sends a certificate that contains its public key, the ciphers that the server recognizes, and a connection number.

♦ The client responds with the CLIENT-MASTER-KEY message, which contains the client's choice of ciphers to be used for the

session, and a key that may be sent in two blocks. For the
international version, one block is encrypted with the server's
public key, and the rest of the key is sent in the clear. This
keeps the encryption key length under the 40 bits that the
U.S. Government currently allows to be exported.

The CLIENT-FINISH method is then sent, which is the session
ID encoded with the current key.

♦ SERVER-VERIFY, which is then sent, consists of the challenge
data in the SERVER-HELLO message encrypted with the
session key.

♦ If authentication between the two parties is desired, this is
when it occurs with an exchange of certificates.

♦ The session master key is then used to create two new keys for
the session. One is created and used by the client, and the
other one is created and used by the server. This adds
additional security to the session.

1.7 SET AND INTERNET-BASED COMMERCE: THE UNDERLYING CONCEPTS OF ERROR-HANDLING

♦ ♦

It seems obvious that SET has the potential to become a major
force in the commerce of the near future. Companies doing
business on the Web have already shown that people will indeed
do business using payment cards over the Internet, as long as they
have a reasonable expectation of security. SET can only widen
merchant acceptance of this payment method by increasing
consumer confidence in the overall system. When the impulse
click of a button in a computer program will translate into an

immediate sale for someone, business will flow to those who capture these buyers.

But we must remember that SET is just a technology, not a product. It's called an "underlying technology" because it's something that can be built on. SET is a roadmap, and the actual driving must still be done. As we'll see in Chapter 7, even the SET development community sees different scenarios evolving for SET. While "true" SET transactions are that of the payment card variety endorsed by the payment card associations, what will stop the eventual use of SET-like technology in private nets, each with its own trust networks—or a common belief in one certificate authority? Nothing, I think. So, the second order effects of SET's introduction into the financial community may be as interesting as the primary ones.

Many of the low-level functions (especially the cryptographic ones) in SET are probably best handled by most programmers with toolkits. Vendors will be selling various toolkits for cardholders, merchants, and payment-gateway applications, which will be created as a result of SET formalization. These toolkits save coders the time and effort of having to "re-invent the wheel" for each individual application. In a cryptographic situation, there's also the added effort of having to ensure that the written code performs the intended cryptographic functions with a wide range of input, the so-called certification process. A good way to jump-start a programmer's effort, toolkits bring a validated and certified functionality for one known and stable price. Of course, all toolkits will not be created equal. Some toolkits will just generate and parse messages, while others will be able to enforce idempotency (failing safely) and the security cross-checking that SET requires.

But the use of toolkits or other higher-level application programming interfaces (API), cannot relieve the competent programmer from the responsibility of having to understand the details of SET. A toolkit alone does not an application make. The programmer has to understand the ebbs and flows of SET transactions and how they will affect the program under construction. When an error condition occurs, the entire process must be understood in order to isolate the error from the overall system. Just knowing the API calls alone won't help to figure out the traffic, packet by packet.

Understanding and using SET in a computer program doesn't mean that an application's designer can ignore user actions and rely upon protocol to make things right. SET is a great way to help process certain kinds of user actions (like buying or selling something with a payment card) and totally useless in other situations. It is not a panacea; it's a way to structure electronic business so that all participants can communicate in an agreed upon manner without unproductive effort.

Let's jump back to a word that was glossed over a few paragraphs ago. If an operation can be performed any number of times without causing harm, that operation is said to be *idempotent*. For SET, this describes the manner in which a recipient responds to a SET message. One of the critical design objectives of SET was that messages could be resent without penalty to the overall transaction, since some messages will always be lost or misdirected in transit during operation. SET (and the programs implementing SET) must be robust enough to allow for this eventuality.

For example, a merchant can't be allowed to resend a payment authorization request message that should only be sent once per transaction. While SET incorporates transaction identifiers to evaluate necessary responses, it's still the programmer's responsibility to build reality checks into the code and adhere to them. The idempotency of SET is an essential characteristic of the rational design of any program that uses SET. If I can get on that soapbox one last time, I think that blindly using any toolkit to "do" SET via incantations of various spells can only lead to problems. There are too many possible error-inducing situations in the real world when money is involved.

SET handles errors by first trying to classify them. Duplicate messages are detected by examining plaintext information found in the SET MessageWrapper (the highest level of information transmitted in SET). If a received message is obviously a retransmit, the reaction of the receiver must depend on the state of the transaction to that point as well as on the number of duplicated messages. If a system detects a "spam" attack, duplicate messages may be ignored.

Corrupted (non-parsable) messages are conceptually easy to handle. For example, if enough data have been received to determine the RRPID (a SET term that stands for Request/ Response pair ID, an individual transaction's statistically unique ID) of the transmitted SET message, a simple request for retransmission will cleanup the situation. If the corruption is such that nothing can be parsed, ignoring the message is the only safe response.

If a message is malformed, or differs after parsing from what is expected, SET will return an error message to the originator, who will deal with the situation and retransmit if indicated.

Lastly, if authentication tests fail, an error message is returned to the message originator. The message should be both delayed and generic so that details about the failure will not feed a possible attack.

1.8 THE SET BUSINESS PLAN

Card issuers defined seven major business requirements for SET. According to the *SET Business Plan*, SET should

1. Provide confidentiality of payment information and enable confidentiality of the order (merchandise) information that is transmitted along with the order's payment information

2. Ensure integrity for all transmitted data

3. Provide authentication that a cardholder is a legitimate user of a branded payment card account

4. Provide authentication that a merchant can accept branded payment card transactions through its relationship with an acquiring financial institution

5. Ensure the use of the best security practices and system design techniques to protect all legitimate parties of an electronic commerce transaction

6. Ensure the creation of a protocol that is neither dependent on transport security mechanisms nor prevents their use

7. Facilitate and encourage interoperability across software and network providers

Let's think about how these requirements can be met by SET. Confidentiality should be ensured by SET's use of message encryption, and payment information integrity can be protected by the use of cryptographic "hashing" and "digital signatures." (The details of these cryptographic methods will be described later.) The linking of cardholders and merchants to specific accounts is addressed by the use of digital signatures and certificates (the specifics of certificate use will be described later). Interoperability means that SET can run on any hardware system that operates a financial gateway system as well as on a PC. Because it is not dependent on any transport security plan (like S-HTTP or SSL), SET is forced to generate its own security when it is needed. If additional security is wrapped around a SET session, so much the better, but SET does not require this in order to assure confidentiality.

The responsibility of those who are implementing SET is to meet the admirable and lofty goals of the business plan. And, as one engineer will tell another, this is a nontrivial task. Time to undertake it.

1.9 THE SCHEMA OF SET

SET, as we shall see, is basically a process that operates under a fixed set of rules. The last section identified what happens in a general way when failure occurs. Now, let's consider the general successful case of a normal SET transaction.

It is routine in the assessment of a dynamic system to analyze the fluctuations from the given initial rest state of the system. SET's initial rest state depends on how one views it. Since SET is an electronic analog of the existing financial credit card system, one may say that the true rest state of SET is when none of the participants (cardholder, merchant, payment gateway) exist in a SET-authorized state and need to be initialized. This is as if one did not have a payment card in the physical world and needed to obtain one.

This initiating authorization process is not the routine rest state of SET. Consider it more as an initialization phase leading to the routine rest state.

One of the basic tokens used in SET is a data structure called an X.509 Version 3 certificate, which is issued and signed by a certificate authority (CA). This certificate is analogous to a driver's license issued by the Department of Motor Vehicles (a driver's certificate authority, if you will). The certificate is a token that, when presented, provides assurance that certain background steps were taken before the certificate (driver's license) was issued. If the issuance process is stringent enough, the token may be used for other purposes not directly related to the original issuance purpose (such as proving age to get into a bar).

These certificates are used in SET as a token of trust in that they bind an identity of a party to a certain public key. As we shall see in Chapter 2, a public key is a way of encoding/decoding messages from an entity that possesses a private key mathematically associated with the public key. To start the process, a cardholder issues a /**CInitReq** message (via their SET software package) to a CA. This message identifies what the cardholder wants to get back (a message exchange public key, so that encryption can be done in subsequent messages along with a registration form) and contains identifiers for certificates already in the cardholder's possession.

The CA's response message (/**CInitRes**) provides the registration forms, the certificates requested, and a list of certificates that the CA deems revoked (the /**CRL** or Certificate Revocation List). This allows the cardholder to remove invalid or out of date certificates that may be in their possession before attempting to undertake a SET transaction.

When the customer fills in the form it will contain financial information; this part of the form is encrypted with *strong* methods (such as technology from RSA Data Security, Inc.). The cardholder also includes his or her public keys to be certified in the /**CertReq** message, which is then sent to the CA. The CA verifies the extracted financial information with the issuer of the payment card, and then generates a certificate that includes the cardholder's public keys. There is also a secret value shared between the cardholder and CA included in the /**CertRes** message that is used in later processing. The cardholder now possesses a certificate that can be used for SET transactions.

We must make a few assumptions for our routine rest state. Those assumptions include the existence of an omniscient and infallible certificate authority for cardholder, merchants, and payment gateways that has properly issued and signed a valid X.509 Version 3-style certificate to each of the involved parties.

Let's also assume that a cardholder has made all his or her shopping decisions by some method. It really doesn't matter to SET how a cardholder shops, only that he or she has done so. For our purposes, the routine transaction begins when the cardholder wants to pay for the goods.

The cardholder's software program (usually called the "wallet" in continuation of carrying physical world terms to cyberspace) begins the purchase by sending a /**PInitReq** message to the merchant. The merchant responds with a /**PInitRes** message that contains small versions of the certificates that the merchant holds along with a /**TransID** that is carried through the transaction sequence. The certificates the merchant has are those that the cardholder would need to complete the transaction, such as the public keys of the merchant and payment gateways.

The next transaction message pair contains fairly complex information. The cardholder issues the /**PReq** message, which contains both payment instructions (/**PI**) and order information (/**OI**). /**OI** identifies the merchandise, and the /**PI** contains financial information, such as the card data and purchase amount. In one of the most elegant features of SET, the /**PI** is encrypted at this point, using the payment gateway's public key. (The card information is first directly encoded using strong 1024-bit encryption technology.) This means that the merchant has no way to obtain the financial data. It is readable only by the gateway.

The /**OI** consists of /**OIData** followed by a SET signature. A dual
signature is composed of the *hash* (a "one way" operation that
reduces an arbitrary set of data values to a fixed length number
such that hashing a given input will always produce the same
output) of /**OIData** added to the hash of /**PIData** (the data of
the /**PI** once the payment card data has already been encrypted),
and then a hash taken of the result. The resulting hash is then
signed to come up with the dual signature. This dual signature
establishes that /**OIData** and /**PIData** were signed together and
at the same time. A dual signature doesn't mean that there are
two signatures involved, but that there are two items linked by the
same signature.

Also appended with the dual signature (forming the SET dual
signature) is the XOR (exclusive OR) of the /**OI** hash and the
/**PI** hash. Including this XOR allows someone who has the
plaintext of either the /**OIData** or the /**PIData** to confirm the
signature that links the two.

The /**PReq** that the customer issues is the functional equivalent
to the payment card imprint slip used in physical transactions.
The customer signs it differently, but it is used by the financial
system as the token of indebtedness for the amount charged. SET
uses /**PReq** as it's core message, with the other messages acting to
support this basic one.

The merchant now has order information and financial
information. It can decrypt the /**OI** and extract the /**PI**. It also
runs a check on the customer's certificates to see if they are valid.
Before returning the /**PRes** response message to the cardholder,
the merchant can perform the authorization step or defer it.
/**PRes** contains codes indicating to the cardholder what steps the
merchant took before it responded.

If authorization is deferred, the merchant sends a message
informing the customer. The customer can then later inquire
about the status of the order by issuing a /**InqReq** message to the

merchant. /**InqReq** embeds the transaction identifier inside it so that the merchant can identify the queried transaction. A response called /**InqRes** is returned by the merchant, which contains much the same information as /**PRes**; that is, the transaction status and result codes for a specific transaction. Multiple /**InqRes** messages may be generated for the same transaction.

To authorize a transaction, the merchant sends the /**AuthReq** message to the payment gateway/acquirer (the two terms are sometimes used interchangeably, but the gateway does not have to be the eventual financial acquirer of the charge). /**AuthReq** has order information from the merchant (along with a hash of the order) and the still-encrypted /**PI**. The acquirer can decrypt the /**PI** and compare the hash of the /**OI** in it with the hash of the /**OI** submitted by the merchant. If they match, the acquirer can attest that the cardholder and merchant agree on what the order consists of without knowing the exact composition of the order. It has only the un-reversible hash, not the details of it. This feature of SET should reassure those who are concerned about tracking buying habits on a grand scale.

Once the acquirer has checked everything for consistency, it performs a financial authorization from the card issuer by means outside the scope of SET. Those means vary by card brand and policy, but will usually return a yes/no response. These authorization methods generally utilize a special secure financial network that the issuer has established.

If a merchant elects to capture the sales immediately, the /**AuthRes** from the gateway/acquirer contains a capture code and transaction amount. Otherwise, a token of the capture is returned that contains the authorized amount and IDs for the capture. This encrypted token can only be used by the acquirer for later batch processing, which usually occurs at the end of the business day.

The merchant, upon getting a go-ahead via the /**AuthRes**, fulfills the order and ships the goods to the customer.

If the merchant uses batch processing of the captured transactions, it will bundle all the captokens it has amassed during the day and issue a /**CapReq**. The /**CapReq** goes to the acquirer who strips out the various authorized amounts and credits the merchant's account. A /**CapRes** is then issued, signed, and encrypted with a completion code indicating how the capture process has been performed.

These basic operations constitute a routine SET transaction. While there are other messages in the SET universe, these are the ones used for most transactions. It can be seen from these brief descriptions that SET does not cover all electronic shopping possibilities. In fact, there are many areas of electronic commerce that SET 1.0 takes pains to ignore. The framers of SET wish the marketplace to determine shopping protocols, for example. SET remains concerned with replacing the current card/paper payment system with a more efficient electronic payment system that functionally mimics the existing arrangements. It seems that SET not only successfully recasts a paper system for a paperless age, but improves on it.

Chapter 2

• • •

CRYPTOGRAPHY BASICS

The medium is the message.

—Marshall McLuhan

In this chapter, we'll look at cryptography as it applies to SET. Because we are going to cover a lot of ground fairly rapidly, you might want to investigate one of the many excellent books on this subject for a fuller approach.

2.1 WHAT CRYPTOGRAPHY DOES

• •

Cryptography, in general, does two things: it encodes (encrypts) and decodes (decrypts) information. It encrypts something by taking an original "plaintext" message and, via the use of some operation or transformation, converts it into an encrypted "ciphertext." The ciphertext is then transmitted by the sender (who is also the encryptor) to the receiver. The receiver performs the inverse of the transformation (decryption) to convert the ciphertext back to the original message. While the message is in transit, it cannot convey information to other parties who may intercept it.

Of course, not all encryption schemes are equal. Some have a greater resistance to "attack" (an attempt to get the plaintext from the ciphertext) than others. Some are computationally easier to implement than others. Let's consider some current encryption schemes.

2.2 SECRET-KEY CRYPTOGRAPHY

"Symmetric" cryptography uses the same "key" (which may be any sort of data structure) to encrypt a message as to decrypt it. That is, the sender and receiver share an identical key which they both must keep secret from others in order to maintain security of the message. The assumption of symmetry forces the encrypting transformation to be the inverse of the decrypting one given the same key. This kind of encryption can be expressed in a number of schemes.

One way this kind of cryptography could be expressed would be a simple substitution cipher, where the linked transposition of letters ("a" for "z," "b" for "y," etc.) becomes the key shared by the message parties. The Usenet standard "rot 13" method is a substitution cipher where the encrypted letter is 13 positions after the plaintext letter. Another kind of secret key could be derived from a user-supplied "password" that is fed to an appropriate algorithm.

The widely used Data Encryption Standard (DES, described in FIPS PUB 46-1) is also a secret-key system, and is used inside SET. Interestingly, it is widely assumed within the "cypherpunk" community that DES is not as secure as its 56-bit long key would seem to indicate. Indeed, this cipher-hacking group believes that a "backdoor" to DES was designed in the standard for use by the government in surveillance efforts. Both IBM (DES's inventor) and the government have long denied the existence of such a backdoor. To bolster this defense, DES has withstood a sophisticated attack developed by Biahm and Shamir called "Differential Cryptanalysis" that has cracked similarly designed ciphersystems.

DES data is encrypted in 64-bit blocks. Data is encrypted through a 16-round scrambling process that divides that data into two halves. One half (32 bits) is scrambled and then passed through a random function called the "s-box." The other half then modifies the s-box-processed data. It's like shuffling a deck of cards, cutting the cards at an arbitrary point in the deck and then reshuffling. The s-box design takes six-bit values (there are eight s-boxes used in practice) and turns them into 4 bits. In this way 48 bits from the 56-bit key are reduced to 32 bits. The s-box function is highly nonlinear, but 16 passes through it do scramble the data, according to Biahm and Shamir. Evidently any computational biases present in one pass through it are canceled out by the next pass, and so on.

Since DES uses bit-shifting (both left and right) to get its results, it implements well on digital processors (most of which can implement such a shift in one instruction between values in the registers of the processor). It's also computationally fast. DES has become the standard encryption used by the government for nonclassified information since 1977, and is described in FIPS 81. There are several DES modes, but SET only uses the Cipher Block Chaining (CBC) mode described above.

Secret-key methods are functionally unusable when the situation calls for many untrusted partners to share information without divulging information to each other, because managing the secret keys becomes a monumental task. This is because only two parties can share the same secret key, and as the number of parties grows, the number of required secret keys grows exponentially. There are better ways to handle this situation, as we shall see.

2.3 PUBLIC/PRIVATE KEY CRYPTOGRAPHY

Public-key cryptography was first identified by Diffie and Hellman in 1976. Encryption and decryption in this method involve two different keys, the public key and the private key. A user gives out his or her public key to other users, and keeps the private key secret. Data encrypted with a public key can be decrypted only with the corresponding private key. This kind of encryption is called asymmetric, because the keys for encoding and decoding are different.

Diffie-Hellman encryption is resistant to attack to the extent that the large prime number resists factorialization. If one obtained the factors of that large prime number, backtracking to the factor pair (the public and private key pair) used for DH encryption is possible, especially with a computer doing the grunt work. Still, for the first time, one could publicly give out a key that, when used for decrypting, could verify that a message came from the possessor of the private key. This was a major advance in ease of use over most secret-key systems.

Diffie and Hellman even figured out a key-agreement algorithm that allowed two people with public keys to create a secret key to be used for a message-transference session. Simplified, the typical implementation of key agreement involves a two-phased key-agreement algorithm:

♦ Sender S sends a message to Receiver R initiating the key-agreement protocol.

♦ S and R independently perform a first phase of some key-agreement algorithm, and send the result of that phase to one another.

♦ S and R independently perform a second phase of the key-agreement algorithm, after which they arrive at a common agreed-upon secret key.

In this manner, S and R can establish a working secret key for encryption of the current messaging session without any trust being established beyond that. Much like a "one-time pad" cipher, the secret key is used only for the one session and then discarded.

Sometimes a "nonce" is used between two parties as a way to defeat a "dictionary" attack, in the way that a "challenge" is used to prevent a playback attack. This nonce is some field data that is changed by one party, and repeated by the other in the response message. This simply shows one party that the other party is really listening to them.

2.4 RSA: THE MEN AND THE COMPANY

♦ ♦

In 1978 R. L. Rivest, A. Shamir, and L. Adleman extended the concept of Diffie and Hellman to exponentiation modulo the product of two prime numbers, instead of just one. (The difficulty of breaking RSA encryption is generally considered to

be equal to the difficulty of factoring integers that are the
product of two large prime numbers of approximately equal
size.) To appreciate this popular implementation of the concept
of Diffie and Hellman, we need a quick review of modulus
arithmetic. In arithmetic modulo, a number n works the same
way as in the arithmetic that we are all used to, except that the
range of numbers that express it are limited to the range $n-1$. If
the arithmetic operation produces a result greater than n, the nth
count becomes 0, and the remainder expressed. For example,
arithmetic modulo 5 has 0, 1, 2, 3, and 4 as the digits available to
it, and 3 hours after 10:00 AM is 1:00 PM, not 13:00 AM.

The RSA algorithm may be broken down into several steps. First,
two large (large enough so that they occupy 200–1000 bits in
binary notation) prime numbers are chosen. Let's call them p
and q. There are several mathematical tests that can be used to
establish whether or not p and q are prime. (A prime number, as
you remember from school, can be divided without remainder
only by itself and 1.)

Multiply the primes together to obtain n; that is, $(pq = n)$. Choose
the secret key s so that the greatest common denominator of s
and the product of $(p-1)$ and $(q-1)$ is 1. The public key $k = 1/k$
mod $(p-1)$ $(q-1)$. (Euclid's algorithm may come in handy here
for calculating the inverse.) The pair of n and k form the public
key, while the n and s pair form the secret key.

To encrypt, the message is first converted into a number less than
n, which we will call m. Encryption is done in blocks of m length,
and is performed by computing m raised to the kth power mod n.
To decrypt, we compute the expression (m raised to the kth
power mod n) raised to the sth power mod n. To raise m to the kth
power by multiplying m by itself k times would be computationally
intensive. Fortunately, there is a simpler way that lends itself to
digital computation:

♦ Start with m and k. Establish a counter j that is initially 1, and then marches through the bits starting with the least significant bit. Initialize an answer variable a as 1. Repeat the loop that follows until j has counted through all the bits in k.

♦ Is bit j of k equal to one? If so, $a = (a \times m)$ mod n
  Set $m = m$ squared mod n.
  Increment j and go to top of loop

♦ At the end of the incrementing, $a = m$ raised to the k mod n.

Rivest et al patented this computational concept and started selling object code of this function that could be incorporated into computer programs. Their company, called RSA Data Security, has developed other cryptographic products, notably the MD2 and MD5 algorithms (described in RFCs 1319 and 1321) for making a message-digest hash. Hash functions are public (so that a receiver could obtain them easily) and one-way; that is, given a hash value, it's not feasible to recreate the original data from the hashed result alone (see 2.3.4).

RSA sells its encryption object code under the BSAFE name (the current version is 4.0) and it is available for C programs on most major platforms. Programming examples for the kit are available from RSA. RSA encryption is widely used throughout the current SET process, and use of its licensed code modules should be considered by any programmer undertaking a SET project.

RSA also publishes the PKCS (Public Key Cryptography Standards) series of notes about RSA techniques. #7 and #10 of the series on RSA envelopes is highly relevant to SET and its underlying technology.

Other companies may offer encryption algorithms for SET in the future. A Canadian company, Certicom, has recently licensed Terisa Systems to develop a SET toolkit based on its Elliptic Curve

Cryptography. ECC is based on the difficulty of the elliptic logarithm problem. The problem may be stated: Given an elliptic curve over a finite field along with two points on that curve (P and Q), determine a method to find an integer k such that $Q = kP$. In cryptography, Q would be the public key and k the private key. Certicom asserts that a key size of 110 bits is as cryptographically secure as an RSA key of 512 bits, and that a 160-bit key is as secure as an RSA key of 1024 bits. There are features that recommend both approaches. ECC may be faster in signature-generation, but RSA is faster in signature-verification. The appropriate use of these encryption technologies will be up to the marketplace, because even though SET is currently implemented using RSA techniques, the protocol itself allows for alternative cryptography methods.

2.5 HASHING AND DIGITAL SIGNATURES

A message-digest hash results from the reduction of a variable length message into a fixed length (for most situations it's usually 128 bits). The hash function gives different results for each message and so produces a unique value for the hash of the message. SET uses 160 bits for its hash length, and the Secure Hash Algorithm (SHA-1, described in FIPS 181-1) as its method. In general, MD2 or MD5 would be the code engine that computes the hash on the fly ("stream processing") in a computer program. If you then encrypt the resulting hash of a message with your private key, you get what RSA calls "the digital signature" of a message. There are other ways to make a digital signature, but we will use the RSA method for purposes of discussion.

The digital signature is the result of binding someone's private key via encryption to a specific message-digest hash, thereby binding the person (by extension) to that specific message. In the

RSA method, to verify that a person has signed a message with his or her private key, one decrypts the encoded message digest (which has been sent along with the message) using the public key of the sender to get the message hash. If that hash is the same as the one that the receiver then performs on the message, the receiver can be sure that (1) the sender encrypted the digest with his or her private key, and (2) the message did not change in transmission.

It's important to remember that the presence of a digital signature does not imply anything about the state of the message to which it is linked. A signature links a sender to a message, it doesn't authenticate the message itself. The message may be left in plaintext, and thus any receiver of the message can verify that it was indeed sent by the purported sender. If the message is encrypted in some way (say with a secret key), only those possessing the key can decode the message, perform a hash operation on the plaintext to get a digest, compare the digest to the encrypted digest (decoded using the sender's public key), and thus determine the validity of the digital signature.

2.6 DIGITAL CERTIFICATES AND ENVELOPES

The section above makes some sweeping assertions about how someone can be linked to a message. But anyone can operate a keypair-producing computation in an untrustworthy manner. How can we know that the public key shown actually belongs to the purported sender? Where are the safeguards to prevent impersonation?

There aren't any. Impersonation is based on a false gaining of trust, a pretension. It could be a technically accurate ruse, one of the kind that unattended computer-based systems usually do fall prey to. The way around this problem is to bring in a trusted third party in an "out-of band" manner that can bind a public key to a uniquely identified entity. The mechanism that binds the public key is called a "certificate." A certificate is a token produced by some "certificate authority" with responsibility for that certificate. The token is actually a series of ASCII characters that can be used as input for later cryptological purposes.

SET participants have to make an initial decision about whom to trust that affects the entire relationship from that (initial) point on. One can "trust" a bank, a brand, an acquirer, or some other financial entity. Exactly how that entity will get the initial certificate to the cardholder will depend on that brand's policy. By accepting that certificate, a party indicates their trust in the entity that digitally bound itself to the certificate.

It works both ways. You can identify yourself to some other party using the same mechanism as they use to identify themselves to you. A cardholder's signature certificate would bind the cardholder's public key to their card's primary account number (PAN). The PAN itself is encrypted within the certificate in a manner that allows decoding only by the Cardholder Certificate Authority (CCA), the cardholder, and the card's issuer (or the acquirer's third parties, like a payment gateway system). The CCA functions as the trusted third party in this situation. (Of course, for the truly paranoid among us, there could also be bogus CAs. There would then have to exist a higher-level certification authority, and so on; until one hit the Root—or top—level of trust. These would be the people who actually hold the Root Certificate that all SET participants agree is trustworthy in a tamper-proof hardware setup.)

Certificate Revocation Lists (CRLs) are the method a Certificate Authority has to use to cancel or invalidate existing certificates as things change. A potentially large data structure, a CRL must be passed among the parties of a transaction for verification steps. To avoid having to transmit this large structure many times, smaller "thumbprints" of the certificates contained in the CRL are used. (A thumbprint is the hash of a certificate or CRL and is the data structure usually attached to a message.) A receiver can use it to check if it already possesses the certificate or CRL the thumbprint represents. Thumbs are computed by performing the SHA-1 hash of the DER-encoded structures **UnsignedCertificate**, **UnsignedCertificateRevisionList**, and the **UnsignedBrandCRLIdentifier**. The hash is computed over the tag-length-value of the encoded structure. (Certificates and their management issues will be dealt with in Chapter 5.) An important thing to remember is that digital signatures can work to bind someone's private key (by being able to decrypt with the public key we consider the message to have been encrypted by the private key) to a message. That message can be countersigned by someone else, like a CCA, to form a certificate. Of course, even without a countersignature, the message can still convey information of other kinds.

Dual-key encoding needs to start its mathematical operations from some initialization vector, or random sequence of numbers, to provide the best possible security. Pseudo-random number generator (pRNG) programs can provide these initializing values, or random human actions like the time between hitting keys can be used to provide them. pRNGs are a topic of controversy amongst the "sci.crypt" newsgroup on the Internet, where most of the serious cipher-lovers hang out, and the consensus seems to be that they work, up to a point.

The problem is that pRNGs may also require an initial seed value to generate randomized numbers. Providing these seed numbers can be a problem for the designer. Netscape suffered some public embarrassment when an observer discovered that the time of day was being used as a seed value in Navigator 2.0. (Knowing the seed value allowed an easier computational attack on the encrypted messages that Navigator was generating.)

For very secure situations, many sci.crypt folk prefer other types of RNGs, such as physical radiation-decay emission counters. That sort of hardware is obviously impractical in the SET universe, but it behooves the designer using encryption to consider carefully where his or her "random" seeds come from. (Eastlake, Crocker, and Shiller's RFC 1750 "Randomness Recommendations for Security" should be consulted for further details on randomization of seeds.)

SET also implements digital dual signatures. Dual signatures link two messages to different people such that the message parts can only be read by the intended recipient, yet provide a way to check the authenticity of the message.

A dual signature is generated by creating a message digest (hash) of both plaintext messages individually ($H(m1)$ and $H(m2)$), concatenating these digests into one value [m3], and then taking the hash of that value [$H(m3)$]. Encrypting $H(m3)$ with the signer's private key provides the dual signature. A recipient can verify the message by computing the message digest of the message sent to it, concatenating it with the sender-provided message digest of the other message, and computing the result. This should equal the decrypted dual signature.

Dual signatures link two messages in one functional unit, yet keep the information content compartmentalized. In SET, dual signatures link an order message sent to a merchant with the card payment information for the acquirer that has been sent by the cardholder. When a merchant sends an authorization request to the acquirer, it includes the card payment information (including the card account number) that was sent to it by the cardholder and the message digest of the order information. The acquirer then uses the message digest supplied by the merchant and computes the message digest of the payment information supplied by the cardholder to check the authenticity of the overall transaction.

A digital envelope is a way to encrypt data and to send the key for that encryption along with the data. Most enveloping schemes use a symmetric method to encrypt the data, and an asymmetric one to encrypt the key.

SET uses a method called Optimal Asymmetric Encryption Padding (OAEP), modified by Matayas and Johnson's hashed-data technique, along with its encryption techniques. OAEP assures that all bits of public/private key-encoded data are equally attack-resistant. In SET, OAEP is applied prior to encrypting the DES key using the public key of an envelope's receiver.

In 1993, Johnson, Matayas, and Wilkins described a symmetrical algorithm for tunneling information while providing for the confidentiality of that information. Called the CDMF (for Commercial Data Masking Facility), it scrambles data based on DES-like techniques using a 40-bit key. Because of the short key length, it is considered a masking technique rather than an encrypting one. CDMF may be used in SET to mask acquirer to cardholder information when passing through the merchant. CDMF is a "place-holder" technique that will eventually be replaced by something cryptoanalytically stronger, like DES.

2.7 AN INTRODUCTION TO ASN.1

ASN.1 (it stands for Abstract Syntax Notation One) is a formal notation used to describe the generalized elements of a system in the application and presentation layers of the CCITT/OSI data framework. While a full and complete description of the notation would take up much of this book, elements of it must be understood to follow the discussion and notation that will follow.

Encoding rules in ASN.1 are algorithms that determine the bit-pattern representation during transfer for any data structure that can be written down using the language. Distinguished Encoding Rules (DER) are used in SET, since the basic rules (BER) may sometimes cause two dissimilar structures to share the same bit-pattern during transfer, which would be disastrous in a system that uses hashes. DER, a subset of BER, guarantees that unique strings produce unique encoded bit patterns when hashed.

ASN.1 compilers are sold that can generate the DER-encoded messages, given SET's ASN.1 specifications. It is expected that programmers will use these to develop SET-enabled applications. Open Systems Solution's (OSS) compiler was used in the development of SET and is commercially priced.

2.7.1 Datatypes and OIDs

An ASN.1 datatype is built up from several primitive data types (INTEGER, REAL, BOOLEAN, NULL) using only three main construction mechanisms: repetition (SEQUENCE OF and SET OF), alternatives (CHOICE), and field lists (SEQUENCE and SET). Names can be assigned to types with the assignment (::=) operator.

"Simple" datatypes have no components. There are also structured types that have components, tagged types which can be derived from other types, and "other" types that include the CHOICE and the ANY type. Once an ASN.1 data type has been defined, it can be used in the definition of other ASN.1 data types exactly as if it were a primitive data type, and such types can be defined before use or after. This, of course, implies that forward references in a datatype are acceptable. Recursion is also allowed.

Every ASN.1 type other than CHOICE and ANY possesses a tag. The tag consists of a class and a non-negative tag number. Types in ASN.1 are the same in the abstract, if and only if their tag numbers are the same.

Tags (also called "object-identifiers" when applied to objects) may be of four classes:

1. Universal: the type is the same regardless of the application. X.208 defines these types.

2. Application: the type has a specific meaning in an application. The tag value may be equivalent in two different applications, yet vary in meaning.

3. Private: the types whose meanings are specific to the enterprises.

4. Context specific: the type's meaning is specific to a given structured type. Context-specific distinguishes between component types with the same underlying tag within the context of a given structured type.

Some "simple" data types (along with their universal tags) are: INTEGER [2], BIT STRING[3] (a string of ones and zeroes), OCTET STRING [4] (a string of 8-bit values, each of which is an octet), NULL [5], OBJECT IDENTIFIER [6] (a sequence of integer components that identify an object), SEQUENCE [16], SET[17], PrintableString[19] (a string of printable characters), IA5String[22] (a string of ASCII characters), and UTCTime [23] (a Greenwich-meantime value).

ISO and ITU-T (the international bodies) have recently adopted ISO/IEC 9834-7 and ITU-T X.666, which provide for an international registration authority (RA). The ID arc for this RA is {joint-iso-itu-t (2) internationalRA (23)}.

MasterCard and Visa have indicated that they will apply for an object identifier for use by SET applications under this arc as soon as the registration authority is named. The ultimate definition of {id-set} will be of the form:

```
id-set OBJECT IDENTIFIER ::= { joint-iso-itu-t(2)
internationalRA(23) set(x)}
```

The {id-set} arc has been divided as follows:

    0   content type
    1   message extension
    2   field
    3   attribute
    4   algorithm
    5   policy
    6   module
    7   certificate extension
    8   brand
    9   vendor
    10 national market

Let's consider each type individually.

Content type: OIDs with the prefix {id-set contentType (0)} are used to identify data elements that are globally defined for use by SET applications. Also, they identify each of the SET data structures that can be signed or digested.

Message extension: OIDs with the prefix {id-set msgExt (1)} are used to identify message extensions that are globally defined for use by SET applications.

Field: OIDs with the prefix {id-set field (2)} are used to identify registration form fields that are globally defined for use by SET applications.

Attribute: OIDs with the prefix {id-set attribute (3)} are used to identify attributes that are globally defined for use by SET applications.

Algorithm: OIDs with the prefix {id-set algorithm (4)} are used to identify algorithms that are globally defined for use by SET applications. All algorithms currently used by SET have externally defined object identifiers.

Policy: OIDs with the prefix {id-set policy (5)} are used to identify policies that are globally defined for use by SET applications.

Module: OIDs with the prefix {id-set module (6)} are used to identify SET ASN.1 modules. ASN.1 uses the module concept extensively. Definitions may be imported and exported (as well as grouped) by a module.

Certificate extension: OIDs with the prefix {id-set certExt (7)} are used to identify certificate extensions that are globally defined for use by SET applications.

Brand: OIDs with the prefix {id-set brand (8)} are used to identify payment card brands. Each payment card brand manages the assignment of OIDs beneath its brand OID. It is strongly recommended that the next level under the brand OID follow the conventions described below under Private OID management. The assignment of brand OID values is roughly based on the values assigned to the brand by ISO using the shortest BIN prefix that is uniquely assigned to the brand.

Vendor: OIDs with the prefix {id-set vendor (9)} are used to identify SET application vendors. Each vendor manages the assignment of OIDs beneath its vendor OID. It is strongly recommended by the SET architects that the next level under the vendor OID follow the conventions described below as Private OID management. The assignment of vendor OID values is made on a first-come first-served basis.

National market: OIDs with the prefix {id-set national (10)} are used to identify national market information. Each national market manages the assignment of OIDs beneath its national market OID. It is strongly recommended by the SET architects that the next level under the national market OID follow the conventions described below under Private OID management. The assignment of national market OID values corresponds to ISO-3166 numeric codes.

Private OID management: Each payment brand, vendor, and national market manages its own arc. However, it is strongly recommended by the designers of SET that the next level in that arc follow the same conventions as followed by the {id-set} arc:

0   content type
1   message extension
2   field
3   attribute
4   algorithm
5   policy
6   module

Note: no brand, vendor, or national market is permitted to define new certificate extensions for use within SET.

2.7.2 Data Structures and Cryptography Operators

We'll use ASN.1 to define some of the basic cryptography used in SET. First, let's define some basic data structures in SET notation.

Tuple. **{A,B,C}** A tuple groups zero or more data elements. The elements may be messages or documents. The above notation means the tuple containing **A**, **B**, and **C**, which may, in turn, be tuples.

Component. Let **T**= **{A,B,C}**. **T.A** is one component of **T**, as are **T.B** and **T.C**.

Ordered concatenation. **A|B|C** stands for an explicit ordered concatenation of **A**, **B**, and **C**. **A** before **B** before **C**.

Optional. **[A]** means that **A** is optional. Though not mandatory, the notation implies that **A**'s presence or lack of presence may still be evaluated in some manner at another point in the datastream.

Selection. **<A,B,C>** means that one and only one of the choices **A**, **B**, or **C** shall appear. You have to select one of them.

Optional selection. **[<A,B,C>]** Either none of the choices or one of the choices **A**, **B**, or **C** may appear here.

Multiple Instantiation. **{A+}** is simple. It's a tuple that contains one or more instances of **A**. So is **{A*}**. That tuple allows no instances of **A**. But **{[A]+}** means a tuple containing one or more instances of **A** in an ordered array where each instance of **A** is optional and can be null. (If I think too long about this construct, my head starts to hurt.)

Hashing. **H(t)** is a 160-bit SHA-1 hash of tuple **t**. SHA-1 is the Secure Hash Algorithm developed by NIST that is very much like RSA's MD-4.

HMAC (t,k) is a 160-bit keyed-hash of tuple **t** using **k** as the key. This uses the 160-bit SHA-1 hash.

Linkage. **L(t1,t2)** means that a link or reference pointer to **t2** is included with **t1**. This expression would be equivalent to the tuple **{t1,DD(t2)}**. Linkage is not symmetric; it does not link **t2** to **t1**.

DigestedData. **DD(t)** 160-bit SHA-1 hash of tuple **t** embedded in a PKCS Digested Data sequence.

See Figure 2.1 for a graphic overview of the DigestedData construct.

Signature. **S (s,t)** This is a signed message, the signature of entity **s** on tuple **t**, including the plaintext of **t**. The default signature

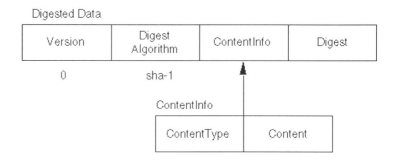

Figure 2.1. DigestedData construct

algorithm of SET is RSA with the SHA-1 hash. This is the same as the PKCS#7 SignedData.

> *encryption flow.* Initialize and load data fields depending on the message's type. Transform data fields (version, algorithm identifier, content type) that are to be signed into their DER equivalent, and take the SHA-1 hash of the DER fields giving the message digest. Encrypt the encoded authenticated attributes (content type and message digest) using sender's private key giving the result of **Encrypted Digest**. Append data, certificates, and CRLs followed by signer information.
>
> See Figure 2.2 for a graphic overview of the SignedData structure.
>
> Signed SET messages will contain the CRLs and certificates necessary for verification, unless the sender has previously sent thumbprints to indicate he or she already has them.

$S(s,t)$. This is the signature of **s** on tuple **t**, not including the plaintext of **t**. It is similar to the PKCS #7 External Signature.

Asymmetric encryption. **E(r,t)** Encrypt **t** with a fresh symmetric key **k**, then insert **k** in an RSA digital envelope for entity **r** under OAEP.

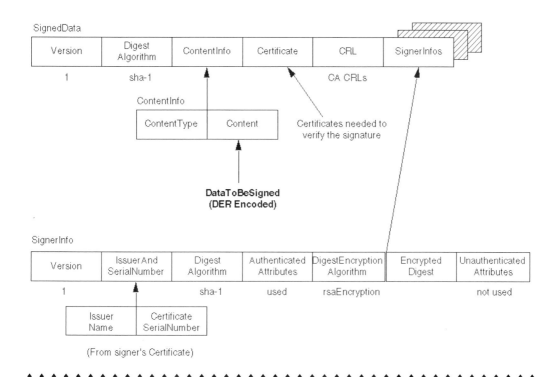

Figure 2.2. SignedData Structures

This is equal to encrypting **OAEP (k)** using the public key of entity **r**, taken from the certificate in tuple **r**. (Corresponds to PKCS #7's EnvelopedData.)

> *encryption flow.* Initialize and load fields into message. Transform data to the DER equivalent. Generate a new DES (symmetric) key, then encrypt the DER result with it using DES-CBC. Add data content type and algorithm identifier to front of encrypted data. Initialize envelope buffer and OAEP buffer with symmetric DES key previously generated. Process envelope buffer with OAEP; then encrypt buffer using public key of **r**. Initialize recipient buffer with RSA algorithm identifier and attach encrypted envelope and encrypted message data. Another way to state the process is to encrypt **t**

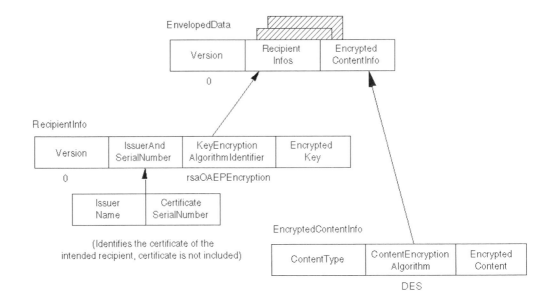

Figure 2.3. EnvelopedData Structures

with the DES key **k**, then insert **k** in a PKCS #7 envelope for entity **r** under OAEP.

Figure 2.3 gives an overview of the data structures involved in the EnvelopedData type of PKCS #7.

Integrity Encryption. **EH(r,t)** Similar to the above, but the RSA envelope contains **OAEP({k,H(t)})** when a signature is not available. To check integrity, rehash **t** and check for a match against **H(t)** in the envelope.

encryption flow. Initialize and load fields into message. Transform data to DER equivalent. Generate a SHA-1 hash of DER result. Generate a new DES (symmetric) key, then encrypt the DER result with it using DES-CBC. Add data content type and DES algorithm identifier to front of encrypted data. Initialize envelope buffer and OAEP buffer with symmetric DES key and the hash previously generated. Process envelope buffer with OAEP; then encrypt buffer using public key of **r**. Initialize recipient buffer with RSA algorithm identifier and attach encrypted envelope and encrypted message data.

Symmetric Encryption with a provided key k. **EK(kd,t)** Uses the tuple **t** using secret key **k** and encryption algorithm **d**.

> *encryption flow.* Initialize and load fields into message. Transform data to DER equivalent. Symmetrically encrypt message using **k** as the secret key via either DES or CDMF (DES stripped down to a 40-bit key length) depending on the message type. Initialize result buffer with data content type and algorithm identifier, and append encrypted message.

Simple Encapsulation with Signature. **Enc (s,r,t)** Signed and then encrypted. Like a PKCS #7 SignedData encapsulated in EnvelopedData.

> *encryption flow.* Use the Signature operator and sign **t** using the private key for **s**. Add this to **t**. Using Asymmetric Encryption, encrypt the resultant using the public key of recipient **r**.

Simple Encapsulation with Signature and provided key data. **EncK(kd,s,t) = EK(kd, S(s,t)}.** A provided key **k** and encryption algorithm **d** encrypts a signed message.

> *encryption flow.* Use the Signature operator to sign **t** using the private key for **s**. Add this to **t**. Using Symmetric Encryption, encrypt the resultant using the secret key **k**.

Extra Encapsulation with Signature. **EncX (s,r,t,p)** This is a two-part message with the first part (**t**) symmetrically encrypted and the second part (**p**) in the extra slot of **EX** where OAEP data usually resides.

encryption flow. **p** has a fresh random nonce (**EXNonce**) for each encoding. Append the contents of **p** to **t**. Use the Signature operator to sign the result using the private key of **s**. Add the results to **t** getting **t1**. Use the Extra Asymmetric Encryption operator to store **p** in the extra slot of OAEP, then encrypt **t1** using **r**'s public key. If **p** is embedded in an **SO** signature instead of the **OAEP** data, the **SO** signature is computed over the DER-encoded form of **p**, then **t** and **SO** (**s**,{**t**,**DER**(**p**)} are placed into the **DES** protected part of the message which is encrypted with the **DES** key **k**.

Simple Encapsulation with Signature and Baggage. **EncB(s,r,t,b)** **b** is the baggage.

encryption flow. Compute baggage's SHA-1 hash and add to **t**, giving **t1**. Sign **t1** using the Signature operator and the private key of **s** and add result to **t1** giving **t2**. Using the Symmetric Encryption operator, encrypt **t2** using public key of recipient **r**, giving **t3**. Add **b** to **t3** to finish.

Extra Encapsulation with Signature and Baggage. **EncBX(s,r,t,b)**. **EX** encrypted two-part signed message with baggage.

encryption flow. Compute baggage's SHA-1 hash and add to **t** giving **t1**. Sign **t1** using the Signature operator and the private key of **s** and add result to **t1** giving **t2**. Using the Extra Asymmetric Encryption operator, store **b** in the extra slot of OAEP and encrypt **t2** using the public key of recipient **r** giving **t3**. Add **b** to **t3** to finish.

Linked Single Extra Encapsulation with Dual Signature. **EncDXL2(s,r,t1,t2,p2)** This construct is used in the Purchase Request with Order Information (**t1**) from cardholder to merchant. **t2** and **p2** are the Payment Information. See 2.6 for more on dual signatures.

2.7.3 Some Cryptographic Hygiene

Let's insert some cryptographic hygiene into the previously discussed OID structures. To do that, we have to step back and consider what the overall rules are. Data being signed must be authenticated by the signature.

The PKCS #7 SignedData structure includes support for authenticated attributes to accompany a signature. These attributes are used to authenticate the content as well as the data. SET signatures include two authenticated attributes: contentType and messageDigest. In addition, the content of data that is protected by a message digest (without a signature) must also be identified.

As an example, consider the signature of the data element *Stuff*. The SHA-1 digest of the DER encoding of the structure is computed. An authenticated attributes data structure is computed by placing the object identifier *id-set-stuff* into contentType and the digest into msgDigest. The SHA-1 digest of this data structure is computed and the result encrypted using the signer's private key; it is this encrypted digest that is placed in the *encryptedDigest* field of the SignedData structure. The object identifier *id-set-stuff* identifies the content—that is, what piece of data is authenticated.

Table 2.1 shows the SET message (or component of a message), the content, and the contentType for digested data.

Table 2.2 shows the SET message (or component of a message), the content, and the contentType for signed data.

Table 2.3 shows the SET message (or component of a message), the content, and the contentType for enveloped data.

Table 2.1. SET Message for Digested Data

Message/Data Structure	Content	Content Type
AuthReq	PI	id-set-content-PI
AuthRes	AuthResBaggage	id-set-content-AuthResBaggage
AuthRes	PANToken	id-set-content-PANToken
AuthRevReq	AuthRevReqBaggage	id-set-content-AuthRevReqBaggage
AuthRevRes	AuthRevResBaggage	id-set-content-AuthRevResBaggage
AuthToken	PANToken	id-set-content-PANToken
CapReq	CapTokSeq	id-set-content-CapTokSeq
CapReq	PANToken	id-set-content-PANToken
CapRevReq	CapTokSeq	id-set-content-CapTokSeq
CapRevReq	PANToken	id-set-content-PANToken
CapToken	PANToken	id-set-content-PANToken
CertReq	AcctInfo	id-set-content-AcctInfo
CredReq	CapTokSeq	id-set-content-CapTokSeq
CredReq	PANToken	id-set-content-PANToken
CredRevReq	CapTokSeq	id-set-content-CapTokSeq
CredRevReq	PANToken	id-set-content-PANToken
HOD	HODInput	id-set-content-HODInput
HOIData	OIData	id-set-content-OIData
HPIData	PIData	id-set-content-PIData
OIDualSigned	PIData	id-set-content-PIData
OIUnsigned	PIDataUnsigned	id-set-content-PIDataUnsigned
PIDualSigned	PANData	id-set-content-PANData
PI-OILink	OIData	id-set-content-OIData
PIUnsigned	OIData	id-set-content-OIData
PIUnsigned	PANToken	id-set-content-PANToken
RegFormReq	PANOnly	id-set-content-PANOnly
RootKeyThumb	SubjectPublicKeyInfo	id-set-rootKeyThumb

Table 2.2. SET Message for Signed Data

Message/Data Structure	Content	Content Type
AcqCardMsg	AcqCardCodeMsg	id-set-content-AcqCardCodeMsg
AuthReq	AuthReqTBS	id-set-content-AuthReqTBS
AuthRes	AuthResTBS	id-set-content-AuthResTBS
AuthRes	AuthResTBSX	id-set-content-AuthResTBSX
AuthRevReq	AuthRevReqTBS	id-set-content-AuthRevReqTBS
AuthRevRes	AuthRevResData	id-set-content-AuthRevResData
AuthRevRes	AuthRevResTBS	id-set-content-AuthRevResTBS
AuthToken	AuthTokenTBS	id-set-content-AuthTokenTBS
BatchAdminReq	BatchAdminReqData	id-set-content-BatchAdminReqData
BatchAdminRes	BatchAdminResData	id-set-content-BatchAdminResData
CapReq	CapReqTBS	id-set-content-CapReqTBS
CapReq	CapReqTBSX	id-set-content-CapReqTBSX
CapRes	CapResData	id-set-content-CapResData
CapRevReq	CapRevReqTBS	id-set-content-CapRevReqTBS
CapRevReq	CapRevReqTBSX	id-set-content-CapRevReqTBSX
CapRevRes	CapRevResData	id-set-content-CapRevResData
CapToken	CapTokenData	id-set-content-CapTokenData
CapToken	CapTokenTBS	id-set-content-CapTokenTBS
CardCInitRes	CardCInitResTBS	id-set-content-CardCInitResTBS
CertInqReq	CertInqReqTBS	id-set-content-CertInqReqTBS
CertReq	CertReqData	id-set-content-CertReqData
CertReq	CertReqTBS	id-set-content-CertReqTBS
CertRes	CertResData	id-set-content-CertResData
CredReq	CredReqTBS	id-set-content-CredReqTBS
CredReq	CredReqTBSX	id-set-content-CredReqTBSX
CredRes	CredResData	id-set-content-CredResData
CredRevReq	CredRevReqTBS	id-set-content-CredRevReqTBS
CredRevReq	CredRevReqTBSX	id-set-content-CredRevReqTBSX
CredRevRes	CredRevResData	id-set-content-CredRevResData
InqReqSigned	InqReqData	id-set-content-InqReqData
Me-AqCInitRes	Me-AqCInitResTBS	id-set-content-Me-AqCInitResTBS
PCertReq	PCertReqData	id-set-content-PCertReqData
PCertRes	PCertResTBS	id-set-content-PCertResTBS
PInitRes	PInitResData	id-set-content-PInitResData
PISignature	PI-TBS	id-set-content-PI-TBS
PRes	PResData	id-set-content-PResData
RegFormRes	RegFormTBS	id-set-content-RegFormResTBS
SignedError	ErrorTBS	id-set-content-ErrorTBS

Table 2.3. SET Message for Enveloped Data

Message/Data Structure	Content	Content Type
AcqCardMsg	AcqCardCodeMsgTBE	id-set-content-AcqCardCodeMsgTBE
AuthReq	AuthReqTBE	id-set-content-AuthReqTBE
AuthRes	AuthResTBE	id-set-content-AuthResTBE
AuthRes	AuthResTBEX	id-set-content-AuthResTBEX
AuthRevReq	AuthRevReqTBE	id-set-content-AuthRevReqTBE
AuthRevRes	AuthRevResTBE	id-set-content-AuthRevResTBE
AuthRevRes	AuthRevResTBEB	id-set-content-AuthRevResTBEB
AuthToken	AuthTokenTBE	id-set-content-AuthTokenTBE
BatchAdminReq	BatchAdminReqTBE	id-set-content-BatchAdminReqTBE
BatchAdminRes	BatchAdminResTBE	id-set-content-BatchAdminResTBE
CapReq	CapReqTBE	id-set-content-CapReqTBE
CapReq	CapReqTBEX	id-set-content-CapReqTBEX
CapRes	CapResTBE	id-set-content-CapResTBE
CapRevReq	CapRevReqTBE	id-set-content-CapRevReqTBE
CapRevReq	CapRevReqTBEX	id-set-content-CapRevReqTBEX
CapRevRes	CapRevResTBE	id-set-content-CapRevResTBE
CapToken	CapTokenTBE	id-set-content-CapTokenTBE
CapToken	CapTokenTBEX	id-set-content-CapTokenTBEX
CertReq	CertReqTBE	id-set-content-CertReqTBE
CertReq	CertReqTBEX	id-set-content-CertReqTBEX
CertRes	CertResTBE	id-set-content-CertResTBE
CredReq	CredReqTBE	id-set-content-CredReqTBE
CredReq	CredReqTBEX	id-set-content-CredReqTBEX
CredRes	CredResTBE	id-set-content-CredResTBE
CredRevReq	CredRevReqTBE	id-set-content-CredRevReqTBE
CredRevReq	CredRevReqTBEX	id-set-content-CredRevReqTBEX
CredRevRes	CredRevResTBE	id-set-content-CredRevResTBE
PIDualSigned	PIDualSignedTBE	id-set-content-PIDualSignedTBE
PIUnsigned	PIUnsignedTBE	id-set-content-PIUnsignedTBE
RegFormReq	RegFormReqTBE	id-set-content-RegFormReqTBE

2.7.4 SET Private/Public Key Summary

Table 2.4 summarizes private/public key pair usage in SET.

Table 2.4. Private/Public Key Pair Usage

	Public/Private Key Pair	Usage
1.	Cardholder message signature	sender signs, recipient verifies
2.	Merchant message signature	sender signs, recipient verifies
3.	Merchant key-exchange	enveloping & recovery of symmetric encryption key
4.	Payment gateway message	signature sender signs, recipient verifies
5.	Payment gateway key exchange	enveloping & recovery of symmetric encryption key
6.	Cardholder CA message	signature sender signs, recipient verifies
7.	Cardholder CA key-exchange	enveloping & recovery of symmetric encryption key
8.	Cardholder CA certificate	signing & verifying cardholder public key certificates
9.	Merchant CA message	signature sender signs, recipient verifies
10.	Merchant CA key-exchange	enveloping & recovery of symmetric encryption key
11.	Merchant CA certificate	signing & verifying merchant public key certificates
12.	Payment gateway CA message signature	sender signs, recipient verifies

Table 2.4. Private/Public Key Pair Usage (continued)

◆ ◆

	Public/Private Key Pair	Usage
13.	Payment gateway CA exchange	enveloping & recovery of symmetric encryption key
14.	Payment gateway CA certificate issuing	signing & verifying payment gateway public key certificates
15.	Payment gateway CA CRL	signing & verifying payment gateway public key CRLs
16.	Geo-political CA certificate issuing	optional
17.	Geo-political CA CRL	optional
18.	Brand CA certificate	signing & verifying dependent public key certificates
19.	Root CA certificate	signing & verifying brand public key certificates
20.	Root CA CRL	signing & verifying brand public key CRLs

2.8 SET EXTENSIONS

◆ ◆

To allow for changes within SET as business conditions warrant, an extensions field has been added to the end of certain SET protocol data units. The following protocol data units (PDUs) have an extensions field added: **MessageWrapper, PInitReq, PInitResData, PIHead, InstallRecurData, OIData, HODInput, PResPayload, AuthReqPayload, SaleDetail, AuthResPayload,**

AuthRevReqData, **AuthRevResData**, **CapReqData**, **CapPayload**, **CapResData**, **CapResPayload**, **CapRevOrCredReqData**, **CapRevOrCredReqItem**, **CapRevOrCredResData**, **CapRevOrCredResPayload**, **PCertReqData**, **PCertResTBS**, **BatchAdminReqData**, **BatchAdminResData**, **BatchStatus**, and **TransactionDetail**.

Note: The convention of printing a formal PDU name in boldface will be continued throughout the rest of the book.

An extension consists of three components: an object identifier, a criticality flag, and data. The object identifier uniquely identifies the extension. This permits SET applications to recognize an extension and process the data contained within that extension.

The data component provides the additional information that necessitated the definition of the extension. The layout of the data (the ASN.1 code) will be defined by the organization creating the extension.

The criticality flag indicates whether or not the recipient must understand the extension to process the message containing the extension. The criticality flag is a boolean value. An extension is considered critical if it is TRUE; otherwise, the extension is considered noncritical. Note that the default value for a critical flag is FALSE.

When an extension is critical, recipients of the message must recognize and be able to process the extension. If the application does not recognize the object identifier in the extension or does not know how to process the data, it will not process the message and will reject it with an error code of unrecognizedExtension.

When an extension is noncritical, recipients who cannot process the extension may ignore the extension and process the rest of the message.

An information object set has been created for each PDU that contains an extension. These sets define the extensions that are permitted to be processed in the PDU. Each of these sets ends with an ASN.1 extension marker ("...") which indicates that additional extensions may be defined that the application does not recognize. Application developers supporting specific extensions will have to add their list of supported extensions after this extension marker. A comma must separate the extension marker from the information objects that follow it.

Also note that organizations defining an extension must register the object identifier and the data content of the extension with the payment card companies (or their designate) prior to deploying software that transmits messages (including test messages) over an open network.

Extensions must conform to certain procedural rules to be considered for inclusion in the SET protocol. Data fields that are defined to appear within the data block (DB) of the OAEP block should never appear within the data of any extension. Such data would be considered sensitive, and should never be transmitted in the clear. Similarly, it is never considered correct to put the PAN into the definition of an extension. It is permissible, however, to put the first six digits of the **PAN**, the Bank Identification Number (BIN), into the data of an extension.

Again, data that is always encrypted by the protocol must not appear in an unencrypted form in an extension. For example, transaction amounts are always encrypted and so cannot appear unencrypted in an extension. The following PDUs contain extensions that are not encrypted: **MessageWrapper**, **PInitReq**, **PInitResData**, **OIData**, **PResPayload**, **InqReqData**, **PCertReqData**, and **PCertResTBS**. The payment card companies will be the final arbiters of whether a given data element may appear in its unencrypted form within a message.

The payment card companies will also reserve the right to disapprove the use of any extension that contains data that may compromise the integrity of the SET protocol. For example, any extension that contains more than six digits of the **PAN** will not be approved for use in a SET message.

Information exchanged between cardholder and merchant outside the SET protocol is collectively referred to as the order description. The **OD** is still important to SET because the digital signature of the cardholder on the purchase request is generated over the hash of the **OD**.

To be able to reference additional information within the SET protocol, extensions can be added to the **HODInput** field. Since this field is not transmitted within the SET message, the cardholder's software should place the list of extension object identifiers that were processed as part of the hash in the order information field. The object identifiers must be listed in the same order within the order information field as they appeared in the computation of the hash.

To verify the hash, the merchant must independently build the data of the extensions that are declared by the cardholder in the order information and put the extensions into his or her copy of **HODInput**. In order for the hash to verify, the extensions must appear in the same order that the cardholder software arranged them.

An additional private certificate extension (see Chapter 6) has been added for SET payment gateway certificates. This certificate extension will list the object identifiers of the message extensions that the gateway can process in payment instructions. Cardholder software can use this information to ensure that no unrecognized critical extensions are put into the payment instructions (in **PIExtensions** or **SRExtensions**).

2.8.1 Extensible PDU Descriptions

To help the designer decide which PDU is best extended for a specific application, a brief description of each extensible PDU follows.

MessageWrapper. The message wrapper is the main SET PDU. It carries every SET message (including the Error message). An extension would be appropriate in the message wrapper under either of two conditions: the data in the extension is general-purpose information about SET messages or the contents of the message are encrypted and the extension contains nonfinancial data that does not require confidentiality. The message wrapper is not encrypted so this extension must not contain confidential information.

PInitReq. The purchase initialization request carries enough information about the cardholder's selection of a card for payment for the merchant software to select an appropriate payment gateway certificate. The purchase initialization request is not encrypted so this extension must not contain confidential information.

PInitResData. The purchase initialization response carries copies of data from the purchase initialization request and the merchant and payment gateway certificates. The information from the request is copied into the response because the response is signed by the merchant; the signature allows the cardholder to ensure that the request was received by the merchant intact. The purchase initialization response is not encrypted so this extension must not contain confidential information.

PIHead. The payment instructions carry information from the cardholder to the payment gateway. The data in an extension to the payment instructions must be financial and should be important for the processing of an authorization by the payment gateway, the financial network, or the issuer.

InstallRecurData. The split/recurring data is a component of the payment instructions that is copied into the authorization token and **HODInput**. The data in an extension must be financial and should relate to the processing of subsequent authorizations by the merchant and the payment gateway. The split/recurring data is not transmitted to the issuer.

OIData. The order information carries information to link the purchase request to the prior shopping and ordering dialogue between the cardholder and the merchant. The data in an extension should relate to the merchant's processing of the order. The order information is not encrypted so this extension must not contain confidential information.

HODInput. The hash of the order description provides a secure linkage of the shopping/ordering dialogue and the purchase request. All information in the hash must be exchanged between the cardholder and the merchant out of band to SET before the purchase request is sent.

PResPayload. The purchase response carries information about the processing of the purchase request by the merchant. The purchase response is not encrypted so this extension must not contain confidential information.

InqReqData. The inquiry request carries enough information about the purchase request for the merchant to locate the transaction and return the current transaction status. The inquiry request is not encrypted so this extension must not contain confidential information.

AuthReqPayload. The authorization request carries information from the merchant necessary for the payment gateway to produce an authorization request message that can be processed by the acquirer or financial network for transmission to the issuer. The data in an extension to the authorization request must be financial and should be important for the processing of an authorization (or subsequent capture) by the payment gateway, the financial network, or the issuer.

SaleDetail. The sale detail carries information from the merchant necessary for the payment gateway to produce a clearing request message (for payment) that can be processed by the acquirer or financial network for transmission to the issuer. The data in an extension to the sale detail must be financial and should be important for the processing of a capture request by the payment gateway, the financial network, or the issuer.

AuthResPayload. The authorization response carries information from the payment gateway regarding the processing of the authorization request. The data in an extension to the authorization response must be financial and should be important for the processing of the authorization response or a subsequent authorization reversal or capture request by the payment gateway, the financial network, or the issuer.

AuthRevReqData. The authorization reversal request carries information from the merchant necessary for the payment gateway to produce an authorization reversal request message that can be processed by the acquirer or financial network for transmission to the issuer. The data in an extension to the authorization reversal request must be financial and should be important for the processing of an authorization reversal (or subsequent capture) by the payment gateway, the financial network, or the issuer.

AuthRevResData. The authorization reversal response carries information from the payment gateway regarding the processing of the authorization reversal request. The data in an extension to the authorization reversal response must be financial and should be important for the processing of the authorization reversal response or a subsequent capture request by the payment gateway, the financial network, or the issuer.

CapReqData. The capture request carries information from the merchant necessary for the payment gateway to produce clearing request messages (for payment) that can be processed by the acquirer or financial network for transmission to the issuer. The data in an extension to the capture request must be financial and should be important for the processing of a capture message by the payment gateway, the financial network, or the issuer. The data in this extension applies to every item in the capture request; data related to a specific item should be placed in an extension to **CapPayload**.

CapPayload. The capture request payload carries information from the merchant necessary for the payment gateway to produce a clearing request message (for payment) that can be processed by the acquirer or financial network for transmission to the issuer. The data in an extension to the capture request payload must be financial and should be important for the processing of a capture message by the payment gateway, the financial network, or the issuer. The data in this extension applies to an individual item in the capture request; data related to the entire capture request message should be placed in an extension to **CapReqData**.

CapResData. The capture response carries information from the payment gateway regarding the processing of the capture request. The data in an extension to the capture response must be financial and should be important for the processing of the capture response or a subsequent capture reversal or credit request by the payment gateway, the financial network, or the issuer. The data in this extension applies to every item in the capture response; data related to a specific item should be placed in an extension to **CapResPayload**.

CapResPayload. The capture response payload carries information from the payment gateway regarding the processing of the capture request. The data in an extension to the capture response payload must be financial and should be important for the processing of the capture response or a subsequent capture reversal or credit request by the payment gateway, the financial network, or the issuer. The data in this extension applies to an individual item in the capture response; data related to the entire capture response message should be placed in an extension to **CapResData**.

CapRevOrCredReqData. The capture reversal or credit request carries information from the merchant necessary for the payment gateway to reverse a prior clearing request message (for payment) or to issue a credit request that can be processed by the acquirer or financial network for transmission to the issuer. The data in an extension to the capture reversal or credit request must be financial and should be important for the processing of a capture reversal or credit by the payment gateway, the financial network, or the issuer. The data in this extension applies to every item in the capture reversal or credit request; data related to a specific item should be placed in an extension to **CapRevOrCredReqItem**.

CapRevOrCredReqItem. The capture reversal or credit request payload carries information from the merchant necessary for the payment gateway to reverse a prior clearing request message (for payment) or to issue a credit request that can be processed by the acquirer or financial network for transmission to the issuer. The data in an extension to the capture reversal or credit request payload must be financial and should be important for the processing of a capture reversal or credit by the payment gateway, the financial network, or the issuer. The data in this extension applies to an individual item in the capture reversal or credit request; data related to the entire capture reversal or credit request message should be placed in an extension to **CapRevOrCredReqData**.

CapRevOrCredResData. The capture reversal or credit response carries information from the payment gateway regarding the processing of the capture reversal or credit request. The data in an extension to the capture reversal or credit response must be financial and should be important for the processing of the capture reversal or credit response. The data in this extension applies to every item in the capture reversal or credit response; data related to a specific item should be placed in an extension to **CapRevOrCredResPayload**.

CapRevOrCredResPayload. The capture reversal or credit response payload carries information from the payment gateway regarding the processing of the capture reversal or credit request. The data in an extension to the capture reversal or credit response must be financial and should be important for the processing of the capture reversal or credit response. The data in this extension applies to an individual item in the capture reversal or credit response; data related to the entire capture reversal or credit response message should be placed in an extension to **CapRevOrCredResData**.

PCertReqData. The payment gateway certificate request carries information to identify certificates that the merchant desires. The payment gateway certificate request is not encrypted so this extension must not contain confidential information.

PCertResData. The payment gateway certificate response carries copies of the certificates that were requested by the merchant. The payment gateway certificate response is not encrypted so this extension must not contain confidential information.

BatchAdminReqData. The batch administration request carries information from the merchant to control capture batches. The data in an extension to the batch administration message must be financial and should be important for the processing of the batch administration request.

BatchAdminResData. The batch administration response carries information from the payment gateway regarding the processing of the batch administration response. The data in an extension to the batch administration response message must be financial and should be important for the processing of the batch administration request. Information regarding the processing of the request itself should appear in an extension to **BatchAdminResData**; information regarding the status of a batch should appear in an extension to **BatchStatus**; information regarding detail for an item within the capture batch should appear in an extension to **TransactionDetail**.

Chapter 3

• • •

SET PAYMENT PROCESSES AND TRANSACTIONS

This is how it goes. A certain Dembscher owed Beethoven fifty florins, and when the composer, who was chronically short of funds, reminded him of the debt, Dembscher heaved a mournful sigh and said, "Muss es sein?" To which Beethoven replied, with a hearty laugh, "Es muss sein!" and immediately jotted down these words and their melody. On this realistic motif he then composed a canon for four voices.

—Milan Kundera, *The Unbearable Lightness of Being*

To understand the SET system, various subsystems and processes must be considered. We will look at an overview of a number of the major payment processing transactions to understand the data flow as a whole. In other words, we're going to follow the money.

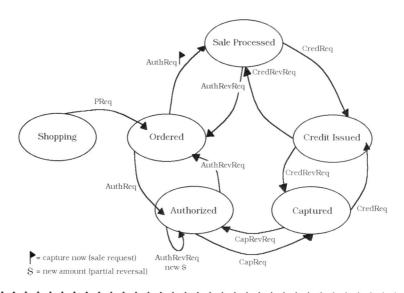

Figure 3.1. Business flows

The major transaction sets to be described right now are
Cardholder Registration, Merchant Registration, Purchase
Request, Payment Authorization, and Payment Capture. There
are other transactions in SET that are not directly part of
payment processing. They include Certificate query, Purchase
Inquiry, Batch Administration, Sale Transaction, Authorization
Reversal, Capture Reversal, Credit, and Credit Reversal. These
transactions perform housekeeping functions and will be
detailed later. Right now, we will examine the larger picture of
how SET moves and flows as it works.

3.1 CERTIFICATE AUTHORITY FUNCTIONS

Certificates, as has been noted before, help to assure all the
parties in a transaction that their partners are, indeed, who they

purport to be. A Certificate Authority has several primary functions in the certificate chain, including to receive registration requests, process and approve (or reject) them, and issue certificates.

Certificates contain information that, after being processed, can establish their own validity and origin. Validation is the process of mapping each certificate to the CA that issued it. This validation proceeds to the Root level.

Depending on the business model, Issuers may elect to perform all the CA functions themselves or contract some or all of them out. An independent registration authority may process certificate requests for multiple card issuers, for example. A number of companies (like GTE or Verisign) are eager and ready to perform such tasks for financial institutions.

3.2 CARDHOLDER REGISTRATION

Let's follow how a cardholder would register herself with a Cardholder Certificate Authority (CCA) so that she might participate in SET transactions with merchants. Unless she has certificates that can be traversed to the Root CA, merchants will refuse any SET attempts she makes.

Passing keys between parties can be interesting and is subject to an implicit negotiation of encryption algorithms. When a CA or Payment Gateway is prepared to encrypt data back to an End Entity, its certificate will list one or more symmetric encryption algorithms that it supports, in order of preference. The End Entity that wants to have data encrypted should select the first algorithm for the list that it supports and randomly generate a key. This key is passed to the CA or Payment Gateway in a request message.

1. The registration process begins when the cardholder's computer sends an initiate request (**CardCInitReq**) to the CCA. The CCA then generates a response (**CardCInitRes**) and signs it. The CCA certificates (key-exchange and signature) are attached to the message.

2. The certificates are verified by the receiving cardholder's computer, along with the CCA's signature, by traversing the trust chain to the Root key. If correct, the cardholder encrypts a registration form request (**RegFormReq**) with a randomly generated secret (symmetric) key. The secret key is encrypted along with the card account number using the CCA public key-exchange key, and transmitted back to the CCA.

3. The CCA decrypts the symmetric key and the **PAN** (cardholder's primary account number) using the private key of the key-exchange pair. The decoded symmetric key is then used to decrypt the registration form request (**RegFormReq**). The CCA may issue a referral response at this point if it does not have the correct form, but can indicate a location where it may be found. The CCA otherwise finds the correct form for the specific card Issuer, and then signs it. The response (**RegFormRes**) is then sent to the cardholder.

4. The cardholder gets the registration form and traverses the trust chain to the Root key, thereby validating the CCA's certificate used to sign the response. The CCA signature is decrypted with the CCA public signature key and compared to a computed hash of the registration form. The cardholder's software then creates a public and private signature key pair, if it has not already done so. The registration form (**RegForm**) sent by the CCA is filled in by the cardholder and used to generate a certificate request (**CertReq**). The **CertReq**, the cardholder's public signature key, and a new symmetric key are combined, and the message-digest hash of the resultant message is created. The hash is signed by the cardholder via encrypting it with the cardholder's private signature key. The

resultant message is encrypted with another new symmetric key. This third key is then encrypted along with the cardholder's account information using the CCA's public key-exchange key, and sent back to the CCA.

5. The cardholder/CCA setup has transacted at this point. The CCA still has to decrypt the digital envelope to obtain the symmetric encryption key, **PANData**, and the random number (nonce), but that's pretty much routine processing that can be done inside the application. The follow-on processing, which uses the symmetric key to decrypt the registration request and verifying the signature using the signature key embedded in the message should also sound familiar. If the signature is not verified, processing stops at this point, and the appropriate error message is returned to the cardholder.

Now the CCA must verify the information in the registration request. This sort of information request/retrieval is outside the scope of the SET protocol, so all we can do is assume that the CCA and the card's Issuer have a mechanism to deal with this need. It could be done in-house or subcontracted, but it has to be done within a reasonable time, considering the online nature of the SET transaction. We will assume, for purposes of discussion, that a competent "black box" has been inserted into the system at this point that can generate an approval when requested.

When the information has been verified by the Issuer, the CCA may produce a certificate. The general method of issuing this certificate begins with the CCA combining a random number with the one the cardholder supplied during the setup process. This generates a secret value known only to the CCA, but based on information from the cardholder. A hash is taken of the **PAN**, expire date, and the secret value. This hash is then placed in the certificate to show the link between the certificate and the cardholder's information.

The CCA will then sign the certificate and assign some period of validity to that certificate based on the CCA's policy. This period is likely to be the same as the expiration date of the card, but this is not a requirement.

A response (**CertRes**) containing the random number (not the combined number that was calculated from the two parts) previously generated by the CCA is encrypted using the symmetric key sent by the cardholder. This encrypted **CertRes** is then transmitted to the cardholder.

6. The cardholder's software verifies the certificate by traversing the chain of trust, and then decrypts **CertRes** using the symmetric key it has saved from prior processing. The CCA signature is verified by decrypting it with the CCA's public signature key and comparing it with a hash of the response. The cardholder can then combine the random value generated by the CCA with the random number that it generated earlier in the cycle to get the secret value, which is used to verify the hash in the certificate by the CCA.

At this point, the cardholder possesses a valid certificate that has been signed by a CCA, and can show it to a similarly registered and certificated merchant. In short, the cardholder and the merchant can now conduct SET transactions between them.

3.3 MERCHANT REGISTRATION

Merchant registration is necessary for the same reasons as cardholder registration, since a merchant needs a properly signed certificate in order to process SET orders. The procedure that it goes through closely resembles the one that the cardholder follows, but there are enough differences to warrant a separate delineation.

1. The merchant sends an initiation request (**Me-AqCInitReq**) to the Merchant Certificate Authority (MCA). The MCA identifies the appropriate registration form (from the merchant's financial institution) and then signs it. The form and the MCA certificates are then sent to the merchant in the response (**Me-AqCInitRes**).

2. The merchant's software program verifies the MCA certificate through a traversal of the trust chain, then verifies the MCA signature. The merchant will now need two pairs of asymmetric keys: one for key encryption and one for signatures. The merchant software generates both these key pairs using standard cryptological methods. The merchant completes the enclosed registration form and generates a certificate request (**CertReq**). The **CertReq** includes a copy of both of the merchant's public keys. It's signed, and the resultant is encrypted with a randomly generated symmetric key. The merchant's account data is then put (along with the symmetric key) into the message's envelope and encrypted with the MCA's public key-exchange key.

3. The MCA then decrypts the envelope of the merchant request to obtain the symmetric key, which is then used to decrypt the merchant's registration request. The merchant signature is verified with the signature key in the message, because even if it can be decrypted using the public key, it was signed (encrypted) with the private key. If the signature cannot be verified, all processing stops and an error message is returned to the merchant.

   The MCA now must verify the information that the merchant provided in the registration form that he submitted. This process, like that of the cardholder's, is not covered by SET protocol. It will be assumed here that the MCA can contact the acquirer in some manner and validate the information in the registration form. The way this occurs should not affect any of the SET transactions, and will be thought of as an "out-of band" transaction that occurs at this point in the system. If the verification is successful, the merchant certificates are created and signed by the MCA. There must be a validity period established as a component of these certificates. This is usually equal to the length of the contract between the merchant and the acquirer, but can vary according to MCA policy. These certificates are encrypted with a new symmetric key, which is itself encrypted using the merchant's public key-exchange key. The entire message is then sent to the merchant.

4. The merchant decrypts the envelope to get the MCA-generated symmetric key by using its private key-exchange key. The symmetric key is used to decrypt the certificates. The certificates are validated by the usual traversal, and stored for use in transactions.

3.4 PURCHASE REQUEST

Since SET is designed to be a protocol for payment by card, it doesn't come into play in the shopping experience until after customers have completed all the browsing, selecting of goods, and ordering that they are going to do for this session. In a cardholder-centered application, everything up to this step would be controlled by the cardholder-centered program. It makes no difference to SET how customers get to this point, only that they arrive with a card and a specific amount to be paid for with their card. This means that if, for example, installment payments are to be made for merchandise, that arrangement between merchant and cardholder should be finalized before invoking SET. All other ordering functions, including adding on any applicable shipping charges and state tax, must also be completed before SET transactions are begun. Only after the final dollar amount to be paid for with the card is locked down does the Purchase Request phase begin.

From the cardholder perspective, the Purchase Request is the central SET transaction. Most of the customer action that occurs in SET happens in this phase. The cardholder, merchant, and Payment Gateway are linked during this phase, either directly or indirectly. Though it is presented as a seamless flow here, it is quite possible that discontinuities can occur during this phase. Delays may be introduced by the cardholder filling out information or the merchant having to check his stock so that he may fill an order. However, the functional chain outlined remains the same, even if a delay occurs between steps.

1. The purchase request phase begins with the cardholder initiating a request (**PInitReq**) to the merchant. The purpose of this request is to get the merchant and Payment Gateway's certificates.

2. When the merchant gets the **PInitReq**, he or she assigns a unique transaction identifier to the message. The merchant's response (**PInitRes**) is signed. **PInitRes** and the two or more certificates are then sent to the cardholder.

3. The cardholder traverses the certificates to establish their validity, and then saves them for later use. The merchant signature is verified by decrypting with the merchant's public signature key and comparing it with a hash of the response message received. The cardholder's software then creates the Order Information (**OI**) and Payment Information (**PI**) data structures using information that has already been decided from the earlier shopping phase. If the cardholder has an acceptable certificate, the **PI** is signed with that certificate. As will be shown in 4.1.3, signing the **PI** increases the overall security of the transaction.

   Once the **OI** and **PI** have been constructed, a dual signature of the data may be generated by hashing the concatenation of the **OI** and **PI**, and encrypting the dual hash with the cardholder's private signature key. The individual hashes of the **OI** and the **PI** are sent along with the dual signature.

The **PI** is then encrypted by a randomly generated symmetric key. If the cardholder presents a certificate, the key and the encrypted **PI** are then further encrypted with the Payment Gateway's public key-exchange key. The resultant **PI** (along with the **OI**) is then sent to the merchant as **PIDualSigned**. If a certificate is not presented by the cardholder, it is sent as **PIUnsigned**.

4. The merchant verifies the cardholder's signature certificate when he or she first receives the Order Information. It then uses the cardholder's public signature key and the separate **PI** hash (which is concatenated to the **OI**'s hash) to check the dual signature validity.

The merchant then processes the request (including the payment authorization step, which is described in the next section). Although a discontinuity could develop here in the data flow, the merchant may send an optional **PRes** message to the cardholder to indicate that the order is under process.

After the merchant completes the necessary processing, a purchase response (**PRes**) is created, which includes the merchant signature certificate. The **PRes** is then signed and sent to the cardholder. If the transaction has been authorized (see 3.5), then the merchant fills the cardholder's order.

5. When the cardholder receives the merchant's **PRes**, he or she verifies the merchant signature certificate by the usual means. The cardholder then takes some action based on the contents of the response. A message may be displayed, for example. The cardholder may also find out more about the status of the order by sending an **InqReq** order inquiry message.

3.5 PAYMENT AUTHORIZATION

◆ ◆

We glossed over the procedure used by the merchant to authorize a transaction and will look at it in more detail now.

1. The merchant creates an authorization request (**AuthReq**) and signs it. The **AuthReq** is then encrypted with a random symmetric key, which is in turn encrypted by the Payment Gateway's public key-exchange key. The encrypted **AuthReq** (which also includes the encrypted **PI** from the cardholder) is then sent to the Payment Gateway.

2. The Payment Gateway first traverses the received certificates in the usual manner and decrypts the authorization request's envelope with its private key-exchange key to get the symmetric key. This symmetric key is used to decrypt the actual authorization request. The merchant digital signature is verified.

The Gateway then verifies the enclosed cardholder certificates, and then decrypts the first symmetric key and the cardholder's account information with the Gateway's private key-exchange key. The **PI** block is decrypted using the first symmetric key. The dual signature is then verified by decrypting it with the cardholder's public signature key and then comparing it with a hash of the concatenation of the **OI** and **PI** hashes.

The Payment Gateway then verifies that the transaction identifier from the merchant matches the one in the **PI** from the cardholder. If it does, an authorization request is formatted and sent to the Issuer. How this authorization request is sent and formatted may vary from Issuer to Issuer, and is beyond the scope of SET. Once again, we will assume a black-box mechanism between the Payment Gateway and the Issuer that simply returns a "go/no go" to the transaction flow. Note also that a time discontinuity may occur here if the Issuer does not immediately respond to the authorization request.

Consider in the midst of all this automation that someone may have to make a phone call to another person. When an Issuer processes an authorization request, it gives responses: approved, declined, or conditionally declined. This latter result is commonly called a "referral" by the payment card companies. A value of callIssuer(4) in the **RespCode** would be found in this case.

Upon receiving a referral response, a merchant must call a telephone number supplied by the acquirer to get approval for the transaction. The merchant is connected to the Issuer, who might ask questions about the transaction and may convert the referral into an approval by supplying the merchant with an approval code. This, of course, varies according to brand policy.

To carry this further, the merchant software must now allow the user to enter an approval code and process the transaction as though the response code had been an approval(0). Note that the value from the response code should not actually be changed. If the **AuthReq** included **CaptureNow** processing, the entry of the approval code should result in a **CapReq** message being sent to the Payment Gateway.

The merchant software should not generate a new authorization request following a referral response, since it is likely the system will decline the transaction a second time (even if a voice authorization was given). The Payment Gateway software must therefore generate all data necessary for the processing of a capture request (possibly including a capture token) on the **AuthRes** (authorization response) message for a referral response. It must accept a capture request for a transaction with a referral response if the capture request also includes a card-supplied approval code.

Also, if the merchant does not receive account numbers on authorization responses, the acquirer must supply them during the telephone call to the Issuer.

In general, when the Issuer responds; the Payment Gateway generates its own **AuthRes** message. This is made up of the Issuer's response and a copy of the Payment Gateway's signature certificate. The **AuthRes** is encrypted with a new symmetric key (K1). K1 is then further encrypted using the merchant's public key-exchange key.

A capture token may also be included to make later capture processing (such as an end-of-day batch process) easier, and is only included if required by the acquirer. If included, it is encrypted with another new symmetric key (K2). K2 is used to encrypt the capture token and the additional information that the Payment Gateway would need to process a capture request when presented with the token. When all the applicable elements are in place, the encrypted **AuthRes** is sent to the merchant.

3. Upon receipt, the merchant verifies the Payment Gateway's certificates and then decrypts K1 using its private key-exchange key. The Payment Gateway's signature is verified by decrypting with the Payment Gateway's public signature key and comparing it to a hash of the authorization response.

The merchant will save the encrypted capture token (if present), and complete processing of the customer order by delivering the goods or services specified in the order.

3.6 PAYMENT CAPTURE

◆ ◆

After the customer's order is filled, the merchant wants to be paid. SET is flexible enough to allow either multiple capture sessions during the business day or one single batch of captures. It's a business decision made by the merchant.

1. In either case, the merchant creates the Capture Request (**CapReq**), including the final transaction amount, the transaction identifier from the **OI**, and other information. The **CapReq** is encrypted with a new symmetric key (K3) after being signed. K3 is then further encrypted using the Payment Gateway's public key-exchange key. The **CapReq** along with the capture token from the authorization response is sent to the Payment Gateway.

2. The Payment Gateway verifies the merchant's certificates and then decrypts K3 using the Payment Gateway's private key-exchange key. Using K3, the capture request can be decrypted.

If the capture token is present, this is where it would be decrypted using the Payment Gateway's private key-exchange key to come up with K2, which is used to decrypt the token itself. The information of the **CapReq** is then added to that of the token by the Payment Gateway to format a clearing request, which is sent to the Issuer via a payment card system that is outside the scope of SET.

A Capture response (**CapRes**) message is created by the Payment Gateway. **CapRes** includes a signed Payment Gateway signature certificate. The resultant **CapRes** is encrypted with a new symmetric key (K4), which is in turn encrypted with the merchant's public key-exchange key. The **CapRes** is then sent to the merchant.

3. The merchant first verifies the Payment Gateway's certificate and then finds K4 through use of its private key-exchange key. K4 is then used to decrypt the **CapRes**.

The Payment Gateway's signature is first verified, and **CapRes** is then stored by the merchant for any further reconciliation steps with the acquirer.

Chapter 4

• • •

THE SET PAYMENT CYCLE

Trotsky: "Have a seat, please." (To Mrs. Trotsky). "You see? We have very good employer-employee relations here." (To Ramon). "Ramon, did you bury this mountain climber's axe in my skull?"

—David Ives, *Variations on the Death of Trotsky*

In the last chapter, we considered how to get SET working, and how to use it to generate a payment flow. The functionality of SET is predicated on how it synchronizes all the parties to the payment flow, and in this section we will examine the details of the methods that SET uses to synchronize the flow. Assume for the following discussion that all certificates presented in a transaction have been validated.

The typical purchase protocol flow is schematically outlined Figure 4.1.

93

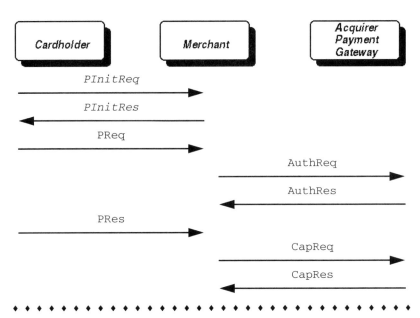

Figure 4.1. Italics indicate that the message pair is optional, and may be used for "wake-up" messages.

This transaction is minimal, with just enough requests and responses to get the transaction as a whole completed. These together constitute the "Big Eight" of SET messages, the basic level of messages that is supported by the SETREF code supplied on the CD-ROM that accompanies this book.

To compare this with a full-blown (all possible messages) transaction, the schematic of the complete case is shown in Figure 4.2. Other ordering of the requests and responses is also permissible.

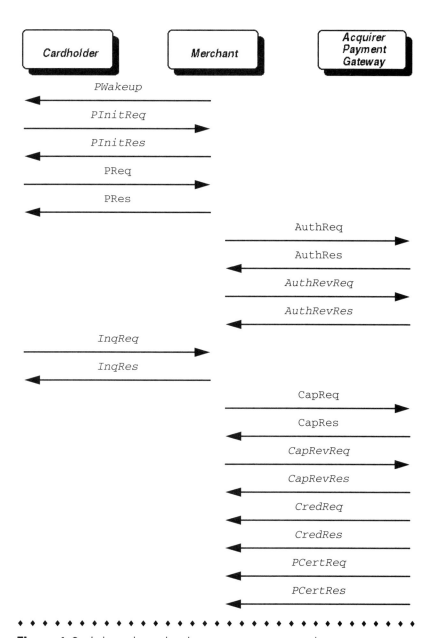

Figure 4.2. Italics indicate that the message pair is optional.

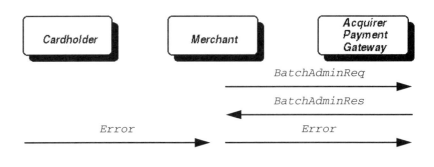

Figure 4.2. Italics indicate that the message pair is optional. (continued)

4.1 PAYMENT FLOW DATA STRUCTURES

Before considering the transaction states in detail, we must define a number of data structures used in the actual transactions. We'll be using SET's Protocol Data Unit (PDU) notation to define the structures and the logical sub-entities. The definitions of PDUs that follow will lay the groundwork for the logical relationships that will be developed later.

4.1.1 MessageWrapper

This is the top-level DER-encoded data structure in SET. It provides information without cryptography, and includes enough plaintext data to make necessary decisions based on which Message is selected. Note that the type of the message may be determined from the DER type-field of Message, which allows certain actions to be taken without decoding the Message.

PDU	Description
MessageWrapper	{MessageHeader, Message, [MWExtensions]}
MessageHeader	{Version, Revision, Date, [MessageIDs], [RRPID], SWIdent}
Version	Currently set to 1 for the first version
Revision	Integer to allow for backward compatibility
Date	Date/time of message
MessageIDs	{[LID-C], [LID-M], [XID]}
RRPID	Request/response pair ID for the cycle, statistically unique by definition
SWIdent	String data as software identifier
LID-C	Cardholder local ID
LID-M	Merchant local ID
XID	Globally unique ID, generated if no **PInitRes**
Message	<PInitReq, PInitRes
	PReq, Pres
	InqReq, InqRes
	AuthReq, AuthRes
	AuthRevReq, AuthRevRes
	CapReq, CapRes
	CapRevReq, CapRevRes
	CredReq, CredRes
	CredRevReq, CredRevRes
	PCertReq, PCertRes
	BatchAdminReq, BatchAdminRes
	CardCInitReq, CardCInitRes
	MeAqCInitReq, MeAqCInitRes
	RegFormReq, RegFormRes
	CertReq, CertRes
	CertInqReq, CertInqRes
	Error >
MWExtensions	Extensions to the MessageWrapper

MessageWrapper Composition

First obtain Message to be sent, enveloped with any needed certificates and CRLs in a PKCS #7 envelope data structure. Insert **Version**, **Date**, and **MessageID**. Insert **RRPID**. If a request, generate a random number and save for later comparison. If a response, copy from request. Insert **SWIdent** that identifies version and vendor of software. Insert Message as ASN.1/DER open type; then DER encode the entire structure and send.

Reception

Decode **MessageWrapper**, leaving **Message** alone. Verify correct version. Check for nonduplication, based on **RRPID**s (if present). If duplicate request and response has been sent, resend it. Discard duplicate messages. Decrypt and verify signatures. Collect any present certificates and CRLs. Decode message via DER; then verify type and **RRPID** (if applicable). Handle **Message** based on message type.

Note that the options given in this data structure consist of almost all the kinds of SET messages that can be used in any SET transaction.

4.1.2 TransIDs

This field provides the information that uniquely defines the transaction and the transaction characteristics the particular message possesses. This tags a transaction so that each of the parties has a convenient identifier. TransIDs are used to match up authorizations and captures, and are created during the first **PInit** or **PReq** Messages that initiate a transaction.

PDU	Description
TransIDs	{LID-C,[LID-M],XID,PReqDate, [PaySysID], Language}
LID-C	Local ID for use by cardholder and their system
LID-M	Local ID for use by merchant and their system
XID	Unique ID generated by merchant. If no **PInitRes**, **XID** is generated by cardholder.
PReqDate	If **PInit** exists, this is generated by merchant. If not, it is generated by cardholder. Start date of transaction.
PaySysID	Used by some card associations to label transaction from authorization onwards.
Language	Language for the whole transaction.

TransIDs Composition

Even though many fields in **TransIDs** are optional according to the formal syntax, they must be filled in if they are available. If a message for the current transaction is available, fill in all fields for which data is present. If a new transaction, generate all required fields.

Reception

If a stored transaction with the same **XID** is present, verify that stored data is consistent with message data. If no **XID** matches, store this message. If any additional fields in the message's **TransIDs** are present, store them. Verify **XID** and **PReqDate** are consistent with versions in **MessageWrapper**.

4.1.3 PI (Payment Instruction)

PI is a very important data structure in SET, for this is the way a card payment is initiated. Data is passed through the merchant to the acquirer in an encrypted form.

Cardholders create **PIUnsigned** and **PIDualSigned**, depending on whether or not the cardholder has a certificate. If signed, the **PI** source is authenticated as well as tested for data integrity. **AuthToken** is a **PI** variant created by the Payment Gateway to support split shipments or recurrent transactions that require additional authorization requests from the merchant.

PDU	Description
`PI`	`<PIUnsigned, PIDualSigned, AuthToken>`

PDU	Description
PIUnsigned	EXH(P, PI-OILink PANToken)
PI-OILink	see PIDualSigned
PANToken	{PAN, CardExpiry, EXNonce}
PAN	Primary Account Number; found on card
CardExpiry	Expiration date on card
EXNonce	New challenge data, foils dictionary attacks

PDU	Description
PIDualSigned	{PISignature, EX(P, PI-OILink, PANData)}
PISignature	SO(C,PI-TBS)
PI-TBS	{HPIData, HOIData}
HPIData	DD(PIData)
PIData	{PIHead, PANData)
HOIData	DD(OIData)
OIData	See 4.3.
PI-OILink	L(PIHead, OIData),
PIHead	PI Header information. See 4.3.
OIData	See 4.3.
PANData	{PAN, CardExpiry, PANSecret, EXNonce}
	PANSecret is shared among cardholder and acquirer and Cardholder CA.

PDU	Description
AuthToken	EncX(P1, P2, AuthTokenData, PANToken)
AuthTokenData	{TransIDs, PurchAmt, MerchantID, [AcqBackKeyData], [InstallRecurData], [RecurringCount], PrevAuthDateTime, TotalAuthAmount, AuthTokenOpaque}
	The first six required and optional fields are copied from a cardholder-produced PIHead.
RecurringCount	Number of recurring authorizations so far
PrevAuthDateTime	Date and time of merchant's last authorizations in this sequence
TotalAuthAmount	Total authorized by all authorizations using this **XID**
AuthTokenOpaque	Defined by Payment Gateway
InstallRecurData	{InstallRecurInd, [IRExtensions]}
InstallRecurInd	<InstallTotalTrans, Recurring>}
InstallTotalTrans	Specified by cardholder for a maximum of permitted Auths. Used for installment payments.
Recurring	{RecurringFrequency, RecurringExpiry}
RecurringFrequency	Minimum days between authorizations
RecurringExpiry	Date after which no authorizations can occur
IRExtensions	Extensions
PANToken	See PI Unsigned

For **AuthToken**, if this is the first authorization, either set **RecurringCount** to 1, or provide **RecurringFrequency** and **RecurringExpiry**. On later authorizations, either increment **RecurringCount** (check if less than **InstallTotalTrans**) or include Recurring information from previous authorization. Verify date against **RecurringFrequency** and **PrevAuthDateTime** and that **RecurringExpiry** is later than current date/time. Fill in remaining fields with **PI** data or data from previous **AuthToken**. Then envelope the data using **EncX** encapsulation with **PANToken** in the extra slot.

4.1.4 Response Data

The results of an authorization request are contained in this dataset, which is found in the **AuthResPayload** structure.

PDU	Description
ResponseData	{[AuthValCodes], [RespReason],[CardType], [AVSResult], [LogRefID]}
AuthValCodes	{ApprovalCode, [AuthCharInd], [Validation Code], [MarketSpecDataID]}
ApprovalCode	Returned on approved authorization
AuthCharInd	Request Custom Payment Service (CPS) processing
ValidationCode	Four byte alphanumeric. Only applies to authorization responses.
MarketSpecDataID	See 4.1.6.
RespReason	Optional indicator for decline
CardType	Enumerated code for type of card used
AVSResult	Address Verification Service response code
LogRefID	Used to match authorization to clearing

4.1.5 CapToken

This token is used by a Payment Gateway for the capture of a transaction. The information is provided by a gateway at the time of authorization. See below for further details of future implementation.

PDU	Description
CapToken	`<Enc(P1, P2, CapTokenData), EncX (P1,P2, CapTokenData, PANToken>` P1 (sender of signature certificates) and P2 (receiver, contains encryption certificates) are Payment Gateways. SET currently supports only the P1 = P2 case; i.e., that they are the same. In the future, P2 could be a second acquirer and would have to support authorization as well as capture to separate gateways.
CapTokenData	`{AuthRRPID, AuthAmt, TokenOpaque}`
AuthRRPID	RRPID from **AuthReq** or **AuthRevReq**
AuthAmt	Actual amount authorized, this may differ from the cardholder's **PurchAmt.**
TokenOpaque	Payment Gateway created and identifiable, used for clearing.
PANToken	See 4.1.3.

4.1.6 SaleDetail

SaleDetail can be generated as part of **CapReq** or **AuthReq** with CaptureNow = TRUE. If **BatchID** is omitted, the default batch is assumed.

PDU	Description
SaleDetail	`{[BatchID], [BatchSequenceNum] [PayRecurInd], [MerOrderNum] [AuthCharInd], [MarketSpecSaleData], [CommercialCardData], [OrderSummary], [CustomerReferenceNumber], [Customer ServicePhone], [OKtoPrintPhoneInd], [SaleExtensions]}`
BatchID	ID for merchant-acquirer accounting
BatchSequenceNum	Sequence number of this item in batch
PayRecurInd	Transaction type, one-byte alphanumeric
AuthCharInd	Requests **CPS** processing, from AuthResPayload
MarketSpecSaleData	`{[MarketSpecDataID], [MarketSpecCapData]}`
MarketSpecDataID	Identifies type of market-specific data In capture requests, this is the value returned in AuthResPayload. For sales requests, the field does not appear.

MarketSpecCapData	**<MarketAutoCap, MarketHotelCap, MarketTransportCap>**
	Market-specific capture data
MarketAutoCap	Car Rental charge description
MarketHotelCap	Hotel/lodging charge description
MarketTransportCap	Travel itinerary
CommercialCardData	**{[ChargeInfo], [MerchantLocation], [ShipFrom], [ShipTo], [ItemSeq]}**
ChargeInfo	**{[TotalFreightShippingAmount], [TotalDutyTariffAmount], [TotalNationalTaxAmount], [TotalLocalTaxAmount], [TotalOtherTaxAmount], [TotalTaxAmount], [MerchantTaxID], [SupplierTaxID], [SupplierReferenceNumber], [MerchantDutyTariffRef], [CustomerDutyTariffRef], [SummaryCommodityCode], [MerchantType]}**
	These fields are all self-evident.
Location	**{CountryCode** (ISO 3166 value), **[City], [StateProvince], [PostalCode]}**

(Note that the same pdu (**Location**) is used for **MerchantLocation**, **ShipFrom**, and **ShipTo**.)

ItemSeq	**{Item +}**
	*1 to 999 item-level detail records; see end of section for description.**
OrderSummary	Description of order
CustomerReferenceNumber	Cardholder assigned reference #
Customer ServicePhone	Merchant's customer service phone #
OKtoPrintPhoneInd	Boolean if OK to print above number, default false

SaleExtensions   Extensions
   **breakout from above PDU:*
Item   **{[ItemOrderDate], Quantity, [UnitOfMeasureCode], Descriptor, [CommodityCode], [ProductCode], [TypeOfSupply], [UnitCost], [NetCost], [DiscountInd], [DiscountAmount], [FreightShippingAmount], [DutyTariffAmount], [NationalTaxAmount], [NationalTaxRate], [NationalTaxType], [LocalTaxAmount], [OtherTaxAmount], ItemTotalCost}**
                     (Each field value is self-explanatory.)

4.1.7 MerTermIDs

MerTermIDs collects the data describing the location of the transaction. It also provides for the identification of the merchant's payment software.

PDU	Description
MerTermIDs	{MerchantID, [TerminalID], [AgentNum], [ChainNum], [StoreNum]}
MerchantID	Copied from Merchant signature certificate implicit in **PInitRes**, or supplied by Merchant
TerminalID	Supplied by Merchant at **AuthReq** time
AgentNum	Supplied by Merchant at **AuthReq** time,6 digit
ChainNum	Supplied by Merchant at **AuthReq** time,6 digit
StoreNum	Supplied by Merchant at **AuthReq** time,4 digit

4.1.8 RRTags

RRTags carries message-identification data. The RRPID serves as a unique identifier for a message.

PDU	Description
RRTags	{RRPID, MerTermIDs, Date}
RRPID	Fresh request/response pair ID for this cycle
MerTermIDs	See 4.1.7.
Date	Current Date

RRPID is generated randomly, and must be globally and statistically unique.

4.1.9 Capture Reversal/Credit Data Structures

Since Capture Reversal and Credit messages are syntactically identical, they share common data structures. They are described here for later reference.

PDU	Description
CapRevOrCredReqData	{**CapRevOrCredRRTags**, [**MThumbs**], **CapRevOrCredReqItemSeq**, [**CRvRqExtensions**]}
CapRevOrCredRRTags	**RRTags** with fresh RRPID for this pair and date
MThumbs	Thumbs of PGwy certificates, CA CRLs, and **BrandCRLIdentifiers** currently held by Merchant cache.
CapRevOrCredReqItemSeq	{**CapRevOrCredReqItem** +}
CapRevOrCredReqItem	{[**TransIDs**], **AuthRRPID CapPayload**, [New Batch ID] **CapRevOrCredReqDate**, [**CapRevOrCredReqAmt**], **NewAccountInd**, [**CRvRqItemExtensions**]}
TransIDs	Copied from prior **AuthRes**
CapPayload	{**CapDate, CapReqAmt**, [**AuthReqItem**] [**AuthResPayload**], [**SaleDetail**], [**CPayExtensions**]}
Cap Date	Date of capture
CapReqAmt	Capture amount requested by Merchant
AuthReqItem	Required if **CapToken** not present
AuthResPayload	Required if **CapToken** not present
SaleDetail	See 4.1.6.
CPayExtensions	Extensions
NewBatchID	Used to re-open a batch that has been closed
CapRevOrCredReqDate	Date request submitted
CapRevOrCredReqAmt	In the case of credit requests, the amount of credit requested, which may differ from **AuthAmt** in **CapToken** and **CapReqAmt** in **CapPayload.** In the case of capture reversals, the amount of the original capture being reversed.
NewAccountInd	Indicates that a new account number is specified in **PANToken**; when this field is set, the new account number overrides the account information in the **CaptureToken** or authorization data retained by the Acquirer. Use of this field is subject to Brand and Acquirer policies.
CRvRqItemExtensions	Extensions
CRvRqExtensions	Extensions

PDU	Description
CapRevOrCredResData	{**CapRevOrCredRRTags**, [**BrandCRLIdentifier**], [**PEThumb**], [**BatchStatusSeq**], **CapRevOrCredResItemSeq**, [**CRvRsExtensions**]}
CapRevOrCredRRTags	Copied from corresponding **CapRevOrCredReqData**
BrandCRLIdentifier	List of current CRLs for all CAs under a brand CA
PEThumbs	If **CapRevOrCredReq.MThumbs** indicates merchant needs new acquirer certs, the thumbprints are found here. The actual **CERT-GKs** are carried in the PKCS#7 data block.

```
BatchStatusSeq              {BatchStatus +}
   BatchStatus                 See 4.6.
CapRevOrCredResItemSeq      {CapRevOrCredResItem +}
   CapRevOrCredResItem          {TransIDs, AuthRRPID, CapRevOrCredResPayload}
      TransIDs                     Copied from corresponding
                                   CapRevOrCredReqData.AuthReqData.AuthTags
      AuthRRPID                 RRPID from corresponding AuthReq or AuthRevReq
      CapRevOrCredResPayload    {CapRevOrCredCode, CapRevOrCredActualAmt,
                                 [BatchID], [BatchSequenceNum],
                                 [CRvRsPayExtensions]}
         CapRevOrCredCode          Enumerated code indicating the capture
                                   reversal or credit status (0=success)
         CapRevOrCredActualAmt  Actual amount
         BatchID                   Batch through which payment is being captured
                                   and settled
         BatchSequenceNum          Sequence number of item in batch
         CRvRsPayExtensions        Extensions
CRvRsExtensions           Extensions
```

4.2 Purchase Initialization

• •

There are two messages usually involved here, although the
messages may be omitted with data provided by offline methods
(such as CD-ROM). If done offline, the challenges will be
omitted.

PDU	Description
PInitReq	{RRPID, Language, LID-C, [LID-M], Chall-C, BrandID, BIN, [Thumbs],[PIRqExtensions]}
RRPID	Statistically unique response/request ID
Language	Language requested by cardholder for this transaction
LID-C	LocalID, a label used by the Cardholder system
LID-M	Same for merchant, copied from any kickoff messages if they exist
Chall-C	Cardholder's signature challenge to merchant
BrandID	Cardholder's chosen brand, "brand[:product]" format
BIN	Bank identification number: the first 6 digits of the card PAN
Thumbs	List of Certificate, CRL, and BrandCRLidentifier Thumbs in cardholder cache
PIRqExtensions	Extensions

PInitReq Composition

Generate random RRPID which identifies response message to request. Insert **Language** and **LID-C**. Generate random **Chall-C**; save to verify correctness in **PInitRes**. From shopping software insert **BrandID**. Optionally, add Thumbs including Root certificate. Invoke Compose Message Wrapper and send.

The Merchant then receives the message from ReceiveMessageWrapper, and saves the **Language**, **BrandID**, and **LID-C** in a database. Optionally, **LID-M** is generated and stored as well. Then generate **PInitRes**.

PDU	Description
PInitRes	S(M,PInitResData)
PInitResData	{TransIDs,RRPID, Chall-C, Chall-M, [BrandCRLIdentifier], PEThumb,[Thumbs], [PIRSExtensions]}
RRPID	Response/request ID
Chall-C	From **PInitReq**
Chall-M	Merchant-generated challenge
BrandCRLIdentifier	List of current CRLs for all CAs associated with a brand
PEThumb	Payment Gateway certificates are sent as signeddata. This thumbprint tells cardholder to use the Certificate whose thumbprint matches this one.
Thumbs	Other thumbprints copied from **PInitReq**
PIRsExtensions	Extensions

PInitRes Composition

The merchant first inserts **TransIDs** into message, along with optional **LID-M**. **Chall-M** is generated and inserted along with **Chall-C**. Current date and time inserted as **PReqDate**. If Gateway Encryption Certificate **CERT-GK**'s thumb has not been received in **PInitReq**, then insert **CERT-GK** into the message signature. Also, send in the signature CA certs and CRL for any Thumbs not received. Include **PEThumb**. Include **BrandCRLIdentifier** if Thumb not received or not current. Include all Thumbs from cardholder into signed portion. Sign and invoke Compose Message Wrapper.

Reception

Cardholder verifies that Thumbs are equivalent to those sent, and that **Chall-C** matches. **TransIDs**, **Chall-M**, and **PReqDate** are evaluated and stored. Use **PEThumb** to match encryption certificate to use for **PReq**.

4.3 PURCHASE ORDER REQUEST/RESPONSE

This pairing is the actual payment pair between cardholder and merchant, and involves the most complex messages (**PReq**) in the SET protocol. **PReq** consists of an Order Instruction (**OI**) directed to the merchant, and a Payment Instruction (**PI**) tunneled through the merchant for the Payment Gateway.

As we noted in 4.1.3, the salted hash of **OD** (Order Description)—gotten by the merchant outside the SET protocol—and **PurchAmt**—also obtained by the merchant outside SET—is included in the **PI**. This hash may also be represented by **H({OD, PurchAmt, ODSALT, [InstallRecurData], [ODExtensions]})**.

Some cardholders will not present certificates for verification. Messages from these cardholders are not signed; instead, the **PIHead** is linked to the **OIData**.

PDU	Description
PReq	<PReqDualSigned, PReqUnsigned>

PDU	Description

PReqDualSigned   EncDXL2(C, P, OIData, PIHead, PANData)
(This can also be expressed as {PIDualSigned, OIDualSigned}.)

PIDualSigned	See 4.1.3.
OIDualSigned	L(OIData, PIData)
OIData	{TransIDs, RRPID, Chall-C, HOD, ODSalt, [Chall-M], BrandID, BIN, [ODExtOIDs], [OIExtensions]}
	All except **ODSalt** and **HOD** (see below) are copied from **PInitReq** and **PInitRes**
	Else they are created by cardholder.
PIData	{PIHead, PANData}
	PANData used only in DualSigned
	PANToken used in unsigned
	See 4.1.3 for definitions of PanData and PanToken.
PIHead	{TransIDs, Inputs, MerchantID, [InstallRecurInd], TransStain, SWIdent, [AcqBackKeyData], [PIExtensions]}
TransIDs	Copied from **PInitRes** else embedded **XID** generated by cardholder
Inputs	{HOD, PurchAmt}
HOD	H({OD, PurchAmt, ODSalt, [InstallRecurData], [ODExtensions]})
OD	Order Description non-SET information between cardholder and merchant
PurchAmt	Non-SET information between cardholder and merchant
ODSalt	Cardholder-generated nonce, prevents dictionary attacks
InstallRecurData	See 4.1.3.
MerchantID	From merchant signature cert
InstallRecurInd	Boolean
TransStain	HMAC(XID, CardSecret)
XID	Software-generated random
CardSecret	Cardholder's secret value sent to CA as nonce and retained
SWIdent	String data identifying vendor and version of software initiating the request
AcqBackKeyData	{AcqBackAlg, AcqBackKey}
AcqBackAlg	From encryption ID in PG cert. Default is CMDF
AcqBackKey	Key for **AcqCardMsg**
PIExtensions	PI extensions

PDU	Description

PReqUnsigned	{PIUnsigned, OIUnsigned}
PIUnsigned	See 4.1.3.
OIUnsigned	L(OIData, PIDataUnsigned)
PIDataUnsigned	{PIHead, PANToken}
PIHead	See previous PDU
PANToken	See 4.1.3.

PReq Composition

PurchAmt and **OD** come from cardholder's shopping phase. If the **PInit** pair were exchanged, **TransIDs** is taken from **PInitRes**. If not, cardholder generates **PReqDate**, **LID-C**, and **XID**. (**LID-M** is included only if received from merchant.) Generate random **RRPID** and store to verify merchant reply. If **PInitRes** exists, insert **Chall-C**; otherwise randomly generate it. Generate random **ODSalt**. Generate **HOD** as digested data of **OD**, **PurchAmt**, **ODSalt**, and **InstallRecurInd**. Insert all into **OIData**. Get **Chall-M** if **PInit** pair exchanged. Include **BrandID** unless already exchanged.

Construct **PIHead** and **PANData**. If the acquirer's certificate will allow only signed cardholder orders, construct **PReqDualSigned**. If not, construct **PReqUnsigned**. Note that a cardholder may possess a certificate, yet send a **PReqUnsigned** if the acquirer's certificate allows it.

For **PReqDualSigned**, construct **PISignature** by storing the digested data of **PIData** as **HPIData**, and **HOIData** from the digested data of **OIData**. The **SO** operator on **HPIData** and **HOIData** will get the signature without the hashes. Link **PIHead** and **OIData** by appending the digested data of **OIData** to **PIHead**. Perform **EX** encryption using PG's public key, including the linkage just computed as ordinary encryption and the **PANData** in the extra slot. Form **PIDualSigned** by concatenating **PISignature** and the EX encrypted data just created. Construct **OIDualSigned** as the linkage of **OIData** and **PIData** by appending digested data of **PIData** to **PIHead**. **PReqDual Signed** is the concatenation of **PIDualSigned** with **OIDualSigned**. Invoke **ComposeMessageWrapper** and send to merchant.

For **PReqUnsigned**, link **PIHead** to **OIData** by appending **OIData**'s digested data. Invoke **ComposeMessageWrapper**. Perform **EX** encryption using PG's public key, including the linkage just computed as ordinary encryption and the **PANToken** in the extra slot. The result is **PIUnsigned**. Form **PiDataUnsigned** by sequencing **PANToken** after **PIHead**. **OIUnsigned** links **OIData** and **PIDataUnsigned** and is formed by appending the digested data of **PIDataUnsigned** to **OIData**. **PReqUnsigned** is constructed as a sequence of **PIUnsigned** and **OIUnsigned**. Send to merchant.

Reception

Merchant processes envelope, and verifies hash or merchant's part of dual signature. If nonsignatured, check **BrandID** is consistent with noncertificate operation. Check for **TransIDs** in database. Verify **Chall-M** if **PInit** pair was used. Store **Chall-C** and other variables for use in **PRes**. Verify **HOD** against newly generated hash of **OD**, **PurchAmt**, and **ODSalt**. Generate **AuthReq** for transmission to the acquirer's Payment Gateway. Notice that a time discontinuity may occur at this point between the receipt of **PReq** and generation of the Purchase Response due to the necessary **AuthReq** processing.

PDU	Description
PRes `S(M,PResData)`	
PResData `{TransIDs, RRPID,Chall-C, [BrandCRLIdentifier],` PResPayloadSeq}	
TransIDs	Copied from **PReq**
RRPID	ID for response/request pair
Chall-C	Copied from **PinitReq**
BrandCRLIdentifier	List of current CRLs for all CAs of a Brand
PResPayloadSeq	`{PresPayload+}`
PResPayload	`{CompletionCode, [Results], [PRsExtensions]}`
CompletionCode	Indicates completion status
Results	`{[AcqCardMsg], AuthStatus, [CapStatus],` `[CredStatusSeq]}`
AcqCardMsg	Copied from **AuthRes**
AuthStatus	`{AuthDate, AuthCode, AuthRatio, [CurrConv]}`
AuthDate	Date of authorization
AuthCode	Enumerated authorization code
AuthRatio	**AuthAmt / PurchAmt**
AuthAmt	See **CapToken**
PurchAmt	See **OIData**

```
        CurrConv              {CurrConvRate, CardCurr} Copied from
                                 AuthResPayload
     CapStatus               {CapDate, CapCode, CapRatio}
       CapDate                  Date of capture
       CapCode                  Enumerated capture code (success = 0)
       CapRatio                 CapReqAmt / PurchAmt
          CapReqAmt               See CapPayload
          PurchAmt                See OIData
     CredStatusSeq           {CreditStatus +} Data only appears if a
                                corresponding CreditReq has been performed
       CreditStatus            {CreditDate, CreditCode,    CreditRatio}
          CreditDate             Date of credit (from
                                 CapRevOrCredReqData)
          CreditCode             Code for status (from
                                 CapRevOrCredRedPayload)
          CreditRatio            CapRevorCredReqAmt / Purch Amt
   PRsExtensions           Extensions to PResPayload
```

PRes Composition

Insert **TransIDs**. Copy **Chall-C** from **PReq**. Insert current
BrandCRLIdentifier. Set **CompletionCode** based on transaction
status. If authorization is complete, insert **AuthCode** from
AuthRes and compute **AuthRatio**. Insert **AcqCardMsg** if received
from Payment Gateway. If Capture complete, insert **CapCode** and
compute **CapRatio**. Sign all data and invoke
ComposeMessageWrapper.

Reception

First, match **Chall-C** in the message against the one that was sent.
Store **BrandCRLIdentifier** and verify that CRLs listed are in the
cache. If not, signature may not be valid; go to error-trapping and
handling. If **CompletionCode** indicates capture is complete, then
report **CapCode** and the quantity (Purchase Amount*CapRatio)
to Cardholder; otherwise interpret and report **CompletionCode**.
If **AcqCardMsg** is present, decrypt and present.

4.4 INQUIRY REQUEST/RESPONSE

Using this message pair, a cardholder can inquire from a merchant the status of a transaction. This is an optional message pair that may be sent at any time after a **PInitRes** has been received or a **PReq** has been sent. Multiple inquiries may also be sent for the same transaction.

PDU	Description
InqReq	<InqReqSigned, InqReqData>
InqReqSigned	S(C, InqReqData)
InqReqData	{TransIDs, RRPID Chall-C2, [InqReqExtensions])
Chall-C2	New challenge generated to merchant's signature

InqReq Composition

Generate **Chall-C2** and combine with **TransIDs**. If a certificate is available, sign concatenation. Invoke **ComposeMessageWrapper**.

Reception/**InqRes** composition. Merchant identifies certificate modality (present or not present). Looks up transaction based on **TransIDs**. Verifies identity in Certificates (if present). Sets **CompletionCode** based on processing stage. If authorization is complete, inserts **AuthCode** and **AuthRatio** from **AuthRes** into message as well as **AcqCardMsg**, if any. If capture is complete, inserts **CapCode** from **CapRes** as well as **CapRatio** into message.

InqRes

Identical in form to PRes; see 4.3.

Reception by Cardholder

Match **Chall-C2** against sent value. If **CompletionCode** indicates completed capture, report **CapCode** and capture amount. If **CompletionCode** shows authorization complete, report **AuthCode** and authorization amount. If neither, report completion status. If **AcqCardMsg** present, decrypt and present.

4.5 GATEWAY CERTIFICATE REQUEST/RESPONSE

◆ ◆

We now go into messages between the merchant and the acquirer's Payment Gateway. The first message pair that must transpire is the **PCertReq/Res** pair. This provides a mechanism to retrieve the Gateway encryption certificates used by the merchant and cardholder. Without this initialization, the merchant and the Gateway would not agree on how to encrypt messages sent between them.

PDU	Description
PCertReq	S(M,{PCertReqData, [PCRqExtensions]})
PCertReqData	{PCertRRTags, [Mthumbs], BrandAndBINSeq}
PCertRRTags	RRTags (Request/response tags include fresh **RRPID** for this cert request, merchant-supplied **MerTermIDs**, and the current date. See 4.1.8.)
MThumbs	Thumbprints (hashes of acquirer certs in cache of Merchant)
BrandAndBINSeq	{BrandAndBIN +} Merchant requested PG certs for these brands if not in **MThumbs**
BrandAndBIN	{BrandID, [BIN]}
BIN	Bank ID No.: first six digits of **PAN**
PCRqExtensions	Extensions

PCertReq Composition

If first message of day (or if first since new private keys received), include the certs as well as the certs in the chain for these new keys. Insert **RRTags** as **PCertRRTags**. Optionally, include **MThumbs** of all certs for this Gateway, for **CRLs**, and for the **BrandCRLIdentifier**. Include **BrandIDs** for which certs are needed. Sign all and invoke Compose MessageWrapper.

Acquirer reception and **PCertRes** composition. Copy **PCertTags** from **PCertReq** into **PCertRes**. Insert corresponding Gateway Encryption Certificate (**CERT-GK**) for **BrandIDs** requested. Include **BrandCRLIdentifier** if needed. Include in **PCertResThumbs**, thumbprints for certs and CRLs being sent in PKCS#7 header.

PDU	Description
`PCertRes` `S(P, PCertResTBS, [PCRsExtensions])`	
`PCertResTBS` `{PCertRRTags, [BrandCRLIdentifierSeq], PCertResItemSeq}`	
`PCertRRTags` `From PCertReq`	
`BrandCRLIdentifierSeq` `{BrandCRLIdentifier +}`	
`PCertResItemSeq` `{PCertResItem +}`	
`PCertResItem` `{PCertCode, [CertThumb]}`	
`PCertCode`	`Enumerated results (0= success,1= unspecified failure, 2 = brand not supported, 3 = unknown BIN)`
`CertThumb`	`Thumb of returned certificate`
`PCRsExtensions` `Extensions`	

Reception

Merchant extracts certificates and matches **CertThumb** to its **PCertCode**.

4.6 AUTHORIZATION REQUEST/RESPONSE

◆ ◆

This set of messages between merchant and Payment Gateway (**AuthReq** and **AuthRes**) enables the merchant to authorize the **PReq** submitted by the cardholder. Since the **PI** in the **PReq** contains the necessary payment card data, the Payment Gateway can use the existing financial networks (which are outside of the SET universe) to complete the authorization process.

PDU	Description

```
AuthReq            EncB (M,P, AuthReqData, PI)
This is equivalent to:
{Enc(M, P, L(AuthReqData, PI)), PI}
   AuthReqData       {AuthReqItem,[MThumbs], CaptureNow, [SaleDetail]}
      AuthReqItem       {AuthTags, [CheckDigests], AuthReqPayload}
         AuthTags          {AuthRRTags, TransIDs, [AuthRetNum]}
            AuthRRTags        Request/response tags. See 4.1.8.
            TransIDs          Copied from OIData
            AuthRetNum        ID for financial system
         CheckDigests      {HOIData), HOD2} (Omitted if PI is AuthToken)
            HOIData           DD(OIData) merchant hash of OIData, compared with
                              cardholder hash of OIData tunneled in PI
            HOD2              DD(HODInput)
               HODInput          H({OD,PurchAmt,ODSalt, [InstallRecurInd]})
                                 From OIData Hash done by merchant, used by
                                 acquirer to verify merchant receipt of OD
                                 and PurchAmt
         AuthReqPayload    {SubsequentAuthInd, AuthReqAmt, [AVSData],
                           [SpecialProcessing], [CardSuspect],
                           [RequestCardTypeInd], [InstallRecurData],
                           [MarketSpecAuthData], MerchData, [ARqExtensions]}
            SubsequentAuthInd  Boolean indicating multiple Auths
            AuthReqAmt         The amount requested
            AVSData            Billing address; not in SET universe
            SpecialProcessing  Enumerated field indicating the type of special
                               processing requested.
            CardSuspect        Indicates merchant questions
                               Cardholder suitability
            RequestCardTypeInd Type of card to be returned in response
            InstallRecurData   See 4.1.3.
            MarketSpecAuthData <MarketAutoAuth, MarketHotelAuth,
                               MarketTransportationAuth>
               MarketAutoAuth     {Duration}
                  Duration           1 to 99
               MarketHotelAuth    {Duration, Prestige}
                  Prestige           Levels are defined by Brand.
               MarketTransportationAuth   Not currently used
               MerchData          {[MerchCatCode], [MerchGroup]}
                  MerchCatCode       Four-byte descriptor code assigned by ANSI
                                     X9.10 to merchant
                  MerchGroup         Enumerated code assigned to merchant
            ARqExtensions      Extensions
```

MThumbs	Thumbs of PG certs,CRLs and **BrandCRLIdentifiers** held in merchant's cache
Capture Now	Boolean TRUE implies capture, else authorize only.
Sale Detail	See 4.1.6.
PI	See 4.1.3.

AuthReq Generation by Merchant

Add new key and certificates received since last gateway message. Put current date/time into **AuthReqDate**. Hash **OD**, **PurchAmt**, **ODSalt** for inclusion. Construct **RRTags**. Compute hash of **OIData**. Compute hash of **PIData** if this **AuthReq** is not based on an **AuthToken**. Compute **Mthumbs**. Construct **AuthReqPayload** based on circumstances. If **CaptureNow** = TRUE, then generate **SaleDetail**. Invoke EncB using **PI** from **PReq** in the baggage, and send.

Reception by Gateway

Decrypt **PI**. If **AuthToken** present, verify that this **AuthToken** has not been previously processed. Verify that **PrevAuthDateTime** is within acquirer's policy range; then reset to current time. Store remaining **AuthToken** variables, and begin processing at **installRecurInd** step. If **PI** is unsigned; make sure that card association rules do not require use of cardholder certificates. Hashes of **OIData** from cardholder and merchant match, also verify **PIHead** and **OIData** linkages. Verify **TransIDs** from merchant and cardholder match. Check if **AuthReqData.CheckDigests.HOD2** = **PIHead.Inputs.HOD**. Verify that **SWIdent** is valid.

If **InstallRecurData** is present, verify date is before **RecurringExpiry**. Store any **AckBackInfo** and ensure encryption key is encrypted in local key. Compare **PIHead.TransIDs** to **AuthReqData.AuthTags.TransIDs**.

PDU	Description
AuthRes	< Enc(P, M, AuthResData, AuthResBaggage), EncBX(P, M, AuthResData, AuthResBaggage, PANToken) >
AuthResData	{AuthTags, [BrandCRLIdentifier], [GEThumb], AuthResPayload}
AuthTags	Copied from corresponding **AuthReq** with **AuthRetNum** filled in
BrandCRLIdentifier	List of current CRLs for all CAs associated with a brand
PEThumb	Cert thumbprints for **CERT-GK**s carried in PKCS#7 data block. **AuthReq.MThumbs** indicates need for certs.
AuthResPayload	{AuthHeader, [CapResPayload], [ARsExtensions]}
AuthHeader	{AuthAmt, AuthCode, ResponseData, [BatchStatus], [CurrConv]}
AuthAmt	Actual amount authorized, used to construct **Results** in **PResPayload**
AuthCode	Enumerated code indicating outcome of authorization processing
ResponseData	See 4.1.4.
BatchStatus	{OpenDateTime, [ClosedWhen], BatchDetails, [BatchExtensions]}
OpenDateTime	Date/time batch was opened
ClosedWhen	{CloseStatus, CloseDateTime}
CloseStatus	Enumerated status of batch close
CloseDateTime	Date/time of close
BatchDetails	{BatchTotals, [BrandBatchDetailsSeq]}
BatchTotals	{TransactionCountCredit, TransactionTotalAmtCredit, TransactionCountDebit, TransactionTotalAmtDebit, [BatchTotalExtensions]}
TransactionCountCredit	# of credits
TransactionTotalAmtCredit	Credit amount
TransactionCountDebit	# of debits
TransactionTotalAmtDebit	Debit amount
BatchTotalExtensions	Message extensions
BrandBatchDetailsSeq	{BrandBatchDetails +}
BrandBatchDetails	{BrandID, BatchTotals}
BrandID	The brand totaled
BatchTotals	Totals
CurrConv	{CurrConvRate, CardCurr}
CurrConvRate	Value with which to multiply **AuthReqAmt** to provide an amount in the cardholder's currency
CardCurr	ISO 4217 country code of cardholder's currency
CapResPayload	{CapCode, CapAmt, [BatchID], [BatchSequenceNum], [CRsPayExtensions]}
CapCode	Completion status of capture item
CapAmt	Actual amount captured by acquirer
BatchID	Merchant-acquirer ID for this settlement batch

```
        BatchSequenceNum      Sequence of this item in batch
        CRsPayExtensions      Contains additional business data
      ARsExtensions         Extensions
   AuthResBaggage      {[CapToken], [AcqCardMsg], [AuthToken]}
      CapToken             See 4.1.5.
      AcqCardMsg           If cardholder has sent AcqBackKeyData, Payment Gateway
                           sends this to merchant, who is required to copy it to
                           PRes and InqRes.
      AuthToken            See 4.1.3.
   PANToken            {PAN, CardExpiry, EXNonce}
      PAN                  Primary Account Number
      CardExpiry           Six-digit expire date (YYYYMM)
      EXNonce              A fresh nonce
```

Gateway Composes AuthRes

AuthDate is derived from current date/time. Copy **AuthTags** from **AuthReq**; update with **AuthRetNum** received in authorization data from payment card financial network. Insert current **BrandCRLIdentifier**, if needed. If **MThumbs** indicates that the merchant needs a new **Cert-GK** to encrypt information to the Payment Gateway, then insert a **Cert-GK** in the PKCS#7 envelope. Insert **PEThumb** into **AuthResData** because **Cert-GK** is not protected by a signature. Fill in **AuthCode**, **AuthAmt**, **RespCode,** and **ResponseData**. Include **CaptureControl** and **CurrConv** if needed. Include **PANToken** if merchant certificate indicates this is needed. Construct optional **AuthResBaggage**. If **PANToken** is included, invoke EncBX encapsulation with **PANToken** in the extra slot, **AuthResBaggage** in the baggage slot, and the rest in the ordinary slot. If not, do the same minus **PANToken**. Send to merchant via **ComposeMessageWrapper**.

Merchant Receives AuthRes

If present, store **BrandCRLIdentifier** with CRLs. Match **PEThumb** encryption (if present) with gateway encryption certs. Process **RespCode** to determine authorization outcome. Save **AuthCode** for successful outcome. If present, save **ValidationCode** and **RespReason**. Verify **AVSResult**, if present, and save **LogRefID**. Process **CaptureControl** if a batch was specified in original request. Save **CurrConv** if present. If capture requested, process **SaleResPayload** by saving **CapCode**, **CapAmt**, and **SettleAmt**. Process **AuthResBaggage** by saving **CapToken**, **AcqCardMsg**, and **AuthToken**.

If **PANToken** is present, encrypt under local key and save. Proceed with Capture and/or Purchase Response, depending on the results of authorization, and the merchant's time frame for return of purchase response.

4.7 CAPTURE REQUEST/RESPONSE

The capture mechanism provides the completion for payment of previously authorized transactions between merchant and Payment Gateway. A single capture message may be made up of multiple capture tokens associated with distinct transactions and their previous authorizations. There are other non-SET methods of capture, but they are outside the scope of this discussion. In the current version of SET, capture must be performed with the same Payment Gateway that authorized the transaction, although this may change in future revisions of the SET protocols.

PDU	Description
CapReq	< EncB (M, P, CapReqData, CapTokSeq), EncBX(M, P, CapReqData, CapTokSeq, PANToken)>

Note: **CapTokSeq** is external "baggage" to avoid superencryption. If **PANToken** is included, it must be a single item due to space limitations in the extra (OAEP) slot of **EncBX**. In turn, in this case, there must be a single **CapItem** and a single **CapToken** in **CapTokSeq** that must correspond to the single **PANToken**.

CapReqData	{CapRRTags, [MThumbs], CapItemSeq, [CRqExtensions]} }
CapRRTags	RRTags
MThumbs	Thumbs of PGcertificates, CA CRLs, and BrandCRLIdentifiers currently held by merchant's software in cache
CapItemSeq	{CapItem +}
CapItem	{TransIDs, [AuthRRPID] CapPayload}

TransIDs	From corresponding **AuthReq**
AuthRRPID	The **RRPID** from corresponding authorization
CapPayload	{CapDate, CapReqAmt, [AuthReqItem], [AuthResPayload], [SaleDetail], [CPayExtensions]}
CapDate	Date of capture
CapReqAmt	Amount requested by merchant
AuthReqItem	See 4.6; required if corresponding **CapToken** not present
AuthResPayload	See 4.6.
SaleDetail	See 4.1.6, required for **CapReq**; optional for other cases
CPayExtensions	Extensions
CRqExtensions	Extensions
PANToken	Must correspond (If present) to the **CapItem** in CapReqData.CapSeq

PDU	Description
CapRes	Enc (P, M, CapResData)
CapResData	{CapRRTags, [BrandCRLIdentifier], [PEThumb], [BatchStatusSeq], CapResItemSeq, [CRsExtensions]}
CapRRTags	From **CapReq**
BrandCRLIdentifier	List of current CRLs for all CAs under a brand CA
PEThumb	If **CapReqData.MThumbs** indicates merchant needs new acquirer certs, here are their thumbprints
BatchStatusSeq	{BatchStatus +}
BatchStatus	See 4.6.
CapResItemSeq	{CapResItem +}
CapResItem	{TransIDs, [AuthRRPID], CapResPayload}
TransIDs	From corresponding **CapReq**
AuthRRPID	**RRPID** from authorization
CapResPayload	{CapCode, CapAmt, [BatchID], [BatchSequenceNum], [CRsPayExtensions]}
CapCode	Completion status of capture item
CapAmt	See **CapToken**.
BatchID	ID of this batch
BatchSequenceNum	Seq # of this item
CRsPayExtensions	Extensions
CRsExtensions	Extensions

PG Reception of CapReq and Sending of CapRes

Process the capture and create **CapResItem** with the amount from the capture processing and success/failure of the item in the associated **CapCode**. Include the **BrandCRLIdentifier** held by PG. Include in **PEThumbs** thumbprints for all Certificates and

CRLs being sent in PKCS-7 header as a result of absent thumbprints in request.

Merchant Receives CapRes

For each **CapResItem**, check the **CapCode** to determine result and record successful captured amounts. If not already sent, send Purchase Response.

4.8 AUTHORIZATION REVERSAL

◆ ◆

AuthRevReq/AuthRevRes message pair is used only to reduce or cancel a previously granted authorization. Thus it is a communication between the merchant and the acquirer's Payment Gateway. It must be sent before capture has been requested. It may be sent multiple times, and so contains a unique challenge and the **TransIDs** of the **PI** to reverse.

PDU	Description
AuthRevReq EncB	(M, P, AuthRevReqData, AuthRevReqBaggage)
AuthRevReqData	{AuthRevTags, [MThumbs], [AuthReqData], [AuthResPayload], [AuthNewAmt], [ARvRqExtensions]}
AuthRevTags	{AuthRevRRTags, [AuthRetNum]}
MThumbs	Thumbs of PG certificates, CA CRLs, and **BrandCRLIdentifiers** currently held by merchant
AuthReqData	Copied from prior, corresponding **AuthReq. TransIDs** are present. Also contains **SubsequentAuthInd**, allowing reversal of recurring Auths. **AuthReqData** is not required in message if **CapToken** generated by Payment Gateway contains all relevant data.
AuthResPayload	Copied from prior corresponding **AuthRes.**
AuthNewAmt	New Auth amount requested must be less than original authorized amount. If zero, the authorization is completely removed. If zero, **CapToken** is always omitted.
ARvRqExtensions	Extensions
AuthRevReqBaggage	{PI, [CapToken]}

```
PI                      Copied from prior, corresponding AuthReq
CapToken                Copied from prior, corresponding AuthRes.
```

Merchant Composes AuthRevReq

Assign current date to **AuthRevDate** and generate **RRTags**.
Establish that the new authorized amount requested,
AuthNewAmt, is less than current authorized amount. Include
MThumbs (omitting those from **AuthReqData**). Copy
AuthReqData saved from earlier **AuthReq** message. Copy
AuthResPayload from previous **AuthRes**. (Payload may be
omitted if data contained in the capture token includes this
data.) Assemble **AuthRevReqData**, omitting **AuthNewAmt** if it is
not greater than zero. Include capture token (if available) and **PI**
in the baggage. Encapsulate and send to Payment Gateway.

PG Receives AuthRevReq

Retrieve transaction record based on **TransIDs**, and store
AuthRevRRPID for response. Verify **AuthRevReqData**. Perform
reversal using payment card financial network.

PDU	Description
AuthRevRes	`<EncB(P, M, AuthRevResData,[AuthRevResBaggage]),`
	`Enc(P, M, AuthRevResData) >`
AuthRevResData	`{AuthRevCode, AuthRevTags, [BrandCRLIdentifier],`
	`[PEThumb], AuthNewAmt, AuthResDataNew, [ARvRsExtensions]}`
AuthRevCode	Enumerated code indicating outcome
AuthRevTags	Copied from corresponding **AuthRevReq**
BrandCRLIdentifier	See composition section
PEThumb	See composition section
AuthNewAmt	May be zero
AuthResDataNew	`{TransIDs, [AuthResPayloadNew]}`
	If **AuthNewAmt** is not 0, acquirer creates a new object similar to an **AuthResData**
TransIDs	Copied from **AuthRevReq**
AuthResPayloadNew	Formally identical to **AuthResPayload** but containing new data. May contain an **AuthToken** for recurring Auth cycles

```
AuthRevResBaggage     {[CapTokenNew] [AuthTokenNew]}
   CapTokenNew            New Capture Token, if AuthNewAmt is not 0. This
                          replaces the CapToken returned in the corresponding
                          AuthRes.
   AuthTokenNew           New token used as the PI in subsequent AuthReqs
```

PG Composes AuthRevRes

Retrieve authorization data from authorization reversal process. Copy **AuthRevTags** from **AuthRevReq**, update with **AuthRetNum** received in authorization data from payment card financial network. Check current BrandCRLIdentifier held by Payment Gateway if thumb for current BrandCRLIdentifier is not current. If **MThumbs** indicates that merchant needs a new **Cert-PE** to encrypt information to the Payment Gateway; then insert a Cert-PE in the PKCS#7 envelope. Also insert a GKThumb into AuthResData since Cert-PE itself is not protected by a signature. Put results from the authorization reversal process into **AuthRevCode**. Populate **AuthNewAm**t with results from the authorization reversal process If authorization is rejected, return the **AuthNewAmt** specified in the preceding **AuthRevReq**. Create **AuthTokenNew** in **AuthRevResBaggage** using values provided in merchant's **InstallRecurData** if **SubseqentAuthInd** was set TRUE in preceding **AuthRevReq**. If **CapTokenNew** and/or **AuthTokenNew** are included, invoke **EncB**. Else, invoke **Enc**.

Merchant Reception of AuthRevRes

Verify that message is fresh by checking dates against **AuthRevReq**'s **TransIDs**. Store **BrandCRLIdentifier** if included. Match **PEThumb** against gateway encryption cert. Save **AuthCode** and **AuthAmt** for forwarding. Save **CapTokenNew** and update database with the new data.

4.9 CAPTURE REVERSAL

◆ ◆

The **CapRevReq**/**CapRevRes** message pair is used to reduce or
eliminate a previously captured amount. The Capture Reversal
Request message may be sent at any time after capture has been
requested by the acquirer's Payment Gateway to change the
amount of capture for a transaction. Changing the capture
amount to zero (which also omits the **CaptureToken**) removes
the capture completely. Since it may be repeatedly sent, it must
contain its own unique challenge and the **TransIDs** from the **PI**
of the transaction. It must be sent the same business day as the
occurrence of the transactions, else the transaction will not be in
the batch queue.

CapRevData.CapRevOrCredReqItems and a single **CapToken** in
CapTokSeq must correspond to the one and only **PANToken**.

PDU	Description
CapRevReq	`<EncB(M, P, CapRevData, CapTokSeq), EncBX(M, P, CapRevData,` `CapTokSeq, PANToken) >`
CapRevData	`CapRevOrCredReqData` (See 4.1.9.)
CapTokSeq	`{[CapToken] +}`

	One or more **CapTokens**; in one-to-one correspondence with
	    `CapRevOrCredReqItem` sequence in
	    `CapRevOrCredReqData.CapRevOrCredReqItems`. (Note that
	    `BatchIDs` in these `CapTokens` need not all be the same.
	    `PANToken`, if present, must correspond with the one and
	    only `CapRevOrCredReqItem` in
	    `CapRevOrCredReqData.CapRevOrCredReqItems`, and the one
	    and only `CapToken` in `CapTokSeq`.)

Merchant Generates CapRevReq

Generate **CapRevData** as described in **CapRevOrCredReqData**.
For each **CapRevOrCred** item in **CapRevOrCredItems**: Populate

an item in **CapTokSeq** as follows: a) If available, populate with **CapToken** for corresponding transaction. b) Else, if unavailable, insert a NULL. The result of this step will be a **CapTokSeq** with a one-to-one, ordered correspondence between items in **CapRevData** and **CapTokSeq**. If **PANToken** is included, only one item may be present in both **CapRevData** and **CapTokSeq**. If **PANToken** is included, invoke **EncBX** encapsulation. Else, invoke **EncB** encapsulation.

Acquirer Reception

Verify **CapToken**. Reject item if not present. Use **CapRevOrCredItem** to perform reversal.

PDU	Description
CapRevRes	Enc(P, M, CapRevResData)
CapRevResData	CapRevOrCredReqData (See 4.1.9.)

Gateway Composes CapRevRes

Gateway receives response(s) from payment card's network and builds **CapRevResData** based on response results. Invoke **Enc** encapsulation and send to merchant.

Merchant Reception

For each **CapRevOrCredResItem**, **CapRevoOrCredCode** is checked to determine result. Successful captured amounts are recorded.

4.10 CREDIT REQUEST/RESPONSE

The **CreditReq/CreditRes** message pair is used to return credit on a previously captured transaction. The **CreditReq** message may be sent at any time and may be used after the reconciliation of merchant account with acquirer. The response message provides the confirmation or denial of the operation.

PDU	Description
CreditReq	<EncB(M, P, CredReqData, CapTokSeq), EncBX(M, P, CredReqData, CapTokSeq, PANToken) >
CredReqData	CapRevOrCredReqData (See 4.1.9.)
CapTokSeq	{[CapToken] +}
PANToken	If present, must correspond with the one and only CredReqItem in CredReqData.CredReqSeq and the one and only CapToken in CapTokSeq

Merchant Composes CreditReq

Include **CapRevOrCredReqData**. Include **CapTokSeq**, consisting of the capture tokens corresponding to the **CapRevOrCredReqItems**. The token sequence must be in the same order in **CapTokSeq** as the corresponding **CapRevOrCredReqItems**. If the merchant has **PANToken**, then it is sent in the "extra" slot and **CapTokSeq** in the "baggage" and **EncBX** is invoked; else invoke EncB with **CapTokSeq** in the "baggage."

Acquirer Reception

Retrieve transaction records based on **TransIDs** and store **CredRRPID** for response. Verify **CapToken**'s presence, else reject. For each transaction, use payment card network to perform the credit function.

PDU	Description
CredRes	Enc(P, M, CredResData)
CredResData	CapRevOrCredResData (See 4.1.9.)

Gateway Composes CredRes

Gateway receives response(s) from payment card's network and builds **CredResData** based on response results. **RRTags** received in request are included. Invoke **Enc** encapsulation.

Merchant Reception

For each **CapRevOrCredResItem**, **CapRevoOrCredCode** is checked to determine result. Successful captured amounts are recorded.

4.11 CREDIT REVERSAL REQUEST/RESPONSE

◆ ◆

This message pair reverses an erroneously processed credit. It is sent from the merchant to the Payment Gateway.

PDU	Description
CredRevReq	< EncB(M, P, CredRevReqData, CapTokSeq),
	EncBX(M, P, CredRevReqData, CapTokSeq, PANToken) >
CredRevReqData	{CredRevTags, [MThumbs], CredRevReqSeq}
CredRevTags	{CredRevRRTags }
CredRevRRTags	RRTags
MThumbs	Thumbs of PGwy certificates, CA CRLs, and
	BrandCRLIdentifiers currently held by merchant's cache
CredRevReqSeq	{CredRevReqItem +}
CredRevReqItem	{TransIDs, CredRevReqAmt, [AuthReqData],
	[AuthResPayload], SaleDetail}
TransIDs	Copied from corresponding
	AuthReq.AuthReqData.AuthTags

```
        CredRevReqAmt     Amount of credit reversal requested
        AuthReqData       Required if CapToken is not present or does not
                          contain needed authorization request data
        AuthResPayload    Required if CapToken is not present or does not
                          contain needed authorization request data
        SaleDetail        See 4.1.6.
CapTokSeq             {[CapToken] +} Note: One or more CapTokens in a one-to-one
                          correspondence with CredRevReqItems in CredRevReqSeq
PANToken              Note: If present, it must correspond to the one and only
                          CredRevReqItem found in CredRevReqData.CredRevReqSeq
```

Mechant Composes CredRevReq

Insert **RRTags** as **CredRevTags**. Optionally, include **MThumbs**. Include one or more **CredRevReqItems**. (Only one is allowed if **PANToken** is included in extra slot of message.) Include **TransIDs** for the reversal transaction, **CredRevreqAmt**, and **SaleDetail** from original capture. For each **CredRevReqItems** optionally include **AuthReqData**, **AuthResPayload**, received during authorization, if information not included in **CapToken**. Include **CapTokSeq**, consisting of the capture tokens corresponding to the **CapRevOrCredReqItems**. The token sequence must be in the same order in **CapTokSeq** as the corresponding **CapRevOrCredReqItems**. If the merchant has PANToken, then it is sent in the "extra" slot and **CapTokSeq** in the "baggage" and **EncBX** is invoked; else invoke EncB with **CapTokSeq** in the "baggage." Invoke **ComposeMessageWrapper** and send to Payment Gateway.

Acquirer Reception

Verify presence of **CapToken**. If not present, reject. For each transaction, use payment card network to perform the credit reversal function.

PDU	Description

```
CredRevRes         Enc(P, M, CredRevResData)
  CredRevResData     {CapRevOrCreditData}
```

Gateway Composes CredRevRes

Gateway receives response(s) from payment card's network and builds **CredRevResData** based on response results. **RRTags** received in request are included. Invoke **Enc** encapsulation.

Merchant Reception

For each **CapRevOrCredResItem** in **CredRevResData**, **CapRevOrCredCode** is checked to determine result. Successful reversal amounts are recorded.

4.12 BATCH ADMINISTRATION

◆ ◆

Some businesses need to do an end-of-day capture of billing transactions. SET allows a batch administration of all the Capture Tokens that have been collected during the day by the merchant into one auditable step. Batch administration processing consists of two messages, a request from a merchant to an acquirer's Payment Gateway, and a response from the acquirer's Payment Gateway back to the merchant. The request may contain actions to open or close a batch and/or request for information about the batch contents. The Gateway's response returns status and merchant-requested information.

PDU	Description

```
BatchAdminReq      Enc(M, P, {BatchAdminReqData})
   BatchAdminReqData    Req { BatchAdminRRTags, BatchID, [BrandAndBINSeq],
                        [BatchOperation], ReturnBatchSummaryInd,
                        ReturnTransactionDetail, [BatchStatus], [TransDetails]
                        [BARqExtensions]}
```

BatchAdminRRTags	**RRTags** with fresh RRPID
BatchID	Batch number for a Brand
BrandAndBINSeq	**{BrandAndBIN +}**
BrandAndBIN	**{BrandID, [BIN]}**
BrandID	ID for brand
BIN	Bank ID No.: first six digits of PAN
BatchOperation	Enumerated value indicating action to be performed on the batch
ReturnBatchSummaryInd	Summary data should be returned in **BatchAdminRes**
ReturnTransactionDetail	**{StartingPoint, MaximumItems, ErrorsOnlyInd, [BrandID]}**
StartingPoint	Zero implies send detail for first group; otherwise **NextStartingPoint** from prior **BatchAdminRes**
MaximumItems	Max items to be returned
ErrorsOnlyInd	Boolean indicating if only items with an error status should be returned
BrandID	A batch may have multiple brands, identify this one
BatchStatus	See next PDU
TransDetails	**{NextStartingPoint, TransactionDetailSeq}**
NextStartingPoint	Zero indicates this is last group; otherwise an opaque value identifies next starting point.
TransactionDetailSeq	**{TransactionDetail +}**
BARqExtensions	Extensions

Merchant Generation of BatchAdminReq

Insert **RRTags** as **BatchAdminRRTags**. Include **BatchID** of target batch. Set **BatchOperation** code. Sign and send to Payment Gateway.

PG reception/BatchAdminRes Generation

Verify the signature and that **RRPID** matches that of the Message Wrapper. Process settlement of all items in the batch. If **ReturnBatchSummaryInd** is true, fill in values in **ReturnTransactionDetail** fields. Actual operations depend on the combination of inputs present.

PDU	Description
BatchAdminRes Enc(P, M {BatchAdminResData})	
BatchAdminResData {BatchAdminTags,BatchID, [BAStatus], [BatchStatus],	
[TransmissionStatus], [SetttlementInfo], [TransDetails], [BARsExtensions]}	
BatchAdminTags	Copied from previous **BatchAdminReq**
BatchID	Individual batch to which this **BatchAdminRes** refers
BAStatus	Enumerated code for batch operation
BatchStatus	{OpenDateTime, [ClosedWhen], BatchDetails, [BatchExtensions]}
OpenDateTime	Date/time of opening
ClosedWhen	{CloseStatus, CloseDateTime}
CloseStatus	Enumerated status code of close
CloseDateTime	Date/time of close
BatchDetails	{BatchTotals, [BrandBatchDetailsSeq]}
	BatchTotals{TransactionCountCredit, TransactionTotalAmtCredit, TransactionCountDebit, TransactionTotalAmtDebit, [BatchTotalExtensions]}
TransactionCountCredit	The number of transactions that resulted in a credit to the merchant's account
TransactionTotalAmtCredit	The total amount credited to the merchant's account
TransactionCountDebit	The number of transactions that resulted in a debit to the merchant's account
TransactionTotalAmtDebit	The total amount debited from a merchant's account
BatchTotalExtensions	Extensions
BrandBatchDetailsSeq	{BrandBatchDetails+}
BrandBatchDetails	{BrandID, BatchTotals}
TransmissionStatus	Enumerated value indicating status from the gateway to the next upstream system
SettlementInfo	{SettlementAmount, SettlementType, SettlementAccount, SettlementDepositDate}
SettlementAmount	Net amount; of type indicated by **SettlementType**
SettlementType	Enumerated amount
SettlementAccount	Merchant's account
SettlementDepositDate	Date credit/debit affects merchant account

```
TransDetails        {NextStartingPoint, TransactionDetail+}
   NextStartingPoint      Zero indicates last group; otherwise opaque value
                          identifying starting point of next group
   TransactionDetail      {TransIDs, AuthRRPID, BrandID, BatchSequenceNum,
                          [ReimbursementID], TransactionAmt,
                          TransactionAmtType, [TransactionStatus],
                          [TransExtensions]}
      TransIDs                   Transaction identifiers from the
                                 authorization/capture processing of
                                 the item
      AuthRRPID                  From authorization
      BrandID                    Brand used for this item
      BatchSequenceNum           Item's sequence within the batch
      ReimbursementID            Enumerated code for item's type of
                                 reimbursement
      TransactionAmt             Amount to be credited/debited to
                                 merchant
      TransactionAmtType         Enumerated code
      TransactionStatus          Enumerated code indicates result of
                                 passing transaction to the next
                                 upstream system
      TransExtensions            Extensions
BARsExtensions        Extensions
```

Merchant Reception

Results of operation recorded along with status. Verify signature
and that the **RRPID** matches that in the Message Wrapper.

4.13 ERROR MESSAGES

Error messages are a way for the application to send messages
about low-level message-formatting or validation failures. This
sort of message has nothing to do with a declined authorization
or other normal business operation. Merchant, Payment Gateway,
and CA software should send an Error message when
encountering a low-level processing error on a SET request
message. Any messages that do not appear to be SET messages
should be ignored.

Cardholder and merchant software should also send an Error
message when encountering a low-level processing error on a
SET response message. The Error message should be sent to a
diagnostic log port if one has been defined for the system that
sent the response. Applications should avoid sending Error
messages on the same port as request messages; however, if no
diagnostic log port is available, the application may send one
Error message per day on the request port. The software may
limit the number of error messages that are sent to mitigate the
effects of denial-of-service attacks.

An Error message must never be sent in response to anything that
appears to be an Error message. A valid SET message will begin
with a tag of [30] and a length for the entire **MessageWrapper**
sequence which will, in turn, contain a tag of [30] followed by the
length of the **MessageHeader** and the content of the
MessageHeader. Also, there will be a tag for the type of message
followed by the length and content of the **Message**. If the tag for
the type of message is 999 (indicating an Error message), a SET
application must never send a response even if the message
appears to be malformed. This is to prevent loops where one
Error message triggers another.

If there is some low-level operating error, the application creates
an Error message and sets the **ErrorCode** to the appropriate
value. If none of the enumerated ones fit the situation, the
unspecifiedFailure (0) is used.

A *nonce* is generated and included in the message. If the *app* does
not support a critical extension, the object identifier for the
extension is included in the Error message. If the Error occurred
due to a certificate, copy the cert's Thumbprint. If it was a
signature verification failure, insert the hash of the cert. Finally,
copy the **MessageHeader** or the entire message (if under
20Kbytes) into the Error message. Sign and send.

PDU	Description
Error	**<SignedError,UnsignedError>**
SignedError	**S(EE,ErrorTBS)**
ErrorTBS	**{ErrorCode,ErrorNonce,[ErrorOID], {ErrorThumb}, ErrorMsg}**
ErrorCode	Enumerated codes for error
ErrorNonce	Ensures signature reliability
ErrorOID	**OID** of critical cert causing error
ErrorThumb	Thumbprint of cert causing error
ErrorMsg	**<MessageHeader, BadWrapper>**
MessageHeader	From message causing error
BadWrapper	From message causing error
UnsignedError	**ErrorTBS** Use only if no signature cert

Chapter 5

• • •

CERTIFICATE MANAGEMENT

To put this more scientifically, I shall say that the reproduction of labour power requires not only a reproduction of its skills, but also, at the same time, a reproduction of its submission to the rules of the established order, i.e., a reproduction of the ruling ideology for the workers, and a reproduction of the ability to manipulate the ruling ideology correctly for the agents of exploitation and repression, so that they, too, will provide for the domination of the ruling class "in words."

—Louis Althusser, *Lenin and Philosophy*

We've considered the use of certificates in both the overview (Chapter 3) and in how they interface with the payment flow (Chapter 4). Let's now look at certificates in a comprehensive way, beginning with the viewpoint of management.

5.1 CERTIFICATE ARCHITECTURE

The architecture of the certificate-management scheme is shown in Figure 5.1.

The nine elements that go into the architecture are defined in relation to each other by their hierarchy of trust. The elements derive trust from the next-higher level, and in turn guarantee the lower elements in the pyramid.

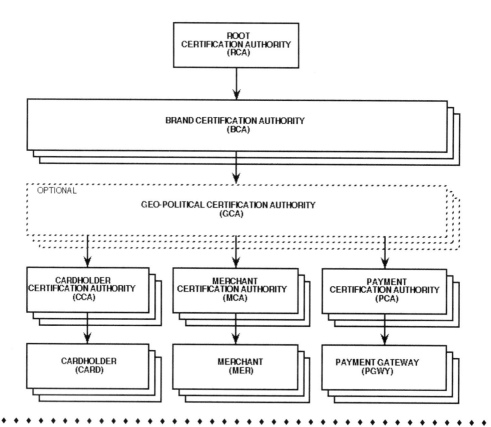

Figure 5.1. Architecture of certificate-management scheme

The Root Certification Authority (RCA) would generally be kept in a secure manner, probably with no net connection available to it at all. As the Root, it is used to issue Brand-level CA certificates as well as new Root certificates. If a compromise of a Brand-level CA certificate should occur, it falls to the Root CA to issue and distribute the CRL identifying the faulty Brand-level CA certificate.

The Brand-level CA allows for each Brand to have a degree of independence in how it manages certificates. The BCA would issue the CA certificates for levels lower than it, as well as manage the issuance and distribution of Brand CRLs for compromised certificates that it originally signed.

The Geo-Political CA (GCA) allows the Brand to distribute responsibility for managing types of certificates to geographic or political regions. Thus, certificate policies can vary from one region of the world to another, depending on local conditions. Again, the GCA manages the CRLs for compromised certificates that it originally signed.

Cardholders get certificates from a cardholder CA (CCA). CCAs can accept requests for certs via e-mail, the Web, or other electronic means, and verify the validity of a request through a relationship with the card issuers. Unlike the other CAs the CCA does not maintain a CRL list of its own. However, it can and does distribute CRLs generated by other CAs. This kind of CA may be operated by any entity that follows the payment card brand's rules.

Merchant CAs are much like CCAs. They are responsible for distributing certificates to a merchant, after the merchant's request has been verified and approved by the acquirer, but do not issue their own CRLs. They do distribute CRLs from other CAs.

Table 5.1. Characteristics of all SET Certificates

Entity	Digital Signature	Key Encipherment	KeyCert Sign	CRL Sign
Cardholder	X			
Merchant	X	X		
Acquirer Payment Gateway	X	X		
Cardholder Certification Authority	X	X	X	
Merchant Certification Authority	X	X	X	
Payment Certification Authority	X	X	X	X
Geo-political Certification Authority			X	X
Brand Certification Authority			X	X
Root Certification Authority			X	X

Payment Gateways are issued certs by the acquirer Payment Gateway CA (PCA). The PCA maintains and distributes CRLs for compromised gateway certificates.

Table 5.1 summarizes all SET certificates and their characteristics.

It should be noted that the CCA, MCA, and PCA will not require three distinct certificates if they are integrated functions. A single signature certificate could contain two or three different Certificate Types.

Also, CAs can combine certificates for signing other certificates as well as signing CRLs. The **KeyUsage** field may contain both the **keyCertSign** and the **offLineCRLSign** privilege or both the **keyEncipherment** and **dataEncipherment**. No other functions, however, may be combined into one certificate.

Table 5.2. End Entity Certificates

X.509 Extension	Cardholder Certificate Signature	Merchant Certificate Signature	Merchant Certificate Key Encryption	Gateway Certificate Signature	Gateway Certificate Key Encryption
AuthorityKeyIdentifier	X	X	X	X	X
KeyUsage	X	X	X	X	X
PrivateKeyUsagePeriod	X	X	X	X	X
CertificatePolicies	X	X	X	X	X
SubjectAltName	O	O	O	O	O
BasicConstraints	X	X	X	X	X
IssuerAltName	O	O	O	O	O
Private Extension					
HashedRootKey					
CertificateType	X	X	X	X	X
MerchantData		X	X		
CardholderCertificateRequired					X
Tunneling					X
SETQualifier	X	X	X	X	X

X = Required; O = Optional

End Entity Certificates have the following required certificate extensions listed in Table 5.2 (and outlined in sections 5.6 and 5.7).

Table 5.3 summarizes the required certificate extensions for CA certificates.

Table 5.3. CA Certificates

X.509 Extension	Digital Signature	Certificate Signature	Key Encryption	CRL Signature	Certificate Signature	CRL Signature
AuthorityKeyIdentifier	X	X	X	X		
KeyUsage	X	X	X	X	X	X
PrivateKeyUsagePeriod	X	X	X	X	X	X
CertificatePolicies	X	X	X	X	X	X
SubjectAltName	O	O	O	O	O	O
BasicConstraints	X	X	X	X	X	X
IssuerAltName	O	O	O	O	O	O
Private Extension						
HashedRootKey					X	
CertificateType	X	X	X	X	X	X
MerchantData						
CardholderCertificateRequired						
Tunneling			X			
SETQualifier	X	X	X	X		

X = Required; O = Optional

5.2 CERTIFICATE ISSUANCE AND REVOCATION

To issue a certificate for a cardholder, the CCA must first receive a request from the cardholder. The cardholder is then sent an encryption certificate that is used to encrypt the PAN that will be sent to the CCA. Once PAN is sent to the CCA, the CCA sends back a specific certificate registration form that is appropriate for the Brand that the customer has specified. The customer completes the registration form, includes his or her public key, and sends it back to the CCA. The CCA then verifies the information supplied via its link with the card issuer, and then generates the certificate and sends it to the cardholder.

The process for issuing a merchant certificate is similar to that for the cardholder. The merchant initiates a request to the MCA, which responds with a registration form, which the merchant fills in and returns with his public key. The acquirer verifies the merchant's information, generates the certificate, and sends it to the merchant.

A Payment Gateway certificate is issued by the Payment Certificate Authority (PCA) and follows the same process as for a merchant.

CA certificate issuance requires a higher level of security due to the obvious fraud potential. This usually involves a hardware token and electronic media. It is outside the scope of SET to describe this issuance process, save to note that it must be trusted by all the SET parties.

Certificate renewal is generally the same as the initial issuance procedure, but may request different information by the issuer.

Certificates may be revoked for a number of reasons. There may be a compromise of the private key, the identification information inside the certificate may change, or there may be a termination of use. Payment Certificate Authority (PCA) Certificate Revocation Lists (CRLs) are distributed to cardholders and show the revoked Payment Gateway certificates. CA CRLs serve the same purpose, but can show unauthorized PG certs created by using a revoked CA certificate.

Cardholders don't have to care about a merchant's certificate status, since the merchant and the cardholder do not share any sensitive financial information. The same holds true from the merchant's viewpoint.

For merchants, use of the CA CRL can show that no CA certificate in the cardholder's certificate path has been revoked. (Because merchants also need to know if a Payment Gateway's certificates are valid, revoked PG certs are included in the CRLs distributed to cardholders, and the revoked CA certs are distributed to merchants in a CRL. Merchants can then derive the PG certs which may have been created using a CA's certificate. Likewise, merchants can use the CA CRL to see if any CA certificate in a cardholder's certificate path has been revoked. Additionally, merchants have relationships with the acquirer which can allow for the supersession and redistribution of PG certificates in a timely manner.

What does a Payment Gateway do to maintain certificate validity? For cardholder information, the PG can check whether or not the cardholder's certificate has been signed by a CA that is listed in a CRL. Also, the PG validates the cardholder-supplied information contained in the Authorization Request (**AuthReq**) step with the issuer. This is another chance to validate that cardholder certificates are current.

For a merchant, the PG can verify that the merchant's certificate path does not include a CA that is listed in a CRL. Additionally, the PG can verify that the merchant maintains a valid relationship with the acquirer.

5.3 CERTIFICATE CHAIN VALIDATION

The hierarchy of trust goes from the End Entities (EE)—the cardholder, merchant, and acquirer Payment Gateway—to the Root Certificate Authority. To validate certificates, the hierarchy must be followed back to the Root CA through the "signature chain."

The SET Root certificate will most likely be distributed within SET software used for a SET application. This cannot be considered a secure means for distribution, so the integrity of the certificate must be verified. One means of verification is to have the user enter a known hash of the Root certificate (itself gotten from a trusted source) and compare it to a hash taken of the supplied certificate.

To validate a Certificate Authority certificate, the following conditions must be satisfied:

1. The issuer name in the End Entity certificate must match the Subject Name in the CA certificate.

2. The **certIssuer** field in the **AuthorityKeyIdentifier** extension of the End Entity certificate must match the **IssuerName** of the signing CA certificate.

3. The **certSerialNumber** field in the **AuthorityKeyIdentifier** extension of the End Entity certificate must match the **SerialNumber** of the CA certificate.

4. The **Validity** dates (certificate and private key) in the End Entity certificate must be within the certificate **Validity** dates of the CA certificate.

5. The **notBeforeValidity** dates in the End Entity certificate must be within the **Validity** field in the **PrivateKeyUsage** extension of the CA certificate.

6. The **BrandIDs**, within the organization name of the subject name of each certificate, must match.

7. The signature verifies.

To proceed with the chain, the following items are validated:

1. The current date is within the certificate **Validity** dates.

2. The **KeyUsage** field of the **KeyUsage** extension is valid for the purpose it was or is to be used.

3. The **BasicConstraints** extension indicates End Entity.

4. The **CertificateType** private extension corresponds with the context in which the certificate is being used.

5. The signature verifies.

After the EE fields have been verified, the following must be validated in the CA certificate:

1. The current date is within the certificate **Validity** dates.

2. The **KeyUsage** field of the **KeyUsage** extension is valid for the purpose for which it was used.

3. The **subjectType** field of the **BasicConstraints** extension indicates CA.

4. The **pathLenConstraint** of the **BasicConstraints** extension is not negative.

5. The **CertificateType** private extension corresponds to the context in which the certificate is being used.

The diagram in Figure 5.2 provides a logical view of the certificate data elements, with an emphasis on the data elements used for signature chain validation. The bold arrows indicate which fields are validated and the arrows show which fields should contain the same value.

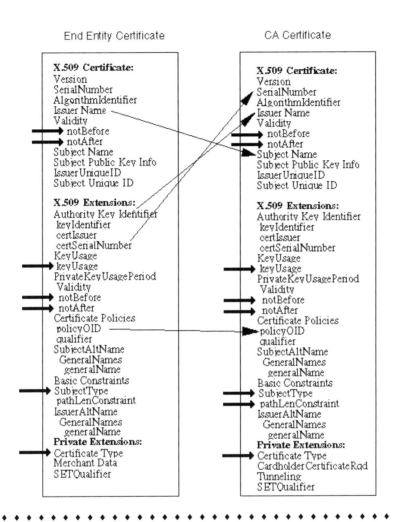

Figure 5.2. Certificate data elements. Bold arrows indicate fields that are validated, thin arrows show fields that should have the same value.

5.4 CERTIFICATE MANAGEMENT PROTOCOLS

This section will detail the protocols used to implement certificate management. (See sections 3.1 and 3.2 for overview.) This lower-level view is centered on the SET messages passed between SET parties as a certificate transaction progresses.

5.4.1 Cardholder Initiation Processing

After the SET application has been started, the cardholder sends a **CardCInitReq** to the CCA, indicating via Thumbprints the certificates, CRLs, and the **BrandCRLIdentifier** (BCI) that it's holding. The CCA responds with a **CardCInitRes** containing any certificates, CRLs, and/or the **BrandCRLIdentifier** that the cardholder will need for signature verification, as well as an encryption certificate to use for subsequent messages.

Note that the process may be initiated via a wake-up message (such as would be sent over the Web to initiate processing), or through a local message such as e-mail.

PDU	Description
`CardCInitReq`	`{RRPID, LID-EE, Chall-EE, BrandID, [Thumbs]}`
`RRPID`	Request/response pair; statistically unique
`LID-EE`	Local ID generated by cardholder
`Chall-EE`	Fresh challenge to prevent replay of message
`BrandID`	Brand ID of requested cert, formatted "brand[:product]"
`Thumbs`	Thumbs of Certs, CRLs, BCI held by EE

CardCInitReq Composition

Insert the stored **BrandID**:Product type from storage or received in WakeUp message. Create the ThumbPrints for each CRL, SET certificate, **BrandCRLIdentifier**, and Root certificate resident in trusted cache, if any.

CCA Reception

RRPID, **Thumbs**, **LID-EE**, and **Chall-EE** are stored for use in **CardCInitRes**.

PDU	Description
CardCInitRes	S(CCA, {RRPID, LID-EE, Chall-EE, [LID-CA], CAEThumb, [BrandCRLIdentifier], [Thumbs]}
RRPID	From `CardCinitReq`
EE-Tags	From `CardCinitReq`
CA-Tags	From CCA
CAEThumb	Thumbprint of CA key-exchange certificate that Cardholder will use to encrypt `ReqFormReq`
BrandCRLIdentifier	List of CRLs to screen received certs against
Thumbs	If sent in `CardCInitReq`, sent back to assure match

CCA Generation of CardCInitRes

Build the "to be signed" data by retrieving the stored **RRPID** and tags, retrieving the Thumbprint, **CAEThumb**, of its data encryption certificate. Then retrieve the **BrandCRLIdentifier**, if it is not specified in the Thumbs received in **CardCInitReq**. Copy the Thumbs from the **CardCInitReq**. Sign everything done so far. As with any SignedData, the certificates and CRLs needed to verify the signature are included in the **CardCInitRes** outside of the "to be signed" data.

Cardholder Reception

Verify that Thumbs match those sent in **CardCInitReq**. Following the receipt of the appropriate certificates, CRLs, and the BrandCRLIdentifer in **CardCInitReq**, the cardholder can securely request a certificate registration form via the **RegFormReq**. **RegFormReq** is encrypted by the cardholder using the certificate sent from the CCA in **CardCInitRes**. If the CCA successfully validates the registration form request, it returns the form in the **RegFormRes**. If the CCA does not have a registration form for the cardholder's request and/or has additional information concerning the service request denial to convey to the cardholder, this is also indicated in the **RegFormRes**.

PDU	Description
RegFormReq	EXH(CA, {RegFormReqData, PANOnly})
RegFormReqData	{RRPID, LID-EE, Chall-EE2, [LID-CA], RequestType, Language, Thumbs }
RRPID	Request/response pair ID
LID-EE	Copied from **CardCInitRes**
Chall-EE2	EE challenge to CA signature
LID-CA	Copied from **CardCInitRes**
RequestType	See Table 5.4.
Language	Desired language for transaction
Thumbs	List of Certs, CRLs and BCIs held by cardholder
PANOnly	Primary Account Number (9 digits), followed by **EXNonce** of size 20.

Table 5.4. Request Types

Request Type	Signature Cert Only	Encryption Cert Only	Both Certs
Cardholder Initial	1	2*	3*
Cardholder Renewal	10	11*	12*

Request Type	Restrictions
2*	Must have a valid signature certificate and must use the corresponding private key to sign the request for an encryption certificate
10	Both the private key corresponding to the certificate being renewed and the private key of the new certificate must be used to sign the renewal request.
11*	Renewal of encryption certificates: The certificate common names of the signature certificate (used to sign the request) and encryption certificate must match. This assumes that the signature and encryption certificates will have the same subject Domain Name.

Table 5.4 indicates options that do not need to be supported in the 1.0 version of SET since cardholder encryption certificates are not required.

Cardholder Generation

Include **RRPID** and freshen up tags. Set **RequestType** and **Language** with these into "Ordinarily Encrypted" data. Send all to the CA, which responds through **RegFormRes**.

PDU	Description
RegFormRes	S(CA, {RegFormResTBS }
RegFormTBS	{RRPID, LID-EE, Chall-EE2, [LID-CA], Chall-CA, [CAEThumb], RequestType, RegFormOrReferral, [BrandCRLIdentifier], [Thumbs]}
RRPID	Request/response pair ID
LID-EE	Copied from **RegFormReq**
Chall-EE2	Copied from **RegFormReq**
LID-CA	Local ID from CA
Chall-CA	CA challenge to requester's signature
CAEThumb	Thumb of CA key-exchange cert which provides the public key used to encrypt **CertReq.** If not present, the certificate identified in **CardCInitRes** is used.
RequestType	Copied from **RegFormReq**
RegFormOrReferral	<RegFormData, ReferralData>
RegFormData	{[RegTemplate], PolicyText}
RegTemplate	{RegFormID, [BrandLogoURL], [CardLogoURL], RegFIeldSeq}
RegFormID	Identifier
BrandLogoURL	URL for .gif file of logo
CardLogoURL	URL for .gif file of logo
RegFieldSeq	{RegField +}
RegField	{[FieldId], FieldName, [FieldDesc], [FieldLen], FieldRequired, FieldInvisible}
FieldId	OID
FieldName	Name of field
FieldDesc	Description of contents
FieldLen	Maximum length
FieldRequired	Boolean
FieldInvisible	Boolean, true = don't display to user; based on **FieldID**

```
     PolicyText            Information to be displayed along with RegTemplate
  ReferralData             {Reason, [ReferralURLSeq]}
  Reason                   Information about the request
  ReferralURLSeq           {ReferralURL +}
     ReferralURL              URLs pointing to referral information, ranked in
                              relevance order
BrandCRLIdentifier   See 5.4.5.
Thumbs               Copied from RegFormReq
```

CCA Generation of RegFormRes

Develop the "to be signed" data first. Copy **RequestType**, **RRPID**, **LID-EE**, **Thumbs**, and **Chall-EE2** from **RegFormReq**. If a cardholder registration form is available as requested, then create **RegFormData**. The **RegTemplate** and associated data are retrieved and included. If the form is not available, include the **Reason** for service denial along with **ReferralLoc**. Sign all the preceding, and send to the cardholder.

Cardholder reception. Strip out **RequestType**, **LID-EE**, and **Chall-EE2** and verify that they are the same as sent. Display **PolicyText** and obtain consent from user, then display registration form. When cardholder has finished form, generate appropriate response (usually **CertReq**). If the **ReferralData** is included, display **Reason** and **ReferralLoc** to the cardholder. Do not generate a **CertReq**, but begin protocol again with **CardCInitReq**.

OID

The **RegField** in the **RegTemplate** of **RegFormRes** is a user-entered field that can be of use to the application beyond simply providing the requestor information. Perhaps the application could save the information for later processing or identity verification at another step of SET. Each kind of field has an associated object identifier (OID) that describes the contents of the field.

The following types of fields are represented as {id-set-field
number}):

> 0   full name
> 1   given name (or first name)
> 2   family name (or surname or last name)
> 3   family name at birth (or maiden name)
> 4   place name
> 5   identification number
> 6   month
> 7   date
> 8   address
> 9   telephone
> 10 amount
> 11 account number
> 12 pass phrase

Descriptions and additional qualifiers for the above fields are
described below. The field qualifiers must appear in the same
order as described.

Full name. The OID {id-set-field fullName (0)} indicates a field
that contains a full name, the given name, and the family name.
This OID may be further qualified to indicate the individual as
follows:

> 0   primary cardholder
> 1   secondary cardholder

Given name. The OID {id-set-field givenName (1)} indicates a field
that contains an individual's given name. This OID may be
further qualified to indicate the individual:

> 0   primary cardholder
> 1   secondary cardholder

Family name. The OID {id-set-field familyName (2)} indicates a field that contains an individual's family name. This OID may be further qualified to indicate the individual:

    0   primary cardholder
    1   secondary cardholder

Family name at birth. The OID {id-set-field birthFamilyName (3)} indicates a field that contains an individual's family name at birth (such as a maiden name). This OID may be further qualified to indicate the individual:

    0   primary cardholder
    1   secondary cardholder

Place name. The OID {id-set-field placeName (4)} indicates a field that contains the name of a place. This OID may be further qualified to indicate the specifics of the place:

    0   birth

This OID may be even further qualified to indicate a place of significance to an individual as follows:

    0   primary cardholder
    1   secondary cardholder

Identification number. The OID {id-set-field identificationNumber (5)} indicates a field that contains an identification number assigned to an individual. This OID may be further qualified to indicate the type of identification:

    0   passport
    1   national identity
    2   voter registration
    3   driver license
    4   business license

This OID may be even further qualified to indicate the nation from which the identification is expected to come by adding the ISO-3166 numeric country code. This OID may be further qualified to indicate a place of significance to an individual:

    0   primary cardholder
    1   secondary cardholder

Month. The OID {id-set-field month (6)} indicates a field that contains a month of significance to an individual. This OID may be further qualified to indicate the significance of the month:

    0   birth

This OID may be even further qualified to indicate a place of significance to an individual:

    0   primary cardholder
    1   secondary cardholder

Date. The OID {id-set-field date (7)} indicates a field that contains a date of significance to an individual. This OID may be further qualified to indicate the significance of the date:

    0   birth
    1   last payment
    2   last transaction
    3   account opened

This OID may be even further qualified to indicate a date of significance to an individual:

    0   primary cardholder
    1   secondary cardholder

Address. The OID {id-set-field address (8)} indicates a field containing an address. This OID may be further qualified to indicate the type of address:

0   home
1   billing
2   prior
3   work

This OID may also be even further qualified to indicate the nation from which the address is expected to come by adding the ISO-3166 numeric country code.

Telephone. The OID {id-set-field telephone (9)} indicates a field containing a telephone number. This OID may be further qualified to indicate the type of number:

0   home
1   business

This OID may be even further qualified to indicate the nation from which the telephone number is expected to come by adding the ISO-3166 numeric country code.

Amount. The OID {id-set-field amount (10)} indicates a field containing an amount. This OID can be further qualified to indicate the type of amount:

0   last payment
1   last transaction
2   account balance
3   line of credit

This OID can also be qualified to indicate the currency code by adding the ISO-4217 currency code.

Account number. The OID {id-set-field accountNumber (11)} indicates a field containing an account number. This OID may be further qualified to indicate the type of account:

0   checking
1   savings
2   card verification code

The card verification code is a number printed on the payment card; because this number is not embossed and does not appear on the magnetic stripe, it is only available to someone with physical access to the card.

Pass phrase. The OID {id-set-field passPhrase (12)} indicates a field containing a pass phrase. Typically this will be exchanged between the individual and the financial institution over a trusted medium of exchange.

Relatives. The relatives of an individual can be specified by adding an additional qualifier to the end of an OID as follows:

0   spouse
1   mother
2   father
3   maternal grandmother
4   maternal grandfather
5   paternal grandmother
6   paternal grandfather

5.4.2 Certificate Logos

The certificate registration process includes optional logos for the brand and the financial institution. Five standard sizes for logos have been defined. The sizes in pixels and the corresponding file names are given in the following table:

Size in Pixels	Name	File Name
32 × 32 or 32 × 20	Extra Small	exsmall.gif
53 × 33	Small	small.gif
103 × 65	Medium	medium.gif
180 × 114	Large	large.gif
263 × 166	Extra Large	exlarge.gif

In order to maintain a constant ratio, designers of an extra-small logo may choose to limit the size to 32 × 20.

Each logo URL specified with the registration form will be either: (1) The name of a directory (ending with a virgule "/") that contains one or more logos named in accordance with the table above (at least one of the following files must appear in the directory: small.gif, medium.gif.); or (2) The name of a file containing a *Small* or *Medium* logo, which may be different from those shown above; however, if one of these names is used, it must be consistent with the size of the icon.

Applications that display logos on the registration form must reserve space for both brand and financial institution logos; at a minimum, the registration form must be able to support *Small* or *Medium* logos. The ability to display logos of larger sizes is at the discretion of the software vendor.

Extra Small logos will never be displayed on a registration form. The color palette of the logos needs to be designed to work within the limited palette of colors typically utilized by most browsers within an 8-bit or 256-color environment or greater (the "Netscape palette").

5.4.3 Merchant/Acquirer Initiation Processing

Let's now consider the case of a merchant or Payment Gateway. The merchant or acquirer Payment Gateway begins the certificate protocol by sending the **Me-AqCInitReq**. The **Me-AqCInitReq** contains the merchant's or acquirer Payment Gateway's bank information, the type of certificate it is requesting, and the certificates, CRLs, and the **BrandCRLIdentifier** that it's holding. The CA responds with a **Me-AqCInitRes**, containing any certificates, CRLs, and the **BrandCRLIdentifier** that the merchant or acquirer will need for signature verification, as well as an encryption certificate to use for encrypting the **CertReq**. After receipt of the **Me-AqCInitRes**, the End Entity may send a **CertReq**.

PDU	Description
Me-AqCInitReq	{RRPID, LID-EE, Chall-EE, RequestType (See Table 5.5), IDData, BrandID, Language, [Thumbs]}
RRPID	Request/response pair, statistically unique
LID-EE	Local ID
Chall-EE	Fresh challenge to prevent replay of message
IDData	<MerchantAcquirerID, AcquirerID>
MerchantAcquirerID	{MerchantBIN, MerchantID}
MerchantBIN	Bank Identification Number or merchant account with acquirer
MerchantID	Established between acquirer and merchant
AcquirerID	{AcquirerBIN, [Acquirer BusinessID]}
AcquirerBIN	Acquirer's Bank ID
Acquirer BusinessID	Business ID of Acquirer
BrandID	BrandID of requested cert, uses brand[:product] format
Language	Language to be used
Thumbs	Thumbprints of Certs, CRLs, and **BrandCRLIdentifier** currently held by EE (including root). EE will check against signed copy in later **Me-AqCInitRes**

Table 5.5. RequestType

Request Type	Signature Cert only	Encryption Cert only	Both Certs
Merchant Initial	4	5	6
Payment Gateway Initial	7	8	9
Merchant Renewal	13	14	15
Payment Gateway Renewal	16	17	18

Request Type	Restrictions
5,8	Must have a valid signature certificate to sign the request for an encryption certificate
14,15,17,18	Renewal of encryption certificates: The certificate common names of the signature certificate (used to sign the request) and encryption certificate must match. This assumes that the signature and encryption certificates will have the same subject Domain Name.
13,16	Both the private key corresponding to the certificate being renewed and the private key of the new certificate must be used to sign the renewal request.

Me-AqCInitReq Generation

Brand information and **Language** are inserted. The thumbprints for each CRL, SET cert, **BrandCRLIdentifier,** and Root certificate in the trusted cache (if any are present) are created. If EE is a merchant, insert **MerchantBIN** and **MerchantID**, else insert **AcquirerBIN**. Send **Me-AqCInitReq** to CA.

Reception

CA retrieves **RRPID**, **BrandID**, **Language**, **Thumbs**, and **IDData**. If **RRPID** is valid, format a **Me-AqCInitRes** containing the appropriate registration form.

PDU	Description
Me-AqCInitRes	S(CA, {RRPID, LID-EE, Chall-E, [LID-CA], Chall-CA RequestType, RegFormOrReferral, [AcctDataField], CAEThumb, [BrandCRLIdentifier], [Thumbs]})
RRPID	Request/response
LID-EE	Copied from **Me-AqCInitReq**
Chall-EE	Copied from **Me-AqCInitReq**
LID-CA	Local ID
Chall-CA	Fresh challenge to prevent replay of message
RequestType	See previous enumeration.
RegFormOrReferral	See previous section.
CAEThumb	Thumbprint of CA key-exchange certificate providing the public key that should be used to encrypt **CertReq**; if this field is not present, the public key used to encrypt **RegFormReq** is used.
BrandCRLIdentifier	Identifies the list of CRLs that the End Entities' software should be screening received certificates against; optional, included if the thumbprints in the **Me-AqCInitReq** do not indicate the valid **BrandCRLIdentifier**
Thumbs	If Thumbs were sent in **Me-AqCInitReq**, the CA sends it back, signed, to EE. EE checks for match against saved value.

Me-AqCInitRes Generation by CA

Build "to be signed" data by copying **RRPID, LID-EE** and **Chall-EE** from **Me-AqCInitReq**. Generate **Chall-CA.** Get Thumb of key encryption cert, **CAEThumb**. If Thumbs in **CardCInitReq** do not include **BrandCRLIdentifier**, then retrieve and include. Copy all other thumbs from **Me-AqCInitReq**. Depending on the **RequestType**, **BINs**, and **Language**, get **ReqTemplate** and **Policy** that are appropriate. Include optional URLs and the **RequestType**, then sign and send to EE.

Reception by EE

Get the **Me-AqCInitRes** message from **Receive MessageWrapper**.
From signed data get **RRPID**, **LID-EE**, **Chall-EE**, **CAEThumb**,
BrandCRLIdentifier, **Thumbs**, **RegTemplate**, **PolicyText**, and
RequestType. Check **RRPID**, **Thumbs**, and **Chall-EE** match those
sent in the **Me-AqCInitReq**. Verify Thumbs match those sent in
Me-AqCInitReq. Display the **PolicyText** and require the user to
acknowledge before generating a **CertReq**.

5.4.4 Generate or Renew Certificate

The EE now enters the information needed by the **RegForm**, and
the SET application sends the **CertReq** message to the CA.
Following validation of the **CertReq**, the generated or renewed
certificate is returned to the End Entity in a **CertRes**.

The Certificate Request (**CertReq**) contains the new public keys,
renewed certificates (if applicable), the filled-in registration
form, End Entity account information, and secret keys to be used
by the CA to encrypt the Certificate Response (**CertRes**), along
with other reference numbers and challenges. The payload of the
message plus a hash of the EE account information is signed
using the private key corresponding to the signature certificate
being renewed (if it exists), and the new signature private key.
The signed data plus the signatures are then encrypted using a
symmetric algorithm. The symmetric key used for this encryption
is OAEP, processed along with the End Entity account
information, and the result is encrypted using a public key
algorithm.

PDU	Description

CertReq
  CertReqData
	<EncX{EE, CA, CertReqData, AcctInfo}, Enc{EE,CA,CertReqData}>
	  {RRPID, LID-EE, Chall-EE3, [LID-CA], [Chall-CA], RequestType,
	    RequestDate, [IDData], RegFormID, [RegForm],
	    [CaBackKeyData], PublicKeySorE, [EEThumb], [Thumbs]}

RRPID	Request/response pair ID, statistically unique
LID-EE	Copied from **RegFormRes** or **Me-AqCInitRes**
Chall-EE3	EE challenge to CA signature
LID-CA	Copied from **RegFormRes** or **Me-AqCInitRes**
Chall-CA	EE challenge to CA signature
RequestType	See table in **Me-AqCInitReq** description
RequestDate	Date of request
EE-Tags3	Fresh challenge
CA-Tags2	From **RegFormRes**
IDData	See 5.4.2. Omit if EE is cardholder.
RegForm ID	Value identifies specific form, CA assigned
RegForm	**{{FieldName, FieldValue} +}** The fieldnames from **RegFormRes**, now accompanied by values filled in by EE's SET program
FieldName	Names of fields from registration form
FieldValue	Values entered by EE
CaBackKeysData	**{CaAlgId, CaKey}** protects the CaMsg
CaAlgId	Symmetric key algorithm identifier
CaKey	Secret key corresponding to the algorithm identifier
PublicKeySorE	**{[PublicKeyS], [PublicKey]}**
PublicKeyS	Public signature key to certify
PublicKeyE	Public encryption key to certify
EEThumb	Thumbprint of entity key-exchange certificate that is being renewed
Thumbs	List of certs CRL, and BCI held by EE
AcctInfo	**<PanData0, AcctData>** If requester is cardholder, use **PanData0**
PanData0	**{PAN, CardExpiry, CardSecret, EXNonce}**
PAN	Primary Acct Number
CardExpiry	Expiration data
CardSecret	Cardholders part of **PANSecret**
EXNonce	Fresh nonce
AcctData	**{AcctIdentification, EXNonce}**
AcctIdentification	Defined by Brand
EXNonce	Fresh nonce

CertReq Generation

If request is for a new or renewed signature certificate or non-cardholder with new or renewed encryption cert, then generate private/public key pair.

Build "to be signed" data by including **RequestType**. Also, if merchant or acquirer, include **IDData** and authentication data. If authentication data is not included, pad field with blanks. For all, include **RegForm**.

Optionally, select from the "tunneling" private extension in the CA key encryption certificate, a common preferred encryption algorithm for the CA to use to encrypt **CAMsg** in the **CertRes**. Include the algorithm ID and a key in **CaAlgID** and **CaKey**, respectively. Send to CA.

CA Reception/Validation of CertReq

Decrypt and verify signature of **CertReq**. If the previously received **RequestType** indicates a new or renewed signature certificate is being requested, verify the signature using the new signature public key contained in **PublicKeyS**. If the previously received **RequestType** indicates a signature certificate is being renewed or an encryption certificate is being requested, verify the signature using the public key within the renewed signature certificate. Get **RequestType**, **IDData**, **RegForm**, **CaBackKeyData**, and the new signature and/or encryption certificates. If **RequestType** indicates renewal, make sure certs have not been renewed before. From the list of **CaBackKeyData**, select the first algorithm that is supported, and use the corresponding **CaKey** for encrypting the **CertRes**.

If the validation fails, the CA prepares a **CertRes** message with the appropriate status. The **CertRes** message is either sent to the End Entity immediately (if the EE is using e-mail), or a **CertInqRes** (which contains the same information as the **CertRes**) is sent in response to a **CertInqReq** (if the EE is using the Web).

If the validation of all fields is successful, processing continues with financial institution authentication. This is outside the scope of SET, but we will assume it proceeds normally and in the affirmative. It may inject some delay into the processing cycle, however.

Let's look at the **CertRes** response that the CA will generate. The **CertRes** contains either the requested certificates or the status of the certificate request. The **CertRes** will be signed and can be encrypted, depending on the data that is included in the message. If the **CertRes** is to contain any cardholder information (such as the currency or a message to the cardholder), the message must be encrypted using a common symmetric (secret key) algorithm supported by both the CA and the EE. If an encryption algorithm cannot be found that is acceptable, the cardholder information will be omitted from the message.

PDU	Description
CertRes	`<S(CA, CertResData), EncK (CaBackKeyData, CertResData)>`
CertResData	`{RRPID, LID-EE, Chall-EE3, LID-CA, CertStatus, [CertThumbs], [Brand CRLIdentifier], [Thumbs]}`
CABackKeyData	Copied from prior **CertReq**
RRPID	Request/response pair
LID-EE	Copied from prior **CertReq**
Chall-EE3	Copied from prior **CertReq**
LID-CA	Copied from prior **CertReq**
CertStatus	`{CertStatusCode,[Nonce CCA], [EEMessage],`
See Table 5.6	`[CaMsg], [FailedItem +]}`
Nonce-CCA	Present if EE is a cardholder; half of shared secret between Cardholder and CCA
EEMessage	Message to be displayed on EE system
CaMsg	`{[CardLogoURL], [BrandLogoURL], [CardCurrency], [CardholderMsg]}`
CardLogoURL	URL for card graphic
BrandLogoURL	URL for brand logo
CardCurrency	Cardholder's billing currency
CardholderMsg	Message for Cardholder
FailedItem	`[ItemNumber,ItemReason]`
ItemNumber	Position of failed item in registration fields
ItemReason	Reason, in text
CertThumbs	The thumbprints of the enclosed, newly generated End Entity signature and or encryption certificates
BrandCRLIdentifier	List of CRL to be screened against
Thumbs	Certs held

CA Generation of CertRes

If the **CertRes** will contain **CaMsg** and if the **CertReq** included a key (**CaBackKeyData**) to encrypt the **CertRes**, the CA generates

Table 5.6. CertStatusCode

Code	Meaning	Source
requestComplete	Certificate request approved	CA
invalidLanguage	Invalid language in initiation request	CA
invalidBIN	Certificate request rejected because of invalid BIN	Issuer or Acquirer
sigValidationFail	Certificate request rejected because of signature validation failure	CA
decryptionError	Certificate request rejected because of decryption error	CA
requestInProgress	Certificate request in progress	CA, Issuer, or Acquirer
rejectedByIssuer	Certificate request rejected by Issuer	Issuer
requestPended	Certificate request pending	CA, Issuer, or Acquirer
rejectedByAquirer	Certificate request rejected by Acquirer	Acquirer
regFormAnswerMalformed	Certificate request rejected because of malformed registration form item(s)	CA
rejectedByCA	Certificate request rejected by Certificate Authority	CA
unableToEncryptCertRes	Certificate authority didn't receive key, so is unable to encrypt response to cardholder	CA

the **CertRes** as Signed Data within Enveloped Data. Include the **CardLogo** URL, **BrandLogo** URL, **CardCurrency**, and/or the cardholder message. If the requester is a cardholder, include **Nonce-CCA**. Compute the thumbs of the EE certificates and **CertThumbs**. Sign the data from all the above steps (collectively called "part 1" later) with the CA signature cert. Include new certs in SignedData structure. Encrypt the signed data, using the selected algorithm and key indicated by **CaBackKeyData** in the **CertReq**. Send to EE via **MessageWrapper**.

The **CertReq** will be signed but not encrypted if any of the following conditions is met:

If the EE is a cardholder and the **CertReq** did not include a key to encrypt the **CertRes**, or a common algorithm is not supported by both the CA and the EE, or the CA does not have a **CaMsg** to transmit, or the CA is returning status in the **CertRes**, or if the EE is a merchant or an acquirer Payment Gateway.

It's important to note that if the CA has a **CaMsg** or **Nonce-CCA** to include in the **CertRes** but does not have a key to encrypt the message, the **CaMsg** and/or **Nonce-CCA** will be omitted from the message. The presence of the key is mandatory for the transmission of these two fields.

EE Reception

If the **CertRes** contains signed data within enveloped data, then decrypt and verify the signature of the **CertRes**, using inverse **EncK** processing and performing symmetric decryption using the algorithm and key that was sent to the CA in **CaBackKeyData**, in the **CertReq**.

If the **CertStatusCode** indicates "certificate request complete," then retrieve the new certificates from the SignerInfo field and validate the signatures. Verify that the **CertThumbs** received match those sent in **CertReq**. If it does, retrieve the **CaMsg**, display the logos and **CardholderMsg**, and store the card currency. Verify that the public keys in the certificate(s) correspond to the private keys. If a cardholder, the following additional steps will be necessary: Compute (**Nonce-CCA** $\oplus$ **CardNonce**) to obtain **PANSecret**. Compute the Unique cardholder ID (defined as HMAC-SHA-1{{**PAN**, **Expiry**}, **PANSecret**}). (This is called "Salted Hash," in the X.509 certificate definitions.) Verify that the result matches the value in the certificate.

If the **CertStatusCode** indicates any status other than "Certificate Request complete," display EEMessage. Should the validation performed by the EE fail for any reason, an Error message is sent to the CA.

5.4.5 Certificate Inquiries

If the certificate is not returned immediately in the **CertRes**, the End Entity can request the status of its certificate request by sending a **CertInqReq** to the CA. The **CertInqRes** will return the certificate if it's ready or will say when it will be ready.

PDU	Description
CertInqReq	S(EE, CertInqReqTBS)
CertInqReqTBS	{RRPID, LID-EE, Chall-EE3, LID-CA}
RRPID	Request/response pair
LID-EE	Copied from **CertRes**
Chall-EE3	EE challenge to CA signature
LID-CA	Copied from **CertRes**

EE Generation of CertInqReq

Include **LID-EE** and **LID-CA**. Generate **RRPID**. Sign with either or both of the private keys corresponding to the renewed or new EE signature certificate.

CA Reception

Using **LID-CA** and **RRPID** as an index, obtain status of certificate. Either send the cert to the EE or update the **CertStatusCode** and return **CertInqRes**.

PDU	Description
CertInqRes	Formatted identical to **CertRes** in 5.4.3.

The field definitions may be found under **CertRes** in the previous section.

CA Generation

The steps are the same as for **CertRes**, as described in the last section.

EE Reception

The steps are the same as for **CertRes**, as described in the last section.

5.4.6 Certificate Revocation/Cancellation

The SET architects made certain assumptions when they designed how to revoke certificates. One of their stated goals was to minimize changes necessary to the existing issuers' payment card system in order to support certificate revocation. Also they wished to maximize reuse of the existing payment card infrastructure.

They also assumed that a cardholder certificate is bound to the payment card account. That is, when a certificate is cancelled, the associated payment card number will be cancelled. When a payment card is lost/stolen or the account is terminated, the certificate is also no longer usable.

When a merchant's certificate is cancelled, only the acquirer needs to know. This is because all payments are authorized via the acquirer. If a cardholder attempts to purchase from a merchant whose certificate has been cancelled, the acquirer will reject the purchase. Furthermore, a person in possession of a compromised private key from a merchant cannot extract payment card numbers directly from cardholder purchase requests since the account numbers are encrypted with the acquirer's public key.

Let's look at the case where a cardholder's private key (and its associated certificate) is compromised necessitating cancellation. The issuer is the key to this process. Since payment requests must go to the cardholder's issuer for payment authorization, the issuer can maintain the cardholder certificate-cancelled status in the context of the payment card hotlists that are currently maintained. So when a payment authorization request is received from the acquirer for an account with a cancelled certificate, the issuer will reject the request because the account number has been cancelled.

The situation differs with a merchant. When merchants terminate their association with a specific acquirer, they can reject all payment requests from that merchant. The acquirer Payment Gateway will either use the existing system to support merchant authentication, or will maintain a local list of merchant certificates that are not to be accepted. In either case, SET needs will cause minimal disruption to the existing ways of doing things.

A Payment Gateway has two certificates: the Key Encryption Certificate (used for encrypting the **PI**) and its signature certificate. Although storage of the private keys depends on the policy of the brand, they are usually stored in hardware modules, with restricted access available.

In the event that one or more of the acquirer's Payment Gateway private keys are compromised (or suspected of compromise), the acquirer must immediately remove the private keys from the acquirer Payment Gateway.

The certificates corresponding to compromised acquirer Payment Gateway private keys will be placed on Certificate

Revocation Lists (CRLs). These CRLs will be generated and distributed by the Payment Gateway CA, as previously outlined. When new certificates are distributed to the acquirer Payment Gateway, merchants will receive them in the same fashion as acquirer certificate renewals. As merchants receive certificates with more recent validity dates, the older certificates are purged from the system. Consequently, the suspect certificate will be effectively removed from the system as soon as a newer acquirer certificate is received by a merchant.

In the event that a CA certificate is compromised, the identity of the compromised CA certificate is included in a CA CRL and distributed to all entities in the system. A list of all up-to-date brand-specific CRLs is contained within the **BrandCRLIdentifier**. An EE will use this to check that it holds valid CRLs. (CRLs are not issued for cardholder and merchant certificates; different mechanisms are used to check the validity of these certificates.)

A CA CRL is distributed via existing messages. For example, the CA distributes the CRL to the acquirer Payment Gateways in the **Me-AqCInitRes** message with each renewal. The CA also distributes CRLs to a cardholder in all downstream response messages. A PG will distribute the CRL to merchants in the **AuthRes** message, since the Thumbs in the **AuthReq** will not include the latest CRL. Also, the merchant distributes the CA CRL to the cardholder in the **PInitRes** or **PRes** when the **PInitReq** or **PReq** Thumbprints do not include one or more of the latest CRLs.

Brand-level CA's manage a **BrandCRLIdentifier** (BCI) used to identify CRLs to be validated. BCI is a signed sequence of CA subject names having CRLs that must be included in the validation of signatures. If the BCI has a CRL as an element, that CRL must be part of the validation chain. Because only one BCI is valid at a time, each new one supersedes the preceding one.

The CAs that can create CRLs and the types of certificates that appear on those CRLs are listed below.

A CRL created by	Contains entries for
Root CA	Brand CA
Brand CA	Geo-political CA, cardholder CA, merchant CA, Payment Gateway CA
Geo-political CA	Cardholder CA, merchant CA, Payment Gateway CA, Payment Gateway

The Brand CA maintains a World Wide Web page on which it keeps the up-to-date BCI and all CRLs referenced by the BCI. CAs and Payment Gateways will regularly download the BCI and CRLs. Cardholder and merchant software can also download the BCI and CRL at their discretion. The web page for retrieving the BCI and CRLs must include at minimum a MIME object containing the PCKS #7 message (as described below). Any other content on this page is at the discretion of the brand.

The PKCS #7 message containing the BCI and CRLs will be encapsulated in a MIME message constructed as follows:

```
MIME-Version: 1.0
Content-Type: application/set-payment
Content-Length: <as appropriate--covering inner MIME>
Content-Transfer-Encoding: binary
MIME-Version: 1.0
Content-Type: application/set-payment; type=BCI-CRL
Content-Length: <as appropriate>
Content-Transfer-Encoding: binary
<PKCS #7 message>
```

The PKCS #7 message included in the MIME header described above is the BCI. Any CRLs referenced by the BCI are included in the CertificateRevocationLists portion of the PKCS #7 SignedData.

Note that the **BrandCRLIdentifier** (further described in 5.8) is defined using the SIGNED type, which does not include certificates and CRLs. **BCIDistribution**, which contains the **BrandCRLIdentifier**, is defined using the S type, which does include certificates and CRLs.

The **BCIDistribution** message created by a brand CA includes the brand CRL signing certificate and all certificates in its trust hierarchy and all CRLs referenced by the **BrandCRLIdentifier** and all certificates necessary to validate the signatures on those CRLs.

A message receiver verifies the signature on the BCI of a message, then checks if BCI's **brandID** matches **brandID** associated with the message. If so, check **validityperiod** is current, check BCI sequence number is not less than the last BCI sequence number in cache, and check for brand-name agreement. Also, check that all applicable CRL numbers against the CRL numbers are included in **BrandCRLIdentifier**. If CRL number is not found, discard this message and log the exception. Save the resultant CRL for chain validation.

It's important to note that updated BCI can be distributed by means other than SET by a Brand-level CA. It may not even be by networked means, if the CA's security concerns do not warrant it.

The message sender will check if the BCI's hash (Thumbprint) matches a Thumbprint that came in the request message. If so, check the BCI's sequence number. If it is the most recent, append the Thumbprint to the response message. If it is not, find the most recent BCI and append that to the response message. Repeat until all relevant BCIs have been examined.

5.5 CERTIFICATE FORMATS

♦ ♦

This section contains a description of the X.509 Version 3 certificate format and certificate extensions used in SET. The certificate format includes the use of public and private extensions to support all SET certificate requirements. See Table 5.7.

5.5.1 Certificate Subject Name Format

The following Object Identifiers (OIDs) shown in brackets are needed for defining items with a format of Name in SET Certificates:

♦ countryName [2 5 4 6]

♦ organizationName [2 5 4 10]

♦ organizationalUnitName [2 5 4 11]

♦ commonName [2 5 4 3]

The ASN.1 notation for the Name OIDs is:

```
id-at-commonName              OBJECT IDENTIFIER ::= { id-at 3 }
id-at-countryName             OBJECT IDENTIFIER ::= { id-at 6 }
id-at-organizationName        OBJECT IDENTIFIER ::= { id-at 10 }
id-at-organizationalUnitName  OBJECT IDENTIFIER ::= { id-at 11 }
```

For a cardholder:

```
countryName=<Country of Issuing Financial Institution>
organizationName=<BrandID>
organizationalUnitName=<Name of Acquiring Financial Institution>
commonName=<Optional-Unique ID>
```

Table 5.7. Basic X.509 Format

Name	Format and Value Restrictions	Description
Version	Integer	Indicates the certificate version. Always less than 3.
SerialNumber	Integer	unique serial number assigned by the Issuer (CA).
Signature .AlgorithmIdentifier	OID and type	Defines the algorithm used to sign the certificate.
Issuer	Name	The field contains the Distinguished Name (DN) of the CA that issued the cert.
Validity .notBefore	UTC Time	Specifies when the certificate becomes active.
Validity .notAfter	UTC Time	Specifies when the certificate expires.
Subject	Name	Contains the Distinguished Name of the entity using the key.
SubjectPublicKeyInfo .algorithm .AlgorithmIdentifier	OID, and type	This field specifies what algorithms can be used with this key.
SubjectPublicKeyInfo .subjectPublicKey	Bit string	Contains the public key provided in the certificate request.
IssuerUniqueID		Not used in SET.
SubjectUniqueID		Not used in SET.
Extensions .extnId	OID format	Contains the extension's OID as defined by X.509, or SET.
Extensions .critical	Boolean; 0 false, 1 true	Each extension description states how this field will be set.
Extensions .extnValue		The extension data.

For a merchant:

```
countryName=<Country of Acquiring Financial Institution>
organizationName=<BrandID>
organizationalUnitName=<Name of Acquiring Financial Institution>
commonName=<Name of Merchant as printed on Cardholder statement>
```

For a payment gateway:

```
countryName=<Country of Acquiring Financial Institution>
organizationName=<BrandID>
organizationalUnitName=<Descriptive Name>
commonName=<Optional-Unique Payment Gateway ID>
```

For the cardholder certificate authority:

```
countryName=<Country of Issuing Financial Institution>
organizationName=<Brand ID >
organizationalUnitName = <Descriptive Name>
commonName=<Optional-Unique ID>
```

For the merchant certificate authority:

```
countryName=<Country of Acquiring Financial Institution>
organizationName=<Brand ID >
organizationalUnitName = <Descriptive Name>
commonName=<Optional-Unique ID>
```

For the payment gateway certificate authority:

```
countryName=<Country of Acquiring Financial Institution>
organizationName=<Brand ID >
organizationalUnitName = <Descriptive Name>
commonName=<Optional-Unique ID>
```

For the geo-political certificate authority:

```
countryName=<Country of organization>
organizationName=<Brand ID >
organizationalUnitName = <Descriptive Name>
commonName=<Optional-Unique ID>
```

For the brand certificate authority:

```
countryName=<Country of Brand>
organizationName=<Brand ID >
organizationalUnitName = <Descriptive Name>
commonName=<Optional-Unique ID>
```

For the root certificate authority:

```
countryName=<Country of Root CA >
organizationName=<SET>
commonName=<Optional-Unique ID>
```

5.6 X.509 Certificate Extensions

SET makes use of several extensions to the X.509 certificate format. In this section we examine the AuthorityKeyIdentifier, KeyUsage, PrivateKeyUsagePeriod, CertificatePolicies, SubjectAltName, BasicConstraints, and IssuerAltName. Some of these extensions are critical to SET usage, while some are not. All contribute in some important way to SET functionality, however.

5.6.1 Authority Key Identifier Extension

A CA may have more than one certificate at one time. It may need different certificates for functionally different purposes, or as key-updating occurs. This extension, which is used to identify which CA certificate must be used to verify the certificate's signature, is non-critical. It contains the following fields: Key Identifier, Certificate Issuer, and Certificate Serial Number (Table 5.8). In SET, the Certificate Issuer and the Certificate Serial Number are always set.

Table 5.8. Authority Key Identifier Extension

Name	Format and Value Restrictions	Description
authorityKeyIdentifier .AuthorityKeyId .keyIdentifier	Octet String	N/A—Not used in SET
authorityKeyIdentifier .AuthorityKeyId .certIssuer	Name	This field contains the Issuer Name of the CA certificate that issued this certificate.
authorityKeyIdentifier .AuthorityKeyId .certSerialNumber	Positive Integer	Contains the serial number of the certificate associated with the private key used to sign this certificate.

5.6.2 Key Usage Extension

The key usage extension indicates that the key may be used for a digital signature, a certificate signature, both data encryption and key encryption, CRL signature or certificate signature, and CRL signature (Table 5.9). This extension, which locks the key's usage down without ambiguity, is a critical extension.

5.6.3 Key Usage Period Extension

The critical extension described in Table 5.10 marks the period that a key is valid by stating a beginning and end time of validity.

Table 5.9. Key Usage Extension

• •

Name	Format and Value Restrictions	Description
keyUsage .keyUsage	0, 5, 6, or {2, 3} or {5, 6} only	This field states whether the public key contained in the certificate may be used for signature verification, encryption, etc.

SET Entity Type	KeyUsage Value	BasicConstraints CA Value	Description
EE	0	EE	Public key may be used to verify message signatures.
EE	2 & 3	EE	Public key may be used to encrypt keys and data in the OAEP envelope.
CA	0	EE	Public key may be used to verify message signatures.
CA	2 & 3	EE	Public key may be used to encrypt keys and data in the OAEP envelope.
CA	5	CA	Public key may be used to verify certificate signatures.
CA	6	EE	Public key may be used to verify CRL signatures.
CA	5 & 6	CA	Public key may be used to verify certificate and CRL signatures.

5.6.4 Private Key Usage Period Extension

This critical extension specifies the period of time that the private key corresponding to the certificate is valid (see Table 5.11).

Table 5.10. Key Usage Period Extension

Name	Format and Value Restrictions	Description
privateKeyUsagePeriod .PrivateKeyUsagePeriod .notBefore	Date and Generalized Time	the start date and time of the private key's validity period
privateKeyUsagePeriod .PrivateKeyUsagePeriod .notAfter	Date and Generalized Time	the end of the private key's validity period

Table 5.11. Private Key Usage Period Extension

Name	Format and Value Restrictions	Description
privateKeyUsagePeriod .PrivateKeyUsagePeriod .notBefore	Date and Generalized Time	the start date and time of the private key's validity period
privateKeyUsagePeriod .PrivateKeyUsagePeriod .notAfter	Date and Generalized Time	the end of the private key's validity period

5.6.5 Certificate Policies Extension

This critical extension delineates the policies that the certificate supports (see Table 5.12). A certificate may contain one or more of the certificate policies which are identified by a unique object identifier with an optional qualifier. Each CA may add one additional policy as a qualifier to the SET Root policy.

Table 5.12. Certificate Policies Extension

Name	Format and Value Restrictions	Description
policy	Object ID	The OID which points to the Root Brand's policy statement. The policy may be obtained from the URL or e-mail address provided in the qualifiers SETQualifier private extension.
policyQualifierId	Object ID	Set to id-set-setQualifier.
qualifier	SETQualifier	• Contains optional qualifiers to the Root policy. • Contains additional optional qualifying policies and their qualifiers.
SETQualifier .policyURL.	IA5String	URL where a copy of the policy statement may be found.
SETQualifier .policyEmail	IA5String	E-mail address where a copy of the policy statement may be found.
SETQualifier .policyDigest	Octet String	The hash of the policy statement, computed using the indicated digestAlgorithm.
SETQualifier .terseStatement	DirectoryString	A statement declaring any disclaimers associated with the issuing of the certificate.
SETQualifier .additionalPolicies .policyOID	Object ID	The OID which points to the CA's policy statement. The policy may be obtained from the URL or e-mail address provided in the associated qualifiers.
SETQualifier .policyAddedBy	Certificate Type	Indicates the CA that the policy corresponds to and that added the policy to the generated certificate.

The following qualifiers to each policy may be included in this extension: policyDigest, terseStatement, policyURL, and policyEmail.

Each of the above items is optional. The policyURL and policyEmail contain addresses where a copy of the policy statement may be obtained. A hash of the policy may be contained in the policyDigest, and its value can be compared with the hashed value of the policy obtained from the URL or electronic mail address. The terse statement, if present, may contain information about the generation and use of the certificate.

5.6.6 Subject Alt Name Extension

This noncritical extension contains one or more of a variety of alternate subject names. The field is included only if the requesting element specifies an alternate name in the request (see Table 5.13).

5.6.7 Basic Constraints Extension

This critical extension indicates whether the certified subject is a CA, End Entity, or both. If it is a CA, the number of sub-CA levels that may be authenticated by the subject is included (see Table 5.14.

Table 5.13. Subject Alt Name Extension

Name	Format and Value Restrictions	Description
subjectAltName .GeneralNames	Name	One or more alternate names for the distinguished name in the certificate; the alternate name may be an e-mail address, a URL, etc.

Table 5.14. Basic Constraints Extension

Name	Format and Value Restrictions	Description
basicConstraints .basicConstraints .cAsubjectType	Boolean	True for all CAs and subordinate CAs; false omitted for End Entities.
basicConstraints .basicConstraints .pathLenConstraint	Integer; only set if the subjectType is a CA	Indicates the number of levels of CAs that this certificate may sign certificates for. For example, a zero in this field means that the CA certificate may only be used to sign EE certificates.

5.7 X.509 SET Private Extensions

This section defines the following private extensions for SET: **HashedRootKey**, **CertificateType**, **MerchantData**, **CardholderCertificateRequired**, **Tunneling**, and **SET Qualifier**.

5.7.1 Hashed Root Key Private Extension

This critical extension only occurs in Root certificates. It contains the Thumbprint (hash) of the next root key. The hash is computed using the SHA-1 hash function, and is used to authenticate the next Root certificate (see Table 5.15).

5.7.2 Certificate Type Private Extension

This critical extension is included in every SET certificate, and identifies which type of certificate is being presented

Table 5.15. Hashed Root Key Private Extension

Name	Format and Value Restrictions	Description
hashedRootKey .DigestedData .digestAlgorithm .algorithm	OID	The OID of the hashing algorithm used over the root key. In SET, SHA-1 is used.
HashedRootKey .DigestedData .digestAlgorithm .parameters		Set to NULL. Not used
hashedRootKey .DigestedData .contentInfo .contentType	OID	Sset to id-set-rootKeyThumb.
hashedRootKey .DigestedData .contentInfo .content		Omitted. Not populated
hashedRootKey .DigestedData .digest .rootKeyThumbprint	Octet String	The hash of the DER encoded subjectPublicKeyInfo. root key

Table 5.16. Certificate Type Private Extension

Name	Format and Value Restrictions	Description
certificateType .certificateTypeSyntax	one value of 0–9 or any grouping of values 3,4, and 5	Specifies what type of element will be using the certificate. This field is based on the type of certificate request received.

(Table 5.16). It is used to distinguish between the different elements. For the following End Entity or CA types, the certificate can have only one type:

♦ Cardholder (CARD)

♦ Merchant (MER)

♦ Acquirer Payment Gateway (PGWY)

♦ Geo-political Certification Authority (GCA)

♦ Brand Certification Authority (BCA)

♦ Root Certification Authority (RCA)

For the following CA types, multiple certificate types are possible. For example, the certificate type can be both a cardholder Certification Authority and a merchant Certification Authority.

♦ Cardholder Certification Authority (CCA)

♦ Merchant Certification Authority (MCA)

♦ Payment Certification Authority (PCA)

5.7.3 Merchant Data Private Extension

An Acquirer needs certain information about merchants. This noncritical extension contains all data needed by the Payment Gateway. Most of this data is obtained from the merchant in the registration form during the certificate-request processing (Table 5.17).

Table 5.17. Merchant Data Private Extension

◆ ◆

Name	Format and Value Restrictions	Description
MerID	Character String; Required	The merchant identification assigned by the Acquirer
MerAcquirerBIN	Numeric String; Required	The BIN used for settlement of the merchant's transactions with the Acquirer
MerCountry	INTEGER	The ISO-3166 numeric country code for the location of the merchant
MerAuthFlag	BOOLEAN: (FALSE) not authorized to receive Cardholder information (TRUE) authorized to receive Cardholder information	Some Acquirers allow certain Merchants to receive additional Cardholder payment information in order to accommodate non-SET business processing of transactions.

The following items may appear more than once to carry information about the merchant in multiple character sets or translated into multiple languages:

Name	Format and Value Restrictions	Description
Language	Character String; Optional	RFC 1766 definition of language
Name	Character String; Required	The name by which the merchant is known to its customers
City	Character String; Required	The name of the city where the merchant is located
StateProvince	Character String; Optional Required	The state or province where the merchant is located
PostalCode	Character String; Optional Required	The postal code for the merchant's location
CountryName	Character String; Required	The name of the country (corresponds to MerCountry)

Table 5.18. Cardholder Certificate Required Private Extension

Name	Format and Value Restrictions	Description
cardCertRequired	Boolean	Indicates whether a cardholderís certificate is required by the brand

5.7.4 Cardholder Certificate Required Private Extension

This noncritical private extension tells whether or not the Payment Gateway will support transactions with cardholders who don't have a certificate (Table 5.18).

5.7.5 Tunneling Private Extension

This noncritical private extension tells if the CA or Payment Gateway supports the "tunneling" of encrypted messages to the cardholder. If so, the extension will delineate a list of supported symmetric encryption algorithms (Table 5.19).

Table 5.19. Tunneling Private Extension

Name	Format and Value Restrictions	Description
Tunneling .tunneling	Boolean	Indicates whether tunneling is supported by the CA or payment gateway
Tunneling .tunnelAlgIDs	Object Identifier	List of symmetric encryption algorithm identifiers that the CA or payment gateway supports

5.8 CERTIFICATE REVOCATION LIST AND BrandCRL IDENTIFIER

The Certificate Revocation List (CRL) is a mechanism defined by X.509 for publicizing and distributing lists of revoked, unexpired certificates. Each CA (except the MCA and CCA) will maintain a CRL. All CAs will distribute CRLs to all the downstream parties that trust them. The BrandCRLIdentifier (BCI) contains a list of all the current CRLs within a given brand. Whenever a CA issues a new CRL, the associated BCI must be updated. The BCI is distributed in all downstream messages. The BCI and the CRLs it identifies are the data for the mechanism that screens certificates and should contain the most up-to-date revocation information.

Each CA in SET is responsible for revoking compromised certificates that it generated and signed. Revocation occurs when the CA places the serial numbers of the compromised certificate on its CRL. The CA is identified within the CRL by its distinguished name, and the CRL is signed by the CA.

Table 5.20 lists the information contained in a CRL.

CRLs are distributed within the CRL field of the PKCS #7 **SignedData**. As we have seen in previous chapters, an entity in the SET protocol shows the CRLs it's holding by putting the Thumbprints in the first upstream (toward the CA) request message. The recipient checks the Thumbprints and includes any missing CRLs in its downstream (away from the CA to the End Entities) response message. Note that the CRL contains only unexpired certificates that have been revoked. As the CRL is updated (and the CRLNumber is incremented by one), expired certificates are removed from the CRL.

Table 5.20. Information in a CRL

◆ ◆

Name	Format and Value Restrictions	Description
CRL .version	Integer; V2	Indicates the CRL version. Always less than 2.
CRL .signature .algorithmIdentifier	OID and type	Defines the algorithm used to sign the CRL.
CRL .Issuer	Name	The field contains the subject DN of the CA that issued the revoked certificate. This field must match the value in the Subject Name in the CA Certificate.
CRL .thisUpdate	UTC Time	Specifies when the CRL was generated.
CRL .NextUpdate	UTC Time	Specifies when the CRL expires.
CRL .revokedCertificates .certSerialNumber	Integer	The serial numbers of the revoked certificates
CRL .revokedCertificates .revocationDate	UTC Time	The date of revocation.
CRL .revokedCertificates .extensions	Extensions	X.509 construct that is not used in SET.
CRL .extensions	Extensions	Two extensions are supported in this field, CRLNumber and AuthorityKeyIdentifier.

A **BrandCRLIdentifier** (BCI) is analogous to a CRL, but is brand-specific. The BCI contains a list of CRL numbers, and is distributed in all downstream response messages. An entity receiving the BCI must verify that it holds all of the CRLs on the list. The BCI is updated every time a CA within the Brand's subtrees updates a CRL. The BCI is signed by the Brand-level CA

Table 5.21. Data Structure of a BCI

Name	Format and Value Restrictions	Description
BrandCRLIdentifier .version	Integer; V1	Indicates the BCI version. Always V1.
BrandCRLIdentifier .sequenceNum	Integer	Monatomically increasing sequence number. The higher the sequence number, the more recent the BCI.
BrandCRLIdentifier .brandID	Name	The BrandID of the BCI.
BrandCRLIdentifier .bciValidity .bciValidFrom	Generalized Time	Specifies when the BCI becomes valid.
BrandCRLIdentifier .bciValidity .bciValidTo	Generalized Time	Specifies when the BCI expires.
BrandCRLIdentifier .crl-ID .issuerName	Name	The IssuerName of a CRL that needs to be used in signature validations.
BrandCRLIdentifier .crl-ID .crlNumber	Integer	The value of the CRLNumber extension of the CRL.
BrandCRLIdentifier .extensions	Extensions	Only AuthorityKeyId extension is used in the BCI. The same restrictions are applied as in its use in CRLs and certificates.
AlgorithmIdentifier .algorithm	OID	
AlgorithmIdentifier .parameters	Null	
Hash	Bit string	The signature over the BCI.

using the private key corresponding to the CRLSign certificate. BCIs are generated on a scheduled interval that is set by the Brand, and may be transferred by means other than SET. Table 5.21 describes the data structure of a BCI.

Another way to express the data structure is in the form of a PDU.

PDU	Description
BrandCRLIdentifier S(CA,UnsignedBrandCRLIdentifier)	
UnsignedBrandCRLIdentifier	{Version, SequenceNum, BrandID, NotBefore, NotAfter, [CRLIdentiferSeq], Extensions}
Version	Version number
SequenceNum	Incremented for each new **BCI**
BrandID	Card brand whose CRLs are contained here
NotBefore	Beginning of validity period
NotAfter	End of validity period
CRLIdentiferSeq	{CRLIdentifer + }
CRLIdentifer	{IssuerName, CRLNumber}
IssuerName	CA of the CRL
CRLNumber	Sequence number of CRL
Extensions	CRL extensions, including CRLNumber extension

Chapter 6

• • •

INTERNET DATA TRANSPORT PROTOCOLS

And I have known the eyes already, known them all—
The eyes that fix you in a formulated phrase,
And when I am formulated, sprawling on a pin,
When I am pinned and wriggling on the wall,
Then how should I begin?

—T.S. Eliot, "The Lovesong of J. Alfred Prufrock"

Secure Electronic Transfer protocol would have no reason for existing if it could not operate over that vast cloud of a network that we call the Internet. But there are different ways to transmit data over the Internet, e-mail or a Web browser, to name two. Even if the message content is the same, the manner in which they are presented and transmitted can differ. First, let's look at the messages sent between cardholder and merchant to see how SET deals with the Internet.

6.1 MERCHANT-CARDHOLDER MESSAGES: INITIALIZATION

◆ ◆

Because SET is a payment transaction, it does not explicitly deal with how the overall SET process is initiated. A payment request could be initiated indirectly by a shopping application or directly by a cardholder using a SET-aware browser. To synchronize the SET transaction, there must be a mechanism to "wake up" all the parties involved. The SET designers came up with a method that works via the Web or e-mail. Although the designers acknowledge that this initiation sequence may be superseded in the future as payment protocols mature and evolve, this one works as an initial way of doing things so that interoperability between SET applications may be assured. The initialization process for a payment request would look something like Figure 6.1.

The minimal SET initiation message is encapsulated using MIME conventions. MIME is an IETF standard (RFC 1521) for describing messages that can carry data of various types. They can carry GIF images, text, or application-specific documents. Such data is conceptually wrapped inside a MIME envelope, which identifies its type and other meta-information, such as length and transfer encoding.

A MIME message contains a header and a body. The body consists of the information content of a MIME message. The header contains meta-information, specifically key-value header fields that describe the associated message content. The header forms the "envelope" of a MIME message, and the body is carried within the envelope.

MIME is a recursive format, which means that a MIME message may be wrapped inside an outer MIME envelope. The inner MIME envelope would describe the content of the inner MIME

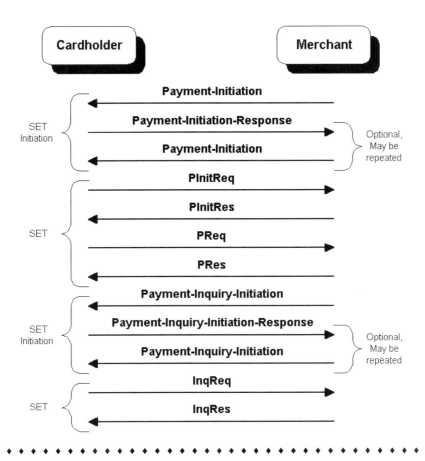

Figure 6.1. Initialization

message, and the outer envelope would describe the inner MIME message as a whole, including the inner MIME's envelope.

A variant of this "MIME-in-MIME" structure is used for encapsulated SET initiation messages. The inner MIME message is the SET initiation message itself, with the inner MIME envelope conveying meta-information appropriate for the particular SET transaction. In a payment request, for example, the inner message body carries the order description, and the **Content-Type** of the inner envelope for a payment request identifies the type of the enclosed order description. The outer MIME envelope describes the SET initiation message itself, with its **Content-Type** identifying the contents as a SET initiation message.

The minimal SET initiation message is described by a MIME type whose overall type is **application**, with a subtype that differs for payment and registration. The specific MIME subtypes are set-payment-initiation for the payment case (**PInitReq** and **InqReq**) and set-registration-initiation for registration (**CardCInitReq** and **CertInqReq**). The different types are used to allow the initiation messages to invoke applications other than the normal payment or registration, although the secondary MIME types may be mapped to the same helper applications as the main SET MIME types.

The advantage of MIME encapsulation is that it allows the message to be identified and processed appropriately by existing MIME-aware applications, such as mail readers and Web browsers. A Web browser could automatically start up a SET helper application to process data identified as a SET initiation message. It's important to realize that initiation messages may not be needed in the electronic mail scenario, where cardholder software is more likely to initiate payment transactions without prompting from the merchant. Similarly, initiation messages are not required in the Web scenario if the cardholder triggers requests directly using his or her SET application rather than indirectly through the merchant's Web page.

Because the initiation message is encapsulated as the body of a MIME message, the outer wrapper message should have a MIME type that triggers the appropriate initiation response mechanism.

In accordance with MIME conventions for a MIME message encapsulating another MIME message, the outer MIME message may be encoded as binary, 7-bit, or 8-bit (if it contains only plain ASCII characters), or as binary. (Binary permits the order description to contain any kind of application-specific data.) For SET initiation messages, the message body should be empty for all cases except that of payment.

The header fields follow the same generic format given by Section 3.1 of RFC 822. Each field consists of a name followed by a colon (":"), a single space (SP, ASCII 20 hex) character, and the value. Field values are terminated by the end of the line (CRLF, ASCII 0D 0A hex). Note that long field values may be expressed using multiple lines. Continuation lines are prefixed with a sequence of at least one linear white space character: space (SP, ASCII 20 hex) or horizontal tab (HT, ASCII 09 hex). An empty line (CRLF alone) separates the header from the body.

The MIME version of a message is indicated by the **Mime-Version** header field. SET implementations support MIME version 1.0 (since it is the version that is currently widely supported) and, when appropriate, indicate MIME version 1.0 in the header field of the MIME message. Single-part MIME alone is required by the designers. Even though some applications may support newer versions of MIME, it cannot be assumed that any other SET participant will support it.

Header fields other than the ones discussed so far are listed in Table 6.1

Other header fields include the **SET-Initiation-Type** field, which specifies the SET message that should be sent by the cardholder in response to the initiation message. The field value is **Payment-Initiation** for a payment request.

If the message is, as in this case, a payment request, the order description (**OD**) is the body of the initiation message. It's important to be aware that the order description may take any form, from plain text to application-specific spreadsheets. All SET

Table 6.1. Header Fields

◆ ◆

Field Name	Required	Field Value
MIME-Version	Yes.	"1.0"
Content-Type	Yes.	See text
Content-Length	No.	The length of the OD.
Content-Transfer-Encoding	Yes.	"Binary"
Content-Language	No.	Determined by the Merchant.
SET-Initiation-Type	Yes.	"Payment-Initiation"
SET-SET-URL	Only if **SET-Response-URL** is omitted.	Determined by the Merchant.
SET-Response-URL	Only if **SET-SET-URL** is omitted.	Determined by the Merchant.
SET-Query-URL	No.	Determined by the Merchant.
SET-Success-URL	Yes.	Determined by the Merchant.
SET-Failure-URL	No.	Determined by the Merchant.
SET-Cancel-URL	No.	Determined by the Merchant.
SET-Diagnostic-URL	No.	Determined by the Merchant.
SET-Version	Yes.	Determined by the Merchant.
SET-LID-M	No.	See text
SET-PurchAmt	Yes.	See text
SET-InstallTotalTrans	No. Mutually exclusive with **SET-Recurring**.	See text
SET-Recurring	No. Mutually exclusive with **SET-InstallTotalTrans**.	See text
SET-Brand	Yes, at least one.	Determined by the Merchant.
SET-Ext-OID	No.	Determined by the Merchant.
SET-Ext-Mandatory	No.	Determined by the Merchant.
SET-Ext-Data	No.	Determined by the Merchant.
SET-Echo-In-Response	No.	Determined by the Merchant.
SET-Echo-In-Request	No.	Determined by the Cardholder.

implementations are required to support plain text, but other encodings may also be supported.

An order description must satisfy MIME requirements, which means that order descriptions typed as text must use CRLF as the line terminator. The final line of an order description typed as text may be terminated with a CRLF, but this is not required.

SET protocol ensures that the customer and merchant have agreed on the order description by including a hash of the **OD** in the **PReq** message. All bytes in the inner message body are hashed, from the first character after the double CRLF that ends the inner MIME header through the end of the body. If a Content-Length field is specified, it must cover exactly the same bytes as are hashed.

Content-Transfer-Encoding specifies the encoding that has been used to prepare the data for transmission. The transfer-encoding field allows binary data to be encoded for transmission through even the most limited mail gateways. One common MIME encoding scheme is Base-64, which translates raw binary data into the 64 most commonly supported characters and back again. But for this type of message (merchant-cardholder), "binary" is used.

The **SET-PurchAmt** field is expressed in terms of the same three components (*currency, amount,* and *amtExp10*) used in the SET payment messages. These components are comma-delimited elements in the field value. The elements must appear in the specified order *(currency, amount, amtExp10)*.

The *currency* value is a numeric ASCII string specifying the three-digit ISO 4217 currency code. For example, a payment denominated in U.S. currency will have a currency value of "840." The *amount* value is a numeric ASCII string representing the amount of the payment, specified in terms of the stated currency. The *amtExp10* value is a numeric ASCII string representing an exponent base 10 such that *Amount* $* (10 ** amtExp10)$ is the amount's value in the minor unit of the specified currency. If the specified currency does not have a minor unit, then *amount* * (10 ** *amtExp10*) is the value in the major unit of the specified currency. If no minor unit of currency applies, *amtExp10* is 0.

For example, U.S. currency has the dollar as the major unit and the cent as the minor unit. Because 100 cents may be multiplied by (10 ** –2) to yield the equivalent amount of one dollar, *amtExp10* is –2. So, the value of $2.50 in U.S. dollars can be expressed as **SET-PurchAmt:** 840,250,–2. This amount is also included with the OD hash in the **PReq** message. If the **SET-PurchAmt** field is not present, the SET application is assumed to have obtained the payment amount through other means.

SET-LID-M is an optional field containing the merchant's label that identifies the current transaction. It may be an order number or other merchant-relevant information that is expressed as an ASCII hexadecimal string. If provided, this value will be converted to binary form and copied into the **LID-M** field of the payment initiation request (**PInitReq**) and subsequent payment messages.

Each initiation message may include one or more URLs that correspond to actions that the application may take in response to conditions that arise while processing the message. The fields listed in Table 6.1, which are of type *url*, must be supported by all applications.

It is important to realize that URLs only apply in a Web environment, and not in an e-mail one.

Initiation messages and their responses must support information that is used by the system generating a message to identify the transaction. Either system involved in the transaction

Table 6.2. URL Fields

◆ ◆

Field name:	Indicates the address to which the recipient should send:	Required or optional?
SET-SET-URL	a SET request message that corresponds to theinitiation message. (Alternatively, a SET initiation response message may be sent to **SET-Response-URL**.)	Required if **SET-Response-URL** is omitted. If this field is omitted, the application should send a SET initiation response message to the **SET-Response-URL**.
SET-Response-URL	a SET initiation response message, as an alternative to sending a SET request message to the **SET-SET-URL**.	Required if **SET-SET-URL** is omitted. If this field is omitted, a SET initiation response message may not be sent.
SET-Query-URL	Used for any subsequent SET inquiry request message	Optional. If this field is omitted, the application should send the inquiry message to the **SET-SET-URL**.
SET-Success-URL	a standard HTTP request upon successful completion of the processing of the current exchange of SET messages.	Required.
SET-Failure-URL	a standard HTTP request upon communications failure or time-out that occurs before the final SET message in the current SET message exchange.	Optional. If this field is omitted, the application should send the HTTP request to **SET-Success-URL** instead.
SET-Cancel-URL	a standard HTTP request if the user indicates that the action corresponding to the initiation message should be canceled.	Optional. If this field is omitted, the application should send the HTTP request to **SET-Success-URL** instead.
SET-Diagnostic-URL	a SET Error message according to the diagnostic log mechanism	Optional. If this field is omitted,the application should send the Error message to the **SET-SET-URL**.

may include information that the other system must repeat in any subsequent initiation message or response. They are of type *text*.

SET-Echo-In-Response	This field may optionally be included in an initiation message. If the field is present, the recipient must copy it to any initiation response message generated.
SET-Echo-In-Request	This field may optionally be included in an initiation response message. If the field is present, the recipient must copy it to any subsequent initiation messages generated.

The prefix **SET-Ext-** in a header identifies a SET message extension that may apply to the processing of the message. Suffixes to this may include **OID** to signify an object-identifier for the content of the message extension, **Mandatory** which is a boolean indicating if the receiving application must include the extension in the corresponsding SET message, or **Data** which contains the value of the extension.

The URL fields may be repeated with different values. If so, they are alternatives which the cardholder's software must resolve. This is useful for the support of multiple protocols. For example, a merchant who supports SET through HTTP and SSL could specify

```
SET-SET-URL:
SET-SET-URL: https://www.merchant.com/payment
```

If HTTP is used, the cardholder's software will use the POST method to send encapsulated SET messages to the **SET-SET-URL** and **SET-Query-URL**. The cardholder software is expected (but not required) to use the GET method with the **SET-Success-URL**, **SET-Failure-URL**, and **SET-Cancel-URL**.

The **SET-Brand** field notes a card brand that is accepted by the merchant, and may be repeated for each brand that the merchant accepts. It is of the form

```
brandId[.product] ["<" url ">"]
```

"BrandId" and "product" are case sensitive.

The **SET-InstallTotalTrans** field authorizes payment in installments (such as split shipments or back orders). The value is a numeric ASCII string specifying the maximum number of permitted authorizations. This field is mutually exclusive with the **SET-Recurring** field. If the **SET-InstallTotalTrans** field is specified, the **SET-PurchAmt** field specifies the total amount of all authorized installments.

The **SET-Recurring** field is used for recurring payments. The field value is a space-delimited two-element list, specifying values for the *recurringFrequency* and *recurringExpiry*. The elements appear in the order *recurringFrequency, recurringExpiry*. The value of *recurringFrequency* is a numeric ASCII string specifying the maximum rate (in days) between authorizations. The value of *recurringExpiry* is an ASCII string specifying the final date, after which no further authorizations are permitted; it follows the ASN.1 syntax for **GeneralizedTime**, with the restriction that local times are not permitted. (This avoids ambiguity when the merchant and cardholder are located in different time zones.) It can be in either UTC time format or the difference between local and UTC times.

The UTC format is a string representing the calendar date and UTC time, in the format YYYYMMDDHHMM[SS[.f[f[f]]]] followed by a literal upper-case letter Z. That is, the string should consist of a four-digit representation of the year, a two-digit representation of the month, a two-digit representation of the day in the month, a two-digit representation of the hour (on a 24-hour clock), a two-digit representation of the minutes after the hour, an optional representation of the seconds after the minute, and a literal upper-case letter Z. If the seconds field is present, it may be followed by fractional seconds which are indicated by either a decimal comma or decimal point, followed by one to three digits.

If the format is different, it would be described in a string representing the calendar date and local time (in the format described above), followed by a representation of the time differential between local and UTC times. The time differential is given by a sign character ("+" or "−") followed by a string in the format of HHMM (two digits for hours followed by two digits for minutes). As an example, if the time difference were 5 hours, the string would be: 199705312106-0500.

An example of a **SET-Recurring** field is **SET-Recurring:** 31 199705312106Z. (This field is mutually exclusive with the **SET-RecurringTotalTrans** field.) If the **SET-Recurring** field is specified, the **SET-PurchAmt** field shall (again) specify the total amount of all authorized installments.

The following is a sample **Payment-Initiation** message:

```
MIME-Version: 1.0
Content-Type: text/plain
Content-Transfer-Encoding: Binary
SET-Initiation-Type: Payment -Initiation
SET-SET-URL: http://www.merchant.com/cgi-bin/doset.exe
SET-Query-URL: http://www.merchant.com/cgi-bin/pay-query.exe
SET-Success-URL: http://www.merchant.com/pay-completion.html
SET-Failure-URL: http://www.merchant.com/pay-failure.html
SET-Cancel-URL: http://www.merchant.com/cancel-order.html
SET-Version: 1.0
SET-PurchAmt: 840 250 -2
SET-LID-M: A53F49
SET-Brand: brand1 <http://www.brand1.com/logo.gif>
SET-Brand: brand2 <http://www.brand2.com/logo.gif>
1 jar of peanut butter
1 jar of grape jelly
1 loaf of white bread
```

Consider that there may be more than one initiation message sent from the merchant to the cardholder when operating in the interactive WWW mode. Let's say that the cardholder hits the "pay button" in his SET-aware Web application. The merchant's server will send the first initiation message to trigger the cardholder's application to send the **PInitReq** message back to the merchant. Standard processing then occurs through the **PRes** message. When authorization for the transaction is completed, the authorization result is returned in the **PRes**, and the transaction comes to a successful conclusion.

6.2 MERCHANT-CARDHOLDER MESSAGES: PAYMENT INQUIRY

There may be a time delay in a transaction authorization. Should that happen in an interactive transaction, the cardholder's software will respond to the second wake up message by sending an **InqReq** (payment inquiry). This allows the merchant to signal the successful authorization. Most of the fields in this wake up message are the same as previously discussed, except for the differences shown in Table 6.3.

SET-LID-M is the merchant's label identifying the transaction. It may be converted into binary and used as the **LID-M** field of the **InqReq.**

SET-LID-C, for example, is an optional field containing the cardholder's label identifying the transaction. It may be used by the cardholder as an order number to associate the payment with other information. It is an ASCII hexadecimal string which is converted to binary form and copied into the **LID-C** field of the payment inquiry request (**InqReq**).

Table 6.3. Wake Up Message Fields

Field Name	Required	Field Value
MIME-Version	Yes.	"1.0"
SET-Initiation-Type	Yes.	"Payment-Inquiry-Initiation"
SET-SET-URL	Only if SET-Response-URL is omitted.	Determined by the Merchant.
SET-Response-URL	Only if SET-SET-URL is omitted.	Determined by the Merchant.
SET-Success-URL	Yes.	Determined by the Merchant.
SET-Failure-URL	No.	Determined by the Merchant.
SET-Cancel-URL	No.	Determined by the Merchant.
SET-Diagnostic-URL	No.	Determined by the Merchant.
SET-Version	Yes.	Determined by the Merchant.
SET-LID-M	Yes.	See text
SET-LID-C	No.	See text
SET-XID	No.	See text
SET-PaySysID	No.	See text
SET-Ext-OID	No.	Determined by the Merchant.
SET-Ext-Mandatory	No.	Determined by the Merchant.
SET-Ext-Data	No.	Determined by the Merchant.
SET-Echo-In-Response	No.	Determined by the Merchant.
SET-Echo-In-Request	No.	Determined by the Cardholder.

Note that if this field is not specified, the cardholder software is assumed to have obtained the value of **LID-C** through other means. Perhaps the cardholder software would ask the cardholder to select which currently outstanding transaction is the subject of the inquiry.

SET-XID is an optional field containing a globally unique ID that identifies the transaction. It is an ASCII hexadecimal string which is converted to binary form and copied into the **XID** field of the payment inquiry request (**InqReq**).

SET-PaySysID is an optional field containing a unique identifier used by some associations for the transaction from the time of authorization onward. It is an ASCII hexadecimal string which is converted to binary form and copied into the **PaySysID** field of the payment inquiry request (**InqReq**).

If this field is not specified, the cardholder software is assumed to have obtained the value of **PaySysID** through other means.

The following is a sample **Payment-Inquiry-Initiation** message:

```
MIME-Version: 1.0
SET-Initiation-Type: Payment-Inquiry
SET-SET-URL: http://www.merchant.com/cgi-bin/pay-query.exe
SET-Success-URL: http://www.merchant.com/pay-completion.html
SET-Failure-URL: http://www.merchant.com/pay-failure.html
SET-Cancel-URL: http://www.merchant.com/cancel-order.html
SET-Version: 1.0
SET-LID-M: A53F49
```

6.3 CERTIFICATE REGISTRATION INITIALIZATION

To initialize the certificate registration process between cardholder and cardholder Certificate Authority (CCA), Web mechanisms similar to those previously discussed are used. (See Figure 6.2.)

The first initiation message (**Registration-Initiation**) triggers the cardholder application, which initiates the registration transaction by sending the **CardCInitReq** message to the CCA. Processing continues through the **RegFormRes**.

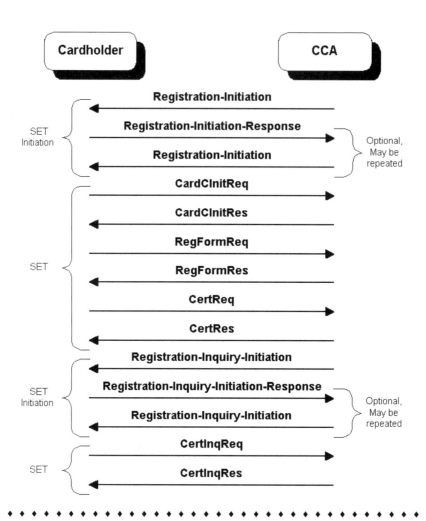

Figure 6.2. Certificate Registration Initialization

The second initiation message (**Registration-Inquiry-Initiation**) is used when the cardholder triggers the certificate inquiry interactively during a Web session with the CCA. In that case, the CCA Web server will send the second initiation message to the cardholder That initiation message again triggers the cardholder application, this time to initiate a registration inquiry (by sending **CertInqReq** to the CCA).

As before, both the initiation messages may not be needed if the transaction occurs by e-mail, or if the cardholder triggers requests directly by using the cardholder application rather than indirectly through the CCA's Web page. The **Registration-Initiation** message header consists of the following:

For certificate registration, the initiation message does not carry a message body. (See Table 6.4.)

Table 6.4. Initiation Message Fields

Field Name	Required	Field Value
MIME-Version	Yes.	"1.0"
SET-Initiation-Type	Yes.	"Registration-Initiation"
SET-SET-URL	Only if SET-Response-URL is omitted.	Determined by the CA.
SET-Response-URL	Only if SET-SET-URL is omitted.	Determined by the CA.
SET-Query-URL	No.	Determined by the CA.
SET-Success-URL	Yes.	Determined by the CA.
SET-Failure-URL	No.	Determined by the CA.
SET-Cancel-URL	No.	Determined by the CA.
SET-Diagnostic-URL	No.	Determined by the CA.
SET-Version	Yes.	Determined by the CA.
SET-Brand	Yes, at least one.	Determined by the CA.
SET-Echo-In-Response	No.	Determined by the CA.
SET-Echo-In-Request	No.	Determined by the Cardholder, Merchant, or Payment Gateway.

The URL fields in the message are defined as in previous messages, but with appropriate URLs for the registration process.

The following is a sample **Registration-Initiation** message:

```
MIME-Version: 1.0
SET-Initiation-Type: Registration-Initiation
SET-SET-URL: http://www.CCA.com/cgi-bin/register.exe
SET-Query-URL: http://www.CCA.com/cgi-bin/query.exe
SET-Success-URL: http://www.CCA.com/register-completion.html
SET-Failure-URL: http://www.CCA.com/register-failure.html
SET-Cancel-URL: http://www.CCA.com/cancel-request.html
SET-Version: 1.0 SET-Brand: brand1 <http://www.brand1.com/
logo.gif>
SET-Brand: brand2 <http://www.brand2.com/logo.gif>
```

Table 6.5. Registration-Inquiry-Initiation Message Fields

Field Name	Required	Field Value
MIME-Version	Yes.	"1.0"
SET-Initiation-Type	Yes.	"Registration-Inquiry-Initiation"
SET-SET-URL	Only if SET-Response-URL is omitted.	Determined by the CA.
SET-Response-URL	Only if SET-SET-URL is omitted.	Determined by the CA.
SET-Success-URL	Yes.	Determined by the CA.
SET-Failure-URL	No.	Determined by the CA.
SET-Cancel-URL	No.	Determined by the CA.
SET-Diagnostic-URL	No.	Determined by the CA.
SET-Version	Yes.	Determined by the CA.
SET-LID-CA	No.	See below.
SET-Echo-In-Response	No.	Determined by the CA.
SET-Echo-In-Request	No.	Determined by the Cardholder, Merchant, or Payment Gateway.

An inquiry mechanism for the registration process is also required in the SET pantheon of messages. The Registration-Inquiry-Initiation message headers are very similar to those that have gone before, with the addiiton of the **SET-LID-CA** field. (See Table 6.5.)

SET-LID-CA specifies the CA's label for an ongoing registration transaction. If provided, this value must be converted to its binary equivalent and copied into the **LID-CA** field of **CertInqReq**.

If this field is not specified, the Cardholder software is assumed to have obtained the value of **LID-CA** through other means. For example, the software could ask the user to select the currently outstanding registration that should be the subject of the inquiry.

6.4 HTTP AND SET: PROBLEMS AND WORKAROUNDS

The World Wide Web (WWW) runs using the HTTP protocol, which allows browsers to request information from, and post data to, a network-based server. In an HTTP session, MIME headers are transmitted along with any other headers following the initial request/response. HTTP supports binary data as the default transfer encoding. This means that SET messages do not have to invoke any MIME transfer encoding, since it's taken care of by the defaults inherent in HTTP.

SET has some functional areas of conflict with HTTP. One is initiation, as has been previously noted. As a matter of security, SET does not allow payment transactions to be initiated by the merchant.

Second, MIME support in a web browser provides a way for the merchant to communicate with the SET payment application, as we have seen in the previous section. But there is not a similar way to pass information back from the SET application to the merchant using a browser.

Third, the minimal merchant/cardholder mechanism described provides for three URLs (**SET-Success-URL**, **SET-Failure-URL**, and **SET-Cancel-URL**), which the cardholder software uses for a smooth transition to the appropriate merchant-controlled WWW page at the end of a payment transaction. For the smoothest transition, the contents of the URLs should replace the merchant page that triggered the payment request. But there is no simple way via HTTP to allow a browser to retrieve any specific page.

Fourth, it may not be feasible for any SET-aware helper application to maintain state by staying "live" through the entire course of a SET transaction. The browser may invoke the helper application for each SET message it receives, rather than pass it to the already active helper.

Fifth, SET software operating over HTTP connections may not receive a timely response. Therefore, SET software needs a way to deal with interrupted connections and session timeouts. Also, there must be limits on the number and frequency of retries for SET software so that it does not spend unlimited time retrying an interrupted connection over a dead communication path.

The SET designers hope that these problems will be resolved through the development of new shopping protocols as well as internal browser support for SET transactions.

If there is no channel for passing data upstream through the browser, SET helper application may be required to initiate connections to the SET-URL and Query-URL. The SET application may need to initiate HTTP POSTs and receive HTTP responses. It will also have to deal with firewall-related issues such as proxy support.

Table 6.6. A Typical HTTP Session

◆ ◆

Step	Action
1	Customer shops at merchant Web site, selects goods, negotiates price, and then selects SET as the payment method. This is the 'shopping' phase.
2	Merchant's server sends the non-SET payment initiation message with the application/set-payment-initiation MIME type to the customer's browser, thus causing it to start a SET helper application. This message contains the OD and amount of the payment.
3	The SET application presents the OD and amount to the user (for verification).
4	If the user approves, the SET application authenticates the customer, then allows him or her to select a card account from the electronic wallet. If the cardholder disapproves the OD or amount, the SET application causes the browser to go to the URL that is given by the Cancel-URL.
5	The SET application records the initial transaction data for later use.
6	The SET application creates a **PInitReq** message, and passes it to the browser via a platform/browser dependent channel. The browser posts the message to the X-SET-SET-URL address with the MIME type application/set-payment.
7	The merchant's application receives the posted message and processes it.
8	The application creates an appropriate **PInitRes** and passes it back to the customer via the server as a response to the customer's post, using the MIME type application/set-payment.
9	The browser passes the **PInitRes** message to the SET application. The SET application extracts the merchant's name and address from the merchant's certificate, shows them to the user, and asks for approval. If given, the SET application then uses the OD and amount and other information to form the **PReq** message. It then updates the records.
10	Using the customer's browser, the SET application posts the **PReq** to an application at the merchant server via the customer's Web browser.
11	The merchant's software processes the **PReq**.
12	The merchant's software forms an appropriate **PRes** and returns it to the customer via the merchant's Web server using the application/set-payment MIME type as the response to the posted **PReq**.
13	The customer's browser passes the **PRes** to the SET application that parses the messages and displays the results.
14	If an error occurred in the processing of the SET protocol, the SET application causes the browser to go to the URL given by the Failure-URL. Otherwise, it causes the browser to retrieve the page given by the Success-URL.

Proxy servers can cache data over many browser sessions. For SET, this means that a private transaction may be mistakenly presented to other users of a proxy server that connects to the same merchant. To avoid this kind of cache problem, merchants and acquirers running HTTP servers offering SET services can use POST instead of GET to collect data from browsers as well as to set page expiration to "immediate."

In spite of all the potential HTTP problems, SET can still transact over the Web. A typical HTTP session might look something like Table 6.6.

6.5 SET AND SMTP: PROBLEMS AND WORKAROUNDS

SET messages passed through e-mail must use the Simple Mail Transport Protocol supported by the Internet. SMTP-based electronic mail has two significant limitations in its ability to support SET transactions: First, not all SMTP servers support 8-bit and binary data. In fact, SMTP must generally assume the lowest common denominator of 7-bit transmissions. Second, SMTP mail delivery does not always occur in a direct source-to-destination fashion. Mail messages usually must pass through several intermediate "relay" hosts and therefore may encounter significant delays. This makes it problematic to support timely interactive communication using e-mail as a transport mechanism.

However, there are workarounds for both these problems. MIME encapsulation provides a way to resolve the binary issue: Each message has a specified transfer-encoding. Base64 is a standard MIME encoding for binary data in nonbinary settings, which

Table 6.7. Typical SMTP SET Transaction

Step	Action
1	Using custom-developed merchant software, the customer shops via a CD-ROM based catalog, selects goods, negotiates price, and selects SET as the payment method. The software develops the order description (OD) and total amount.
2	The customer is authenticated and allowed to choose a card account from his or her electronic wallet.
3	The custom-developed merchant software creates a payment initiation message based on the order description and the amount.
4	The merchant software creates a **PReq** message based on the order description, amount, and the chosen account.
5	The merchant software passes the payment initiation message, **PReq** message, and e-mail address of the merchant to the customer's e-mail application via a messaging API or similar channel.
6	Customer's mail software encodes the messages in base64 and creates a multipart MIME mail message with headers that contain the merchant's e-mail address, message-encoding type (i.e., base64), and message MIME types.
7	Customer's mail software delivers the mail via the Internet.
8	Merchant receives the mail and detaches the payment initiation and SET messages. Merchant records the order information and amount from the initiation message, then decodes the SET message and processes it.
9	Merchant creates a **PRes** message, attaches it to an e-mail message, and sends it back to the customer.
10	The customer's mail reader receives the mail, decodes the SET message back to pure binary form. Based on the message's MIME type, the mail software invokes the SET helper application on the SET message.
11	The SET application displays the results contained in the **PRes** message. It extracts the merchant's name and address from the merchant's certificate, and displays them to the user so that the latter can know what organization signed the purchase response.

allows transmitting SET messages in Base64 encoding to get around the lack of direct binary transmission of files.

To get around the effects of delayed delivery, the SET designers recommend that one "cheat" a bit. The two initial messages (**PInitReq** and **PInitRes**) may be skipped in the e-mail case with one caveat: the cardholder has to provide the transaction-specific merchant values normally provided in the **PInitRes** message. This data may be provided via some other medium or may be created on the cardholder's machine by the SET software that could be supplied by the merchant. Consequently, SET applications must provide a means to manually enter this merchant information in the event that it is provided via some alternative media. The SET designers recommend that all SET software support this **PInit**-less option for the purchase transaction flow. By eliminating these two messages, it is hoped that the time necessary to complete an e-mail-based SET transaction will be decreased.

For the initial message exchange (as in the Web scenario), the merchant and the cardholder should coordinate the order description and the amount of the transaction. The cardholder should include in the initialization mail both the order description and the amount, using the initiation message described earlier. This message is MIME-encapsulated, marked with the SET initialization MIME type, *application/set-payment-initiation*. If it is included in the same mail with the **PReq** message, the mail message is a multipart/mixed MIME message containing the SET message in one part and the payment initiation message in another.

It is envisioned that the typical SMTP SET transaction would proceed as in Table 6.7.

Chapter 7

• • •

THE WORK OF WEB
IN THE AGE OF
ELECTRONIC REPRODUCTION

The adjustment of reality to the masses and of the masses to reality is a process of unlimited scope, as much for thinking as for perception.

—Walter Benjamin,
"The Work of Art in the Age of
Mechnical Reproduction"

"What's with the title of this chapter?" I hear you ask. Walter Benjamin wrote "The Work of Art in the Age of Mechanical Reproduction" in 1936. "Benjamin explores the effect of technology's ability to reproduce art as a manufactured commodity (and, yes, he wrote this before Warhol). Benjamin is laying the groundwork for the post-structuralist theorists who constitute an image as more real than the original that the image leads us to imagine once existed." (Elizabeth Loeb, 1997).

I think what she means is that things seem more real in the catalog than when we get them, which is the kind of abstraction that SET deals with. In any case, SET coud not have been developed without the Internet as a communication glue.[*]

The development of SET could probably not have occurred without using the Internet as a means of communication.

SET was developed by a small group of developers, but disseminated and discussed via a mailing list devoted to the topic. The entire physical world was linked by the abstractions of SET discussed in "set-dev" (as well as "set-discuss") mailing lists, which discussed the ins and outs of SET and how it could be applied. This chapter excerpts some of the discussions that took place over the years of SET development (The names of askers and answerers have been deleted for obvious reasons.)

Q: We are trying to implement SET protocol here in the Czech Republic, and I would like to ask you several questions. Payment Gateway is supposed to send authorization request and capture request through a financial network to cardholder's financial institution. I know that this is not within the scope of the SET specifications. But can someone tell me what needs to be done to establish such a connection, what does the format of such messages look like, and does anyone have such a connection at present?

A: Banks that issue or accept MasterCard or Visa all have such connections. These connections may be made directly to the financial institution or through a third party processor. There are six financial institutions in the Czech Republic that both issue Visa cards and acquire Visa transactions for merchants. You should contact these institutions for information regarding how they are connected to the financial networks.

---

[*] SET is the mechanism that makes the Web image into reality, on a massive scale.

Q: I have a question on the private key duration of the payment gateway. In the paragraph "compromise recovery" it emphasizes the frequent rekey of the encryption key as desirable. On the other hand, in the "Appendix F Recommendations," the private key duration of the payment gateway is specified as one year, which is the same as that of the signature key of a merchant, for example. I know it depends on how the acquirer estimates the risk and the acquirer's policy to decide what length it sets as duration, but is one year too long as a recommendation value? I don't have any quantitative bases, but isn't it desirable that the duration as a recommendation value be a day, or a week, or so?

A1: Today people are using DES and very seldom changing keys for credit card transactions. One year does not seem unreasonable to me. Remember the acquiring sites are normally very secure and the procedures to back up keys often elaborate and time-consuming.

A2: The payment gateway is a particularly sensitive point in SET due to its ability to directly access card information. In addition, there are concerns of key compromise in any system.

My personal feeling is that keys should be changed as often as practical, minimizing exposure and potential compromise. DES keys that change yearly are very likely candidates for compromise given existing technology and the current speed at which an exhaustive key search can be conducted.

Though there is usually very good security at acquiring institutions and their third party processors, payment gateway keys should still be rotated out of production regularly. Though there are no requirements currently under consideration at MasterCard (that I'm aware of), I would feel that a reasonable period of use of key pairs used for payment gateway encryption would be three months. It would follow that signature keys should probably have the same usable life.

Q: I wonder if anyone could explain the following ASN.1 syntax to me:

```
—Cryptographic Parameterized Types—
L { T1, T2 } ::= SEQUENCE {                —Linkage from t1 to t2
   t1   T1,
   t2   DD { T2 }                          —PKCS#7 DigestedData
}

(Found in SetPKCS7Plus)
```

I can't find how it works in my simple "ASN.1 layman manual."

A: L is defined to take two parameters, T1 and T2, that are substituted into the output. So, for example, when you see L {PIHead, OIData} in the protocol, the result is:

```
SEQUENCE {
   t1   PIHead,
   t2   DD {OIData}
}
```

I suspect the reason you can't find this in your layman's guide is because parameterization was introduced into ASN.1 in 1994 after the guide was written.

Q: Does anybody know of an "ASN.1 Decompiler" that, given an ANS.1 datastream, would decompose the datastream into the ASN.1 "primitives" (such as SEQUENCE, INTEGER, OCTET-STRING, etc.)?

A1: Well, after having made SET development a job for institutions which can spend $$$$$ on compilers capable of translating ASN.1/94, I somehow feel that you don't really deserve this hint. In exchange, it would be very much appreciated if the next SET specification could be compiled on public domain ASN.1 compilers like snacc. Many academic institutions which can't afford an OSS (Open Systems Solutions, a commercial ASN.1 compiler used in the reference SET development effort—ed.) compiler will be grateful for this.

Anyway, your problem can be solved with a public domain tool. You can use the library routine DES-parse() of the SSLeay 0.4.5d cryptlib (mutated to ASN1-parse() in SSLeay 0.6.3).

A2: I'd like to thank Carl Ellison and David Balenson for helping me with this question. Attached is David's program, with a few minor modifications.

The text of trval.c that follows has been reproduced on the CD-ROM that accompanies this book.

```
/**********************************************************************
 *
 * trval.c
 *---------------------------------------------------------------------
 *
 * (c)1996, David M. Balenson <balenson@tis.com>
 * Additional changes by Aram Perez, RSA Data Security, Inc.
 * These changes are:
 *    Compile for Win95 using MS Visual C++, V.4.1
 *    Used ANSI function definitions
 *    Capitalized some messages and added more descriptions.
 *    Default is to print the types.
 *    Changed definition of WIDTH to 16.
 *********************************************************************/


#include <stdio.h>
#include <ctype.h>

#ifdef WIN32
#include <string.h>
#include <stdlib.h>
#endif

#define OK 0
#define NOTOK (-1)

/* IDENTIFIER OCTET = TAG CLASS | FORM OF ENCODING | TAG NUMBER */

/* TAG CLASSES */
#define ID-CLASS   0xc0      /* bits 8 and 7 */
#define CLASS-UNIV 0x00      /* 0 = universal */
```

```
#define CLASS-APPL 0x40     /* 1 = application */
#define CLASS-CONT 0x80     /* 2 = context-specific */
#define CLASS-PRIV 0xc0     /* 3 = private */

/* FORM OF ENCODING */
#define ID-FORM    0x20     /* bit 6 */
#define FORM-PRIM 0x00      /* 0 = primitive */
#define FORM-CONS 0x20      /* 1 = constructed */

/* TAG NUMBERS */
#define ID-TAG     0x1f     /* bits 5-1 */
#define PRIM-BOOL 0x01      /* Boolean */
#define PRIM-INT  0x02      /* Integer */
#define PRIM-BITS 0x03      /* Bit String */
#define PRIM-OCTS 0x04      /* Octet String */
#define PRIM-NULL 0x05      /* Null */
#define PRIM-OID  0x06      /* Object Identifier */
#define PRIM-ODE  0x07      /* Object Descriptor */
#define CONS-EXTN 0x08      /* External */
#define PRIM-REAL 0x09      /* Real */
#define PRIM-ENUM 0x0a      /* Enumerated type */
#define PRIM-ENCR 0x0b      /* Encrypted */
#define CONS-SEQ  0x10      /* SEQUENCE/SEQUENCE OF */
#define CONS-SET  0x11      /* SET/SET OF */
#define DEFN-NUMS 0x12      /* Numeric String */
#define DEFN-PRTS 0x13      /* Printable String */
#define DEFN-T61S 0x14      /* T.61 String */
#define DEFN-VTXS 0x15      /* Videotex String */
#define DEFN-IA5S 0x16      /* IA5 String */
#define DEFN-UTCT 0x17      /* UTCTime */
#define DEFN-GENT 0x18      /* Generalized Time */
#define DEFN-GFXS 0x19      /* Graphics string (ISO2375) */
#define DEFN-VISS 0x1a      /* Visible string */
#define DEFN-GENS 0x1b      /* General string */
#define DEFN-CHRS 0x1c      /* Character string */

#define LEN-XTND    0x80    /* long or indefinite form */
#define LEN-SMAX    127 /* largest short form */
#define LEN-MASK    0x7f    /* mask to get number of bytes in length */
#define LEN-INDF    (-1)    /* indefinite length */

int print-types = 1;
int expand-cont = 0;

/*************************************************************************/


int trval(FILE* fin, FILE* fout);
int trval2(FILE *fp, unsigned char *enc, int len, int lev, int* rlen);
```

```
int decode-len(FILE *fp, unsigned char *enc, int len);
int do-prim(FILE *fp, int tag, unsigned char *enc, int len, int lev);
int do-cons(FILE *fp, unsigned char *enc, int len, int lev, int *rlen);

void main(int argc, char** argv)
{
    int optflg = 1;
    int options = 0;
    FILE *fp;
    int r;

    while (--argc > 0) {
        argv++;
        if (optflg && *(argv)[0] == '-') {
/*          if (!strcmp(*argv,"-types"))
                print-types = 1;
            else */ if (!strcmp(*argv,"-notypes"))
                print-types = 0;
            else if (!strcmp(*argv,"-cont"))
                expand-cont = 1;
            else if (!strcmp(*argv,"-nocont"))
                expand-cont = 0;
            else {
                fprintf(stderr,"Unknown option: %s\n", *argv);
/*              fprintf(stderr,"Usage: trval [-[no]types|-[no]cont]
[<file>]\n"); */
                fprintf(stderr,"Usage: trval [-notypes|-[no]cont]
[<file>]\n");
                exit(1);
            }
        } else {
            optflg = 0;
            if ((fp = fopen(*argv,"rb")) == NULL) {
                fprintf(stderr,"trval: unable to open %s\n", *argv);
                continue;
            }
            r = trval(fp, stdout);
            fclose(fp);
        }
    }
    if (optflg) r = trval(stdin, stdout);

    exit(r);
}

int trval(FILE* fin, FILE* fout)
{
    unsigned char *p;
    int maxlen;
```

```
    int len;
    int cc;
    int r;
    int rlen;

    maxlen = BUFSIZ;
    p = (unsigned char *)malloc(maxlen);
    len = 0;
    while ((cc = fgetc(fin)) != EOF) {
        if (len == maxlen) {
            maxlen += BUFSIZ;
            p = (unsigned char *)realloc(p, maxlen);
        }
        p[len++] = cc;
    }
    fprintf(fout, "<Total length = %d>", len);
    r = trval2(fout, p, len, 0, &rlen);
    fprintf(fout, "\n");
    (void) free(p);
    return(r);
}

int trval2(FILE *fp, unsigned char *enc, int len, int lev, int* rlen)
{
    int l, eid, elen, xlen, r, rlen2;

    if (len < 2) {
    fprintf(fp, "Missing ID and length octets (%d).\n", len);
        return(NOTOK);
    }

    fprintf(fp, "\n");
    for (l=0; l<lev; l++) fprintf(fp, ".   ");

    eid = enc[0];
    fprintf(fp, "%02x ", eid);

    elen = enc[1];
    fprintf(fp, "%02x ", elen);

    if (elen == LEN-XTND) {
        fprintf(fp,
          "Indefinite length encoding not implemented (0x%02x).\n",
elen);
        return(NOTOK);
    }

    xlen = 0;
    if (elen & LEN-XTND) {
        xlen = elen & LEN-MASK;
```

```
        if (xlen > len - 2) {
            fprintf(fp, "Extended length too long (%d > %d - 2).\n",
xlen, len);
            return(NOTOK);
        }
        elen = decode-len(fp, enc+2, xlen);
    }

    if (elen > len - 2 - xlen) {
        fprintf(fp, "Length too long (%d > %d - 2 - %d).\n", elen, len,
xlen);
        return(NOTOK);
    }

    switch(eid & ID-CLASS) {
    case CLASS-UNIV:
        fprintf(fp, "[UNIV ");
        break;
    case CLASS-APPL:
        fprintf(fp, "[APPL ");
        break;
    case CLASS-CONT:
        fprintf(fp, "[CONT ");
        break;
    case CLASS-PRIV:
        fprintf(fp, "[PRIV ");
        break;
    }

    fprintf(fp, "%d", eid & ID-TAG);

    if (print-types && ((eid & ID-CLASS) == CLASS-UNIV))
        switch(eid & ID-TAG) {
        case PRIM-BOOL: fprintf(fp, " Boolean"); break;
        case PRIM-INT:  fprintf(fp, " Integer"); break;
        case PRIM-BITS: fprintf(fp, " Bit String"); break;
        case PRIM-OCTS: fprintf(fp, " Octet String"); break;
        case PRIM-NULL: fprintf(fp, " Null"); break;
        case PRIM-OID:  fprintf(fp, " Object Identifier"); break;
        case PRIM-ODE:  fprintf(fp, " Object Descriptor"); break;
        case CONS-EXTN: fprintf(fp, " External"); break;
        case PRIM-REAL: fprintf(fp, " Real"); break;
        case PRIM-ENUM: fprintf(fp, " Enumerated type"); break;
        case PRIM-ENCR: fprintf(fp, " Encrypted"); break;
        case CONS-SEQ:  fprintf(fp, " Sequence/Sequence Of"); break;
        case CONS-SET:  fprintf(fp, " Set/Set Of"); break;
        case DEFN-NUMS: fprintf(fp, " Numeric String"); break;
        case DEFN-PRTS: fprintf(fp, " Printable String"); break;
        case DEFN-T61S: fprintf(fp, " T.61 String"); break;
        case DEFN-VTXS: fprintf(fp, " Videotex String"); break;
```

```
        case DEFN-IA5S: fprintf(fp, " IA5 String"); break;
        case DEFN-UTCT: fprintf(fp, " UTCTime"); break;
        case DEFN-GENT: fprintf(fp, " Generalized Time"); break;
        case DEFN-GFXS: fprintf(fp, " Graphics string (ISO2375)"); break;
        case DEFN-VISS: fprintf(fp, " Visible string"); break;
        case DEFN-GENS: fprintf(fp, " General string"); break;
        case DEFN-CHRS: fprintf(fp, " Character string"); break;
        default: fprintf(fp, " ???");
        }

    fprintf(fp, "] ");

    if ((eid & ID-CLASS) == CLASS-CONT && expand-cont) {
        fprintf(fp, "<%d>", elen);
        r = trval2(fp, enc+2+xlen, elen, lev+1, &rlen2);
        *rlen = 2 + xlen + rlen2;
    } else {
        switch(eid & ID-FORM) {
        case FORM-PRIM:
            fprintf(fp, "Primitive <Length = %d>", elen);
            r = do-prim(fp, eid & ID-TAG, enc+2+xlen, elen, lev+1);
            *rlen = 2 + xlen + elen;
            break;
        case FORM-CONS:
            fprintf(fp, "Constructed <Length = %d>", elen);
            r = do-cons(fp, enc+2+xlen, elen, lev+1, &rlen2);
            *rlen = 2 + xlen + rlen2;
            break;
        }
    }

    return(r);
}

int decode-len(FILE *fp, unsigned char *enc, int len)
{
    int rlen;
    int i;

    fprintf(fp, "%02x ", enc[0]);
    rlen = enc[0];
    for (i=1; i<len; i++) {
        fprintf(fp, "%02x ", enc[i]);
        rlen = (rlen * 0x100) + enc[i];
    }
    return(rlen);
}

/*#define WIDTH 8 */
#define WIDTH 16
```

```
int do-prim(FILE *fp, int tag, unsigned char *enc, int len, int lev)
{
    int n;
    int i;
    int j;

    for (n = 0; n < len; n++) {
        if ((n % WIDTH) == 0) {
            fprintf(fp, "\n");
            for (i=0; i<lev; i++) fprintf(fp, ".  ");
        }
        fprintf(fp, "%02x ", enc[n]);
        if ((n % WIDTH) == (WIDTH-1)) {
            fprintf(fp, "     ");
            for (i=n-(WIDTH-1); i<=n; i++){
                if (isprint(enc[i])) {
                    fprintf(fp, "%c", enc[i]);
                } else {
                    fprintf(fp, ".");
                }
            }
        }
    }
    if ((j = (n % WIDTH)) != 0) {
        fprintf(fp, "     ", j);
        for (i=0; i<WIDTH-j; i++) fprintf(fp, "   ");
        for (i=n-j; i<n; i++){
            if (isprint(enc[i])) {
                fprintf(fp, "%c", enc[i]);
            } else {
                fprintf(fp, ".");
            }
        }
    }
    return(OK);
}

int do-cons(FILE *fp, unsigned char *enc, int len, int lev, int *rlen)
{
    int n;
    int r;
    int rlen2;
    int rlent;

    for (n = 0, rlent = 0; n < len; n+=rlen2, rlent+=rlen2) {
        r = trval2(fp, enc+n, len-n, lev, &rlen2);
        if (r != OK) return(r);
    }
    if (rlent != len) {
        fprintf(fp, "Inconsistent constructed lengths (%d != %d).\n",
```

```
        rlent, len);
        return(NOTOK);
    }
    *rlen = rlent;
    return(r);
}
```

Q: During the cardholder registration process, a hash value is generated as: hash value = hash (account number + expiration date + secret value). The hash value is placed into the cardholder certificate. If the account number, expiration date, and secret value are known, the link to the certificate can be proven. If we would like to maintain the link between (account number, expiration date) and (certificate), a hash value of (account number, expiration date) is enough. Without the secret value, the security and linkage still work. Can anyone tell me what is the purpose of the secret value?

A: The secret value is there to prevent dictionary attacks on the account number. The range of valid expiration dates is small and frequently the exact value can be determined from the validity period of the certificate. One can also determine the issuer from the certificate giving a short list of BINs. It would not be difficult for someone to build a dictionary of all valid account numbers and use that to derive the account number from the hash.

Q: I am trying to compile ASN.1 SET code and have the following problem: My compiler complains about circular references in the ASN.1 code when I try to use it on SetPKCS7Plus. I have full understanding with the compiler because the code is circular. Please look at this: (The compiler I am using only handles the pre-94 asn, so some translation has to be done but my problem lies in interpreting the code below.)

```
1) SupportedContents CONTENT-INFO ::= {
setData                 |
pkcs7Data               |
pkcs7SignedData         |
pkcs7EnvelopedData      |
pkcs7DigestedData
}
```

A: Type SupportedContents is an object of class CONTENT-INFO. Formally, it defines an information object set (a collection of information objects). The "|" operator means UNION. So type SupportedContents is the union of a set of information objects of class CONTENT-INFO.

Q:

```
pkcs7SignedData CONTENT-INFO ::= {
SignedData IDENTIFIED BY signedData }
```

A: Identifier pkcs7SignedData names an object of class CONTENT-INFO. The format of these objects, specified for objects of this class in the definition of CONTENT-INFO, has the form.

```
"{ type IDENTIFIED BY object identifier }"
```

So SignedData is a type that is identified by the object identifier "signedData."

Q:

```
SignedData ::= SEQUENCE {
--
 PKCS#7
    sdVersion          INTEGER { sdVer2(2) } (sdVer2),
    digestAlgorithms   DAlgorithmIdentifiers,
    contentInfo        ContentInfo,
certificates        [0] IMPLICIT Certificates  OPTIONAL,
crls                [1] IMPLICIT CertificateRevocationLists
OPTIONAL,
signerInfos         SignerInfos
}

ContentInfo ::= SEQUENCE {
contentType  CONTENT-INFO.&id({SupportedContents}),
content      [0] EXPLICIT CONTENT-
INFO.&Type({SupportedContents}
{@contentType})  OPTIONAL
}
```

A: Roughly, this reads as follows when decoding data that your application has received:

1st Line:

> "CONTENT-INFO.&id({SupportedContents})" says look in the information object set named SupportedContents, and find the OBJECT IDENTIFIER that matches that in the data to be decoded. If no match is found then error. If a match is found, assign its type (always an OBJECT IDENTIFIER) and value (say, signedData) to this field.

2nd Line:

> "[0] EXPLICIT CONTENT-INFO.&Type({SupportedContents}{@contentType}) OPTIONAL" says look in the information object set named SupportedContents, and find the OBJECT IDENTIFIER value that matched that in the data in the first line. It identifies the type for this component.

For the particular case in your question, ContentInfo would resolve to

```
ContentInfo ::= SEQUENCE {
   contentType  OBJECT IDENTIFIER (signedData),
   content      [0] EXPLICIT SignedData
}
```

But keep in mind that there is a set of possible old-type possibilities that can be carried by type ContentInfo, not just this one.

This notation is the ASN.1:1994 replacement for the ANY DEFINED BY notation that served a similar purpose in older versions of the language. It binds a type to an object identifier. Unlike the ANY DEFINED BY, however, ASN.1:1994 notation allows the protocol designer to define and identify all of the possible combinations of old-type pairs that are supported by the protocol.

The class CONTENT-INFO is defined to be class TYPE-IDENTIFIER, which is described in Annex A of ISO/IEC 8824-2 (ITU-T Rec. X.681) as a "useful information object class." It is defined as follows:

```
TYPE-IDENTIFIER ::= CLASS {
   &id   OBJECT IDENTIFIER UNIQUE,
   &Type
}
WITH SYNTAX { &Type IDENTIFIED BY &id }
```

The "WITH SYNTAX" statement above describes the notation that a protocol designer uses to define objects in this class. (See pkcs7SignedData above.) TYPE-IDENTIFIER is built-in, and requires no definition in the SET protocol, and can be used freely in any module.

The notation "CONTENT-INFO.&Type" is an open type, and if unrestricted, can carry any ASN.1 type, much like the now deprecated ANY. In the example above, it has been restricted to only carry a type that is mapped to one of the unique object identifiers in the information object set SupportedContents.

[The following discussion is critical for an understanding of SET within a wider context. It concerns nonrepudiation—that is, binding both the customer and the merchant to a transaction. In the physical world, the customer signs a charge slip to indicate he or she has agreed to the terms of the transaction. But what is to be done for a cyber transaction? The thread starts out simply enough, and then grows.]

Q: Does SET support nonrepudiation?

A: It is not a requirement for SET to support nonrepudiation.

Q: From a purely technical perspective, of course, SET supports nonrepudiation because it uses digital signatures. However, nonrepudiation is a legal, not a technical construct.

A: In practice, a cardholder's right to dispute is governed by a number of factors including local legislation, payment brand regulations, and the agreement between the issuing financial institution and the cardholder.

Q: How can a card issuer tolerate that the cardholder cannot repudiate a purchase request?

A1: Assume for a moment that all of the laws, regulations, and agreements that apply to the transaction prohibit the cardholder from disputing participation in a transaction containing the cardholder's digital signature. Even so, there will be no way for the issuer to know that the dispute is invalid when the cardholder makes it. This is the case because the issuer does not verify the cardholder's digital signature, the payment gateway (acquirer) does. Therefore, the issuer will send the dispute to the acquirer who would object that the cardholder really did participate and present the digital signature as proof.

A2: Not to be argumentative, but nonrepudiation can be established technically. The formal definition requires that through technical and procedural proofs a party cannot repudiate a transaction. The law may not recognize those techniques and procedures for contractual purposes today but the ABA is working on it.

Digital signatures are part of the solution but not sufficient. Trusted time-stamp is required in a Certificate-based environment. Trusted CA operation is also required.

This topic was developed somewhat under ARPA contract a few years back and can be found in the IOS Report #1 on the host

ests.bbn.com. Aside from some military systems, I know of no
system that provides nonrepudiation today.

A3: As [an ABA Authority Figure—ed.] and a member of the
drafting team for its Digital Signature Guidelines, I suppose I am
one of the people expected to "solve" the nonrepudiation
problem through legal means.

Notwithstanding any technical or procedural proofs, there is no
absolute nonrepudiation, as a legal matter, unless a statute is
enacted to that effect. For consumers in the U.S., there is no
indication that this will happen. The applicable laws governing
credit cards and the consumer use of debit cards specify that the
customer can repudiate any unauthorized transaction, and that it
is left to his bank/issuer to prove that the transaction was actually
performed by that customer or under his authority. Even if
technical means are used to ensure that the customer will always
retain solitary access control to the account (by biometric means,
for example), he can still claim coercion, error with respect to
legal capacity, etc. Where software-based keys are used to confirm
identity and/or authority to enter into a transaction, there are
additional risks of error or fraud associated with initially
obtaining a key and tying it to an identity, as well as the ongoing
association between the key and the identity and/or authority.

In these cases some third party ("trusted" CA, etc.) could step in
and contractually agree to bear all risk of customer repudiation,
but given the relatively low value of the average transaction that
would be unlikely. Additionally, in some countries laws may shift
the risk of loss absolutely to the customer or otherwise prevent
him from repudiating a transaction. To some degree, this is the
direction taken in the U.S. laws governing commercial wire
transfers. If there are any countries contemplating the enactment
of laws that would absolutely bind a person whenever his private
key has been used, I would be most interested in hearing about
them.

A4: I agree with [the previous answerer.] The best that can be done vis-à-vis technical and procedural proofs is to provide essentially prima facie evidence that a document was signed by the individual whose public key was listed in a certificate, and whose identity was bound to that certificate by a CA. But there are a whole host of technical things that could go wrong in the process that are completely independent of [the answerer's] observations regarding duress, legal incompetence, overt fraud, etc.

It might be a thought-provoking exercise, so let me list some of the potential problems that are not always listed as assumptions when someone starts talking about technical nonrepudiation. (I should hasten to say that I know [the previous answerer] reasonably well, and am certain that he is well aware of these various problems. Some of the newcomers to this field may not be as familiar with these issues, however.)

1. Because typically the contents of the certificate (claimed identity) are not included in the digitally signed transaction, there is the implicit assumption that the public/private key pair is unique. But this depends entirely on the methods used to generate the key pair, and as the incident involving a well-known company clearly demonstrated, it is perfectly possible to do an incompetent job of key-generation.

2. Even if the best possible random number sources are used to generate the key pair, if the private key is ever processed in the clear by software, there is an excellent chance that a Trojan Horse program could capture the key and later export it to an unauthorized user. Certainly no one would make any strong claims for the security of the most popular operating systems, including DOS, Windows, and the Macintosh, but even military grade systems could not be considered highly resistant to such attacks unless the key were labeled as a classified object (with appropriate downgrading for the results of encryption or signing), and a Trusted Computing Base that

has been rated at the B3 or higher level of trust is used. The Wang B3 system is one of the few commercially available systems that I know of, but it costs on the order of $40,000, plus another $40,000 for the software development kit and other tools and support. (Not exactly the kind of tool that we would expect the average consumer to use when charging purchases over the Internet.) But at least the principle is sound—consumers should be looking for software that is running on at least a C2-level platform if they want any kind of trust in their software at all.

3. Even if the key is generated in hardware and never leaves the smart card or other container, we cannot be absolutely certain that the key cannot be compromised. It is possible that the onboard processing is not adequately shielded, and that a sensitive radio receiver, perhaps with a small probe that could follow the traces on the card, could pick up a copy of the key as it was being used. And just because a process is implemented in hardware doesn't mean that fallible humans couldn't implement the key-generation or other processes incompetently, or worse yet, design in a deliberate trapdoor. One good thing about software-only processes is that if you pay enough money to get the source code, you can inspect it and recompile it yourself. The closer you get to the raw silicon, the harder this becomes for anyone other than a national laboratory.

A partial answer to this problem is to insist on hardware or software implementations of the cryptographic functions which meet the FIPS 140-1 level 4 standard, which includes protection against some of the more exotic attacks such as x-ray or fiber-optic attacks against locks, electron microscopy, micro-charge sensors, and those attacks involving radiation flooding, low or high voltage, high or low temperatures, and other sophisticated attacks designed to make the crypto algorithm partially fail and thereby permit the kind of partial-analysis attack recently described by Adi Shamir. But even then, because FIPS 140-1 is an unclassified specification, it does not deal with all possible attacks. And although it might be nice to think that only a national laboratory such as NSA could carry out such sophisticated attacks, we should never underestimate the criminal mind or the ingenuity of a determined hacker.

4. Until we get to the point where BOTH a digital signature and biometrics are used, it is impossible to prove by technical methods that the user didn't accidentally or deliberately "loan" his secure hardware token to a friend to use. And even with biometrics we would still have the question of the degree of trust in the hardware/software used to provide the biometric interface, plus the strong possibility of a replay attack. (Fingerprints, or even better, retinal patterns, are great when used at a point of purchase, but difficult to send over a wire without the possibility of a replay attack. At least retinal patterns don't leave latent prints lying around, but as soon as Sears or someone starts collecting a higher grade digitized (not digital) signature, someone else could append it to a document.)

5. Even if we assume absolute perfection in the implementation of the hardware and software used to calculate the digital signature (and we haven't discussed the possibility that a Trojan Horse application presents one version of a document on the screen, but actually signs another), there is still the possibility that something went wrong within the CA's operation. At least in the United States we do not have a national identity card, and anyone who has ever spent much time with teenagers realizes how easy it is to get a fake driver's license that is at least good enough to get into a bar on a busy Saturday night. We might like to think that all of the CAs, and for that matter all of the banks that may be issuing SET credentials, will be absolutely infallible in their decision-making, but some recent personal experiences in trying to open a checking account have convinced me that banks are

not yet invulnerable to human frailties. There is, however, some reason to hope that a regime of licensing and auditing/oversight applied to CAs may provide some additional level of trust in their operations, and for that reason it would be nice if CAs could be rated against some reasonably simple standard.

6. All of these various problems of course exist at every level of the certificate chain. If a consumer's private key could conceivably be compromised, then so could a CA's key. In fact, there might be considerably greater motivation to compromise a CAs key than the consumer's key, since fraud could then be conducted at the wholesale, rather than retail, level.

7. Finally, we have the problem of expired and revoked certificates. It may not be well understood in the technical community, but the fact that a certificate has expired, been suspended, or even revoked, does NOT ipso facto invalidate a digital signature, any more than the digital signature is necessary in order to have a valid, legally binding signature. Remember, even oral contracts can be binding and enforceable—it is just that they are more difficult to prove. So the fact that a certificate has been revoked does not automatically constitute a basis for repudiating the signature; it just makes it more difficult to prove. In particular, if the reason for revoking the certificate is that a particular person has left the company, changed his address, or changed her name, that should not imply that their previous signatures were invalid. It may imply that future signatures were not authorized by the company, but that probably does not relieve the signer of their responsibility for their signature. The question at that point would be whether the relying party made a commercially reasonable assumption in relying on the signature, or even if he was obligated to check the certificate status if there were other mitigating factors, such as a frequent and on-going relationship with either that individual or that company.

8. Most of the discussion regarding nonrepudiation in the
technical community centers around the problem of a known
compromise of a key, and the desire to revoke the certificate
to prevent any further damage. The implicit assumption is
that the user can and should be held liable for all transactions
occurring before the date of the compromise, but not after.
The problem, of course, is that the compromise may not be
discovered until well after the fact, but we would not like to
allow people to write checks in disappearing ink. In addition,
there is the problem that the perpetrator might back-date an
important document, so as to make it appear as if it had been
signed prior to the compromise occurring. In order to prevent
this, a marvelously complex system of CRLs, trusted time-
stamps, etc., has been constructed on paper, but not yet
implemented. But all of this merely provides an indication of
the technical validity of the transaction—it is not a substitute
for a tryer of fact (a judge or a jury) making a judicial
determination after the presentation of the evidence and all
the rebuttals. (But can you imagine presenting all of this to
the average jury? You thought that the juror's eyes glazed over
during all of the DNA evidence in the O.J. Simpson trial—wait
till someone has to explain modular exponentiation, factoring
attacks, Trojan Horse programs, TEMPEST attacks, cryogenic
considerations, radiation flooding, etc.!)

Eventually, we may have some uniformly agreed-to policies
that would apply to both consumers and CAs—a sort of small,
medium, and large level of assurance that everyone will
understand. And once we get to that point it will be much
easier to have a common understanding as to what level of
trust (technical nonrepudiation) to ascribe to a given
transaction. But until that happy day arrives, as it has with
respect to fingerprints, radar guns, ATM machines, and other
now common but once suspect technology, nonrepudiation
will be primarily a legal issue, not a technical one.

And by the way, the foregoing is perhaps the best explanation I can offer for why I believe that the various legislatures that are considering a "short-form" or laissez-faire approach to digital signature legislation are doing their constituents a significant disservice. By abandoning the carefully crafted approach to digital signature legislation advocated by the ABA Digital Signature Guideline and enacted by the State of Utah, and replacing it with a statement that essentially says that a digital signature is the legal equivalent of a written signature, but without addressing the very important public policy issues of who should bear what portion of the risk in exchange for what portion of the reward, they risk opening a Pandora's box of legal problems that will take years to resolve, and will needlessly retard the adoption of a very useful technology. It should be obvious (but often isn't) that if there isn't a meeting of the minds between the subscriber, the relying party, and the CA as to appropriate allocation of the risks and the rewards for using this technology, one or more of the players will simply refuse to participate, and will leave the table. Unfortunately, the technology is sufficiently complex that the average man-in-the-street probably cannot make a well-informed decision by himself. So we can either try to address these various problems in enabling legislation, and try to stave off these problems, or else the corrective measures will come in the form of consumer protection legislation and/or regulation, as they did in reaction to the indiscriminate mailing out of credit cards.

A5: Military law allows that community to define whatever they wish by a mix of governing statutes, and administrative regulations. [A previous reply] asserted that the claims of NR are presented in military contexts. The claims are reasonable, in that highly specialized environment. There is little reason to believe that the conditions of that environment are in any way repeatable or exploitable in nonmilitary environments, other than institutions organized and regulated on pseudo-military lines, like paramilitary police forces, FBI, postal inspectors, U.S. Treasury agents, etc. But all these tend to be given the ability to invoke a priori legal NR provision by virtue of being government-empowered entities, with sovereign immunity from liability when they screw up an actual NR case.

The rest of us have to wait for the court to levy a decision on a contested claim of NR. It doesn't matter how many technical or procedural controls are in place where the ultimate authority is judicial. Fixing the bar at high-grade controls may make the judicial decision easier to obtain, but it's no more an a priori guarantee of NR judgment than with low-grade controls. High-grade controls do make the entire system much more expensive, though, which will slow down actual benefits to real people.

The ISO NR service used in SET asserts, under the authority of the operating regulations of the brands and agreed to by all subscriber and merchant parties, that the technical controls are adequate proof of intent, for the purpose of the payment networks deciding who takes responsibility for satisfying the guarantees of the credit-card system when something goes wrong (at a pretty constant fixed rate, built into the risk management and pricing formula).

There is no assertion that, should a claim be contested in court and not settled merely by the indemnity and guarantee system, and use the statement from SET data unit as evidence, there is any a priori NR, or even that that the control system design is sufficient for fast judicial decision as to whether the evidence is repudiable. In fact, there is major commercial benefit to ensuring the legal route would always be slow, to encourage nonjudicial settlement as per the rules of the operating regulations, which tend to settle 99.9999% of contested transactions.

It was not the purpose of the application of ISO NR to satisfy a legal purpose. ISO NR mechanisms are not tied to legal NR applications; it is quite reasonable to apply the technical provision to commercial third-party guarantee dispute resolution systems upon which VISA/Discover/etc. members' businesses, etc., are based.

SET doesn't want/need the legal NR problem solved, particularly. It's not relevant to SET or the present (plastic) system of credit-card guarantees. It does want ISO NR technology so it can invoke its own dispute-handling mechanism using the signing technology to automate the process—when the current credit-card system is used in the new non-face-to-face environment of the Internet.

Q: Regarding the question of nonrepudiation, I have one curious point. We have been having ATMs for quite a long time. The ATM withdrawal is controlled by the PIN. Have there been a lot of cases where the customer is repudiating the withdrawal (saying that somebody has used his pin)? Or is it that 100% of ATM installations have cameras... I do not think this is true. Hence, where does this leave us? Who acts as the ultimate deciding authority and insures against the loss, if any?

A: I will address the U.S. situation, which is driven by statute. The Electronic Fund Transfer Act (1978) and the Federal Reserve's Regulation E (1980) have long dictated the banks' obligations with respect to consumer ATM claims. Any time a consumer makes a claim to his bank that an unauthorized ATM withdrawal took place, the bank is obliged to promptly investigate the alleged error, determine whether an error occurred, and transmit the results of its investigation and determination to the customer. If an unauthorized withdrawal was made (irrespective of the customer's own negligence in writing down his PIN, etc.), the bank must recredit its customer's account for the amount of the error (minus any statutory customer liability). If the bank determines that no error took place (for example, the customer authorized someone else to make a withdrawal), it may deny the claim, but must make available to the customer all the documents upon which it relied in making its determination.

The bank is kept honest in three ways: (i) Its Reg E compliance procedures and records of claims are regularly reviewed as part of its regulatory agency's consumer compliance examinations; (ii) an aggrieved customer can try to pursue an individual matter with the appropriate bank regulator having administrative enforcement over the Act; or (iii) a customer can bring suit against his bank. If a court finds that "the financial institution knowingly and willfully concluded that the consumer's account was not in error when such conclusion could not reasonably have been drawn from the evidence available to the financial institution at the time of its investigation," then the consumer is entitled to treble damages.

Making a fraudulent claim or an unauthorized withdrawal is, in most if not all jurisdictions, a crime.

Many banks have Reg E claims departments to handle these matters. A large bank will receive claims fairly regularly. To the extent the bank must recredit its customer's account as the result of a claim, it is the insurer against loss. This approach was built into the U.S. law in order to encourage financial institutions to continually improve their computer and telephone-access security procedures and fraud-detection methods, and to provide assurance to bank customers that they would be protected against unauthorized computer access to their bank accounts. (Credit cards have a somewhat analogous set of protections, under Reg Z.) Of course, banks will endeavor to recover their losses under Reg E indirectly, through their interest rate or fee structures.

Cameras may be installed at a bank's discretion, or they may be required under the rules of an ATM network in which the bank participates or a state or municipal law governing security measures that must be taken to protect against crimes that occur near ATM machines. Cameras are not universally used, however.

Q: Are you aware of anyone with an X.500 implementation that supports 750 million certificates?

A: The question of how to distribute cryptographic certificates has been discussed repeatedly over the last five years, and there is still no definitive conclusion as to which way is best (mainly because no one has done it on a sufficiently large scale as yet).

The following is therefore not intended as any criticism of the SET proposal or Visa/MasterCard's intended implementation. After all, [a particular company] was and is a participant and supporter of this system, and I have no intention of shooting myself in the foot. However, because this list is apparently being read by a very wide community, some of whom may be completely up-to-speed on these issues and others who may not be, I'd like to address comments from an architectural perspective. If SET becomes an international standard, as I certainly expect that it will, other companies such as American Express, Discover, etc., may use it, and other applications as well. They might legitimately come to a different conclusion than Visa and MasterCard have on this issue, depending on their particular requirements.

I'll qualify my remarks by saying that I have not personally installed or operated an X.500 system, but as a simple exercise we installed two DEC X.500 Directory Service Agents (DSAs) operating on two minimal configuration DEC Alpha workstations, and we loaded up the entire contents of the telephone directory for [a company's] customers in Downey and Long Beach, California—a total of approximately 100,000 entries. Although we deliberately loaded the Downey numbers on one machine and Long Beach on the other (roughly a 40,000/60,000 split), the interaction between the two machines was almost instantaneous—a query from a Directory User Agent connected to one machine was immediately retrieved by the other machine.

The question of how large a database a single X.500 directory server could support may be beside the point, but I believe that the products currently available from DEC, CDC, Isocor, Marben, the ISODE consortium, as well as some almost-X.500 directories such as Novell's product, could all handle on the order of 20 to 100 million entries on one machine or locally attached cluster of machines and processors, depending on the exact hardware configuration. (Operators are standing by to take your orders!)

Although putting that number of entries on a single machine would probably provide the best performance, whether that would be the most cost-effective design might be another question. This is a speed vs. space vs. transmission time issue, and a definitive conclusion cannot be reached without studying the network topology and design, the sources and sinks of the information, the hardware design, etc.

The real point is that X.500 is a *distributed* directory, and it is not expected or intended that all of the information would ever reside in a single location. Certainly Visa and MasterCard would not have to share the same database, so that cuts the size approximately in half.

Secondly, there wouldn't be a lot of point in replicating all of the certificates of Visa's or MC's U.S. customers in a directory that is located in Europe or Japan, or vice versa. Although people certainly do travel and use their cards in other countries, the percentage using them at any one time must be a fraction of 1%, and those can easily be handled by referencing the directory in the country of origin.

Third, although I don't know how many payment gateways there are in the United States, I suspect that there are at least 10, and maybe closer to 100. In most cases I assume that those payment gateways are operated by Acquiring Banks, who are themselves major Issuing Banks, and therefore might be in a position to deposit the certificates into their own X.500 directories at the time they were created.

By distributing the data across multiple banks or gateways, even as few as 10 for the entire world, the problem can be reduced to a scale that can rather easily be handled by existing technology. If the data were distributed over, say, 100 DSAs, with an average of 7.5 million entries, then we could start talking about implementing the DSAs on garden-variety Pentium processors, at a cost of well under $10K each, or around $1 million total. This is a storage cost of less than 0.13 cents per certificate. In addition there will certainly be some increase in the network costs, but since the certificates do not contain any sensitive information, there is no reason why they cannot be handled over the Internet. The secure Banknet/Visanet networks would not be impacted.

Of course, I doubt that all of those 750 million customers are going to go online with certificates all at once—I don't think that many PCs have been sold. But I assume that the additional revenue that will be generated by that number of people engaging in electronic commerce would make that a very nice problem to have to solve.

There is one final point that I'd like to make. The SET designers have designed the system so that it makes as few assumptions as possible about developments that may not be under their control, e.g., the deployment of a global certificate distribution infrastructure. That is a very reasonable position to take in the early stages of a significant new venture.

But I believe that SET will, by its very existence, create a sufficient critical mass for public key cryptography to allow many other public key systems to develop as well. And those systems are also going to need some way to distribute certificates efficiently.

The electronic shopping phase of electronic commerce will eventually need encryption for privacy, if not digital signatures.

And the electronic distribution of intangible goods is almost certain to require encryption (to protect the product until it is paid for) and digital signatures (to acknowledge receipt in order to get the key to unlock the encrypted product). Software vendors are moving in the direction of digitally signing software in order to protect it from viruses, and that is also going to require certificates. And I haven't even mentioned secure e-mail, which I expect to take off this year.

If all of these applications insist on in-band transmission of certificates, we may end up with a less than optimal solution to the total problem for society. I would therefore recommend that all such applications, including SET, specify the function of retrieving a certificate as a generic function, one that can be satisfied by either an in-band transmission or an out-of-band directory lookup. Hopefully such an approach will let us go either way as this infrastructure emerges.

[Although intermediate programming documentation has been superseded, the following exchange raises an interesting point.]

Q: My reading of page 18 of the August 1 version of Book 3 in reference to the definition of HD and D clearly implies that the hash is of the ciphertext produced by encrypting the plaintext data. This seems convenient, in that you don't have to bother decrypting the data if the integrity check is bad. On the other hand, the 21 June Book 2 is very clear and unambiguous on page 80 and elsewhere that the integrity hash is on the unenciphered plaintext. I think the HD description should be changed to "A 20-byte SHA-1 hash of the data to be DES-encrypted: H(D)." and the D description changed to "The data to be encrypted under the DES key DEK. This data is carried in its encrypted form in the PKCS block, outside of the RSA-encrypted block." or the like.

To make the other interpretation absolutely clear, the HD description should be changed to "A 20-byte SHA-1 hash of the DES-encryption of the plaintext data: H(D)." and the D description should be changed to "The encryption of the plaintext data under the DES key DEK. This ciphertext is carried in the PKCS block, outside of the RSA-encrypted block." or the like.

A1: I believe this ambiguity was raised earlier and the consensus then was to perform the hash on the plaintext. The nonces included in the messages avoid the attacks that are solved by hashing ciphertext. Some hardware vendors we are talking to also prefer hashing the plaintext because it allows them to compute the DES and SHA1 operations in parallel as soon as the plaintext is ready.

A2: The key principle in the design of SET that applies to this message is "signatures must be generated on plaintext data, i.e., before encryption."

This principle can be generalized to account for unsigned messages to be: "integrity hashes must be generated over the unaltered data for which integrity is being ensured." In the case of the OAEP block, the integrity check is actually on the DES-encrypted data; in fact, an integrity check on the plaintext data in this case would not be useful.

Therefore, I believe the specification of SET is internally consistent. I admit that one must be fairly well versed in the design principles to understand that consistency.

Q: When SET is available, will credit card payments be safer in the Internet than in fax or normal mail?

A: I think that depends on what you mean by "safer." If it means "the account number is protected from interception by a third party" then I would find it difficult to say the answer is definitely yes although I can understand the logic of such an answer.

Mail can be intercepted at many places between its origin and destination. The person stealing the mail might do so based on the intended recipient believing that an account number might be inside.

Someone can intercept a fax by tapping into the phone line of either the sender or the recipient. If one tapped the phone line of a merchant and printed off all faxes then one could collect account numbers that way.

In both cases, we are dealing with a targeted attack against a particular cardholder or merchant. SET does protect against similar attacks in the electronic world. However, I do not believe most people worry about attacks against their mail or telephone communications (including faxes) in the same way that they worry about the unknown hacker lurking on the Internet.

If pressed into taking a position as to whether SET over the Internet is "safer than fax or normal mail," I would grudgingly say yes. I do not, however, believe that people should be discouraged from using either mail or fax as a means of transmitting account information to merchants.

Q: Where is the cardholder's cert sent to the merchant and where is the merchant's cert sent to the cardholder?

A: The merchant's cert is sent to the cardholder in **PInitRes**. The cardholder's cert is sent to the merchant in **PReq**.

Q: As I interpret it, the following is included in the #PKCS7 SignedData structure: signedData->certificates. Am I right in the following cases? **PInitReq**: *All certificates needed to verify the message and payment gateway cert that aren't in the* **pInitReq**.*thumbs are sent to the cardholder in the PKCS#7 SignedData structure: signedData->certificates.*

A: Yes.

Q: Or is it only the PGW certificate, tunneled by merchant to the cardholder, that is contained in the signedData in the **PInitRes***?*

A: No.

Q: PReq: *The cardholder sends its cert to the merchant (if it has one) in the **pInitReq**->**pReqDualSigned**->**PISignature**->certificates?*

A: Yes. Don't forget to put in the certs that the gateway will need, as this signature will be checked by the gateway as well, so the gateway will likely need at least the PCA. Just to be safe, I'd throw in the whole chain (except for the root).

Q: *SET defines type Date as "Date ::= GeneralizedTime". Type Date is used in the SET payment messages, in particular for **TransIDs.pReqDate** and **RRTags.currentDate**. Type GeneralizedTime takes values in three forms:*

```
1. Local time only.                      "YYYYMMDDHHMMSS.fff".
2. UTC only.                             "YYYYMMDDHHMMSS.fffZ".
3. Local time and differential for UTC. "YYYYMMDDHHMMSS.fff+-HHMM".
```

The payment gateway should have UTC, in particular if logs are to be aged using RRTags.currentDate as suggested by the SET specification. Local time would also be useful to the payment gateway for logging and also if the brand's payment network requires it. What assumptions can the payment gateway make about the forms of GeneralizedTime it will receive in SET request messages—can the payment gateway assume that form 3 will always be used?

A: No. SET requires DER encoding. DER encoding requires that the UTC only time be used. Note, "trailing" zeros in the (nonfractional) seconds are required, but not in the fractional seconds:

```
19920521000000Z      —correct
19920521000000.Z     —incorrect
19920521000000.0Z    —incorrect
```

Q: *The merchant supplies both its own certificate and the payment gateway's certificate to the cardholder. Must the **MerAcquirerBIN** in the* *merchant's certificate and the **acquirerBIN** in the payment gateway's certificate be identical?*

A: Yes.

Q: Must the organizationalUnitName fields in the merchant's certificate and in the payment gateway's certificate be identical?

A: Yes.

Q: Does ISO 8583 support business purchasing cards?

A1: In the current environment, the implemented versions of ISO 8583 are used for authorization. The ISO 8583 messages that are implemented have extensions that may be used to support purchasing card activity. This is done through the use of the definition of required fields in private data elements. These messages, used for both VIP (Visa) and CIS (MasterCard), are based on the 1987 version of ISO 8583.

Within MasterCard, purchasing card data is defined in the clearing message (INET) where it is maintained as part of the actual posting (with a dollar value) rather than being associated with the authorization message (risk control message).

Under the MasterCard implementation of ISO 8583 : 93 (ISO 8583 1993 version), additional private data elements have been defined by MasterCard for the specific use of purchasing card activity. MasterCard created this message definition three years ago to support new initiatives. I don't think this message format, known as Integrated Product Messages (IPM), is currently available, but the ISO 8583 : 93 is. Check for it through ISO or ANSI ASC X9 Secretariat.

American Express does use ISO 8583 : 93, but I'm not sure whether purchasing card data is defined into their implementation. I think American Express has a clearing message format that is not defined using ISO 8583 and I'm not that familiar with their message formats.

A2: Yes, ISO 8583 will support purchasing cards. There is some additional information this is often included for purchasing card transactions on the clearing request. In Visa's case this information is not passed using ISO 8583 messages since we have our own proprietary message format for clearing.

*Q: Can someone set me straight on how recurring payments are supported? I know that we can indicate recurring payments in the **PReq**, but how are the authorizations and settlements performed? If the goods purchased were for 3 installments billed over 30 days per installment with a total of $90, does the cardholder grant the permission to the merchant to authorize and capture these amounts every 30 days until the last installment? My question is how exactly does it all work?*

A: SET supports both installment and recurring payments. For the installment payment scenario you described, the cardholder's Payment Instructions would contain the following fields:

```
PurchAmt = $90.00–{840, 9000, -2}
RecurringTotalTrans = 3
```

This indicates to the payment gateway that an Authorization Token should be returned for the first and second authorizations, but not the third.

Ultimately, however, the merchant is in control of the number of authorizations/captures and the amount of each of these. The merchant can submit three transactions for the same amount {$30, $30, $30} or for different amounts {$40, $25, $25}. Furthermore, if there is a split shipment, the merchant can turn this into four (or more) authorizations/captures by setting the SubsequentAuthInd to TRUE {$15, $25, $25, $25} or even {$30, $30, $30, $30}. (The last example will undoubtedly result in a dispute from the cardholder.)

The cardholder can indicate a recurring payment (such as for a monthly charge from an Internet service provider with Payment Instructions that contain the following fields:

PurchAmt = $239.40—{840, 23940, -2}
RecurringFrequency = 28—monthly, i.e., the length of the shortest month
RecurringExpirty = December 15, 1997

This indicates that the cardholder is expecting to be charged $19.95 per month each of the next 12 months. The merchant can (will) charge more in any given month if the usage charge exceeds the contract amount.

*Q: I am confused about how fields **AuthNewAmt** and **AuthResDataNew** should be filled in **AuthRevRes** messages in the case of successful and failed reversals.*

A: I am interpreting this question to equate a "failed reversal" with a "declined authorization," i.e., the situation where an issuer says, I won't reverse that transaction. There is no such status to an authorization reversal. The reversal is an advisory message to the issuer from the merchant/acquirer that says "I authorized this transaction, but I no longer intend to complete the transaction as authorized." An issuer may use this information to increase the cardholder's open-to-buy (or not) depending on its own processing rules. However, even if the issuer decides not to change the open-to-buy, it does not "decline" the reversal; it just ignores it.

Note: Not all payment systems support partial reversals. In the event the payment system for the brand in the reversal request does not support partial reversals, the payment gateway should format a response message to the merchant, without sending any message to issuer via the payment system. The result of this is that the cardholder's open-to-buy is lower than it needs to be and the merchant has done all it can to correct the situation.

Q: In the business spec VISA/Mastercard explains the principle of the dual signature. While the functionality is described clearly, I don't see the need for dual signatures. Can someone explain to me why dual signatures are implemented? An example would help. Are dual signatures used for every transaction or just in special cases?

A: Speaking non-authoritatively, on an interesting SET philosophy topic: At a very high level—the only level I understand—I think of the need being satisfied by dual signature constructs in SET as being one in which "business separation" is being enforced—such that, for various items of sensitive data, certain parties in the flow cannot, by design, perform some security primitives—given the data available to them—yet others who are enabled to collect more pieces of the puzzle, perhaps after processing and forwarding by parties without the privilege, will be able to perform such a security critical function, as is their requirement and right.

The organization of the SET flow and the SET dual signature construct reflect a perceived need to separate who amongst the parties (cardholder, merchant, acquirer, attacker) can know a piece of sensitive payment data, given which messages arrive on which channels in a particular order. It's perfectly reasonable to subjectively question if this has real value (over mere technical function).

I would argue that such systemic constructs are part of what SET is offering over and above the traditional payment flows, and represent the value of being part of such service networks which are infrastructural, versus a mere service variation or access method offered by some innovative provider. The SET technical documents are not the place for parties to sell the features of such an infrastructure, obviously, or go overboard on their explanation of the goals for upgrading the payment infrastructure to be capable of this kind of processing, and payment market construction and evolution.

I have seen briefings of the Associations to their members which embrace the bigger message, though. Perhaps consult your acquirer/issuer bank. Traditional Internet flows are not great on consumer privacy (type in your order details and credit card number here, please . . .), are not great on chargebacks or handing over the money promptly (First Virtual), and are not great on price (please pay an extra 1% for the Internet processing facility), or they require a new network gateway (Intuit, Cybercash) and (perhaps) a specialized software program, and are not great on offering more than MOTO rules (for credit activities).

The philosophical need being addressed by SET design, surely, is to ensure the native payment service *system* is available to all as an infrastructure for service delivery, without logically altering the traditional functional and physical distribution of autonomous operations which the banks and other "stakeholders" are used to in the current service delivery infrastructure. The idea is to ensure that the SET framework brings about non-face-to-face credit-oriented payment services without featuring the problems identified above as a consequence of too hasty, too piecemeal, or ill-conceived design, by using applied crypto technology uniformly in a careful messaging flow constructed for bankcard service transactions "in general."

While deploying and evolving the infrastructure, it's vital to not necessarily change the essence of the underlying debt/account-management service, or the relationships within and between association members, as many of the business models assume particular risks and co-marketing costs.

Such features as dual signature are there thus to satisfy a perceived need for an infrastructural upgrade by which more advanced services can be deployed progressively by association members, in the usual highly differentiated manner, and in the usual competitive manner, right across the Internet environment by all players.

As cardholders get more service for potentially less money, they seem to be on the winning curve. As merchants get access to new markets, they win. As payment providers get more throughput they win. As banks service more categories of managed risk, they win.

Try to think of SET as an infrastructural initiative, not merely a standard for translating one data format into another.

Q: What about "web spoofing"—a sort of "man-in-the-middle attack"? Spoofing is when a false merchant makes a WWW shadow copy which buyers could enter without knowing it. In this shadow copy of WWW (were a copy of a legitimate merchant exists), the buyer would enter his address and quantity of a product within a form, but it would be exchanged for something else when it continued to be processed. Does this problem exist or not with SET? If not, why?

A1: First, it is extremely difficult (if not impossible) for a false merchant to participate in a SET transaction since a merchant must have a certificate signed under the brand CA hierarchy. Even if the merchant obtains a certificate, the cardholder still receives a copy of the order information and signs it.

A2: SET addresses the issue by requiring the merchant to sign the **PInitRes** message. To successfully spoof that message, a false merchant would have to know the real merchant's private signature key. (That's one reason why a merchant should safeguard its private keys.)

*Q: I have a question about the specification of **CertReq**. In **CertReq**, S or SO is used. In both data structures, the specification is described as follows: ... WITH COMPONENTS { ..., signerInfos (SIZE(1)) })*

*This means that at least one signerInfo must be included in **CertReq**. And from this follows that issuerAndSerialNumber must be included in **CertReq**. But when an end entity requests for the first time, it doesn't have a certificate, and it can't provide issuerAndSerialNumber. In such a case, what value is to be set?*

A: Issuer is set to the "null DN," which is a SEQUENCE of length 0 (0x30 0x00).

Serial is set to 0.

*Q: The SET Spec seems to allow for multiple authorizations even when not using the **InstallRecurringInd**. However, is it a fair assumption that - ALL- Payment Gateways will support this? Since much of the PG work is for legacy financial systems, this level of support is crucial for merchants with mixed goods types—downloadable goods and hard goods. As you can see, downloadable goods can be performed as a sale transaction (auth with capture) but the hard goods cannot (auth only). For hard goods, capture should only occur after the goods are shipped. Again, will -ALL- PGs support multiple authorizations and captures without using the **InstallRecurringInd**? If not, should this be added to the Spec?*

A: The **InstallRecurInd** is created by the cardholder and indicates that the cardholder expects the merchant to perform multiple authorizations. There are two situations when the cardholder will create **InstallRecurInd**: the cardholder accepts the merchant's offer of four easy payments of $29.95; or the cardholder authorizes the merchant to regularly bill the account, such as monthly charges to an Internet Service Provider.

The **SubsequentAuthInd** is set by the merchant and indicates that the merchant has detected that an additional authorization will be required, such as for a back order. It is possible (although unlikely) for the cardholder to include the **InstallRecurInd** in an authorization request and for the merchant to also set the **SubsequentAuthInd**. All payment gateways that want to be certified as compliant with the SET specification will support both the **InstallRecurInd** and the **SubsequentAuthInd**.

*Q: Let me try to clarify my question. A mixed goods type does not fall into the categories of installment payments, subscriptions, etc., but rather in a category on its own. It more resembles that of back orders because of multiple auths and captures. For mixed goods, the merchant will not (should not) set the SET-Recurring or SET-RecurringTotalTrans in the wake-up message because it doesn't really fall into the categories described above. Since this doesn't occur, the cardholder will not create the **InstallRecurInd**. The question then becomes, can the **SubsequentAuthInd** be used when the **InstallRecInd** isn't?*

A: Yes.

Q: Today, if I buy merchant software to help me accept credit cards over the net, the choice I have in banks is limited by who that software vendor is certified with. Therefore, if I pick the bank first, then that probably limits my selection of off-the-shelf software. After SET, assuming my bank has a SET-compliant gateway, can I select any vendor with SET-compliant merchant software? Or will certain vendors still only be able to support certain, predefined banks?

A: I believe that the image of payment gateways being resident at banks or operated by banks or one per bank, while all possible, are misleading. No doubt they will occur in some instances, but I believe the reality is most gateways will be operated by third parties on third party premises, that most banks will be accessible through a number of gateways, and that many gateways will provide access to a large number of banks.

Q: That is, who has control? The merchant or the vendor? At least for credit-card-based payment infrastructures, the banks have complete control. The merchant servers and the bank-resident payment gateway must interoperate (certified through a rigorous process). The bank supplies its merchant clients with approved point-of-sale software.

A: What you say may be true in principle, but in practice it would be more accurate to replace "bank" with "payment gateway operator" realizing that in some cases these will be the same.

Q: Note the close relationships between the equipment/software supplier and the acquirer, and between the latter and its merchant clients. As a merchant, you are advised to talk to an acquiring bank first.

A: Merchants, of course, need a relationship with an acquiring bank. And it's certainly reasonable to ask the bank for recommendations. But I think in many instances it would also make sense to talk to a gateway operator and see whether they can access your current bank and if not whether they can arrange to. [A company name] goes to great lengths to preserve merchant-bank relationships and has had great success in arranging for banks to accept transactions through our gateway and I don't see why that would change as we add SET support.

I don't think the operation of a payment gateway will be just buying a box and sticking it in a closet. For the same reason that third party credit-card processors have evolved for the non-Internet work, third party specialists with the experience, expertise, staffing, infrastructure, etc., to handle Internet transactions will predominate. It is possible that the world will evolve into a relatively small number of gateway operators with many gateways capable of accessing most banks.

[When is SET not SET? The following discussion brings up the possibility of the private use of SET technology, and answers the question: When is a Brand a Brand?]

Q: In response to "Can some other institution/company take over the role of Visa or MasterCard in the SET model?" [a respected authority] says No. I don't understand this. SET is just a specification, isn't it? It seems to me I could set up a closed SET network of nodes with my mother playing the role of MasterCard. What am I missing? Is there some small print somewhere that says there can't be stand-alone implementations of SET?

A: Yes, SET is just a specification. In theory, you can set up a closed network of nodes with your grandmother as the root, your mother playing the role of MasterCard, and your father playing the role of Visa. However, the messages flowing over your closed network will not be SET transactions under the rules of MasterCard and Visa. If you want your transactions to qualify as SET transactions, the root key used to certify the brand must be endorsed by the brand. You cannot set yourself up as MasterCard or Visa even within a closed network.

Q: Is Wells Fargo a suitable CA for SET?

A1: Yes. In fact, anybody can be a CA for SET. Yes, anybody.

A perfectly reasonable scenario is for a merchant to be the SET CA for his own customers. The merchant issues his own credit and guarantees his own receivables with his savings. The merchant trusts his authentication of his own customers. No bank or bank association need be involved at all. He can run his own SET domain on the Web just like the big guys. He is his own root and his own brand. The SET protocol doesn't care.

Or, as a less realistic example, I could be a SET CA for a simple loan of $1 that I make to you. I verify you are you. I build a cert for you in a two-entry CA (me and you). I sign everything in sight with my own key. I trust myself and my authentication of you so I give you the $1 using the SET protocol. SET isn't based on banking or even money; it is based on trust and its obverse, risk assumption. What we are going to see, I predict, is that affinity groups will set up their own CAs and trust domains. All the stamp collectors in Maine or all the Baptists in Texas. On the Internet anybody can be a brand.

A2: This last statement is exactly correct. And it's what I said. Nouveau brands are perfectly reasonable, as are nouveau banks, and nouveau merchants (and nouveau payment networks). (Consumers are likely to say pretty much the same—demanding, and protected by government regulation on the various providers to manage scams and fraud and world macro-economics.)

Anyone who writes credit to merchants, or offers to manage consumer debt, is part of SET. Provision of credit and financial services tends to be highly regulated by the Federal Reserve, though, in the U.S. (One doesn't see a huge number of Texas Freemen's e-cash deployment out there yet, does one . . . I doubt radical SET will go the same way, even though lending as a legal service is less regulated than those who would establish currencies competitive to the dollar within the U.S.)

But, yes, you've got the right spirit about what SET represents, and what public key crypto does enable due to its scaling properties. SET has the technological capability to be quite revolutionary, though is unlikely to be so in practice, if the history of technology goes as usual. Will SET actually get rid of those COBOL systems soon, though? I doubt it.

As the name suggests, SET technology is a general-purpose transaction technology, not only for projecting a credit card model. Any business model and relationship set you like is quite acceptable.

The original questioner had the right question—what one needs for a viable (nouveau) business model, in all this, is financial guarantees, and providers who accept the various liabilities. Trust is then a function of being able to substantiate the ability to handle the risk, assuming actual losses mount, to governments and then consumers, via branding and recognition.

It's hard to compete with the liquidity or marketing of the VISA members; the number of credit unions becoming VISA members continues to mount, despite the political theory of consumer preference for local lending.

SET is going to be (and for those of us in the middle of it now, is) a lot of fun. It, and its equivalents, will create a million tiny changes in what we all suffer currently, I suspect.

Perhaps someone could do research. What percentage of the 15th century Venetian merchants really underwrote their own credit? And how many sought outside capitalists, risking their own assets as collateral? I suspect the answer is about the same as today.

A3: Being a brand requires more than getting a certificate from some anonymous certificate authority. The trust that cardholders, merchants, and financial institutions place in a brand is earned through years of effort. You must establish a brand image and protect that image when someone tries to take advantage of it. No one other than Visa International will be certified with the name "Visa" as their brand ID on the Internet. I expect MasterCard and American Express will say the same for their brands. On the Internet, only a Brand can be a brand.

A4: From the card association (MasterCard/Visa) perspective, there are no organizations that can play the same role with regard to supporting SET in an infrastructure, a specification for secure commerce, than MasterCard and Visa. The market will ultimately determine the protocols preferred for open-system payments security. But when it comes to actually clearing and settling value owed/paid between cardholders, merchants, issuers, and acquirers on a global basis (hundreds of millions of accounts, tens of billions of transactions), there are no organizations besides the major card brands that can possibly play the same role in building trust, supporting pilots, helping financial institutions gain experience, and generating confidence among their customers, the cardholders.

You can physically go into a merchant now and pay with cash, check, money order, or credit card, and there are systems that support the fair exchange of value behind each one of those payment vehicles. Individuals require flexibility, so it's hard to imagine a robust web-based economy without multiple infrastructures. SET implementation and compliance (read: not mandatory, just compliant) is one system, a path to a solution in which consumers, merchants, and financial institutions can have a high degree of comfort in exchanging value.

The SET protocols are emerging and evolving, as are other methodologies—and the card associations play a role in that process. No one, however, can duplicate (in the time frames necessary for the implementation of web commerce) the networks and relationships of MasterCard or Visa, which are vital to the exchange of about a quarter of the world's commerce.

Q: The BrandID in the SET 1.0 has the type of SETString; a change from the prior DirectoryString. The BrandID is carried in the attribute of organizationName in the subjectName AVAs. In turn the organizationName is the type of DirectoryName in the SET 1.0. Because of the incompatibility, it seems we need to retrieve organizationName as a DirectoryName and manually convert it to a SETString; mapping the PRINTABLESTRING to VISIBLESTRING if necessary. Is this by design? The SET spec is not consistent with the X.509. Do I understand this correctly?

A1: I would suggest that when converting from SetString to DirectoryString:

1. SetString.bmpString always map to DirectoryString.bmpString.

2. If SetString.visibleString contains only PrintableString characters, it should be mapped to DirectoryString.printableString.

3. If SetString.visibleString contains non-PrintableString characters, it should be mapped to

DirectoryString.bmpString. This is done by expanding each one-byte character in SetString.visibleString to a two-byte BMPString character, setting the high-order byte of the BMPString character to zero.

When converting from DirectoryString to SetString:

1. DirectoryString.printableString always maps to SetString.visibleString.

2. If DirectoryString.bmpString contains only VisibleString characters, it should be mapped to SetString.visibleString. This is done by truncating each character in DirectoryString.bmpString to a one-byte VisibleString character, discarding the high-order byte of the BMPString character.

3. If DirectoryString.bmpString contains any non-VisibleString characters, it should be mapped to SetString.bmpString.

A2: Yes, it is by design. All strings defined by SET use the type SETString. There is no incompatibility. PrintableString maps onto VisibleString without any conversion and BrandID must always match a value that appears in the organizationName of a certificate. Therefore, one of the following assignments will work:

```
BrandID.visibleString = organizationName.printableString
BrandID.bmpString = organizationName.bmpString
```

Q: What I do not quite understand is the following: Can anyone just build applications starting from the reference implementation and sell it, or are there any licenses involved?

A: The answers are "yes" and "probably." I'll try to explain. Yes, you are free to build applications starting from the SET reference implementation (SETREF). The one thing you *can't* do with the SETREF code is to resell or redistribute it as a toolkit.

Building final-form SET applications based on SETREF is permitted, however (see the legalese included in the SETREF release notes for details).

On the other hand, SETREF does not come with a cryptographic engine. It is designed to work with BSAFE 3.0, and using BSAFE does require a license from RSA. Of course, you could always supply your own crypto engine, but that would require additional work.

Q: Who would buy a toolkit from Terisa, if there is a free reference implementation of SET available?

A: DISCLAIMER: I work for Terisa Systems, the company that both built SETREF *and* sells a commercial SET Toolkit.

While it is certainly possible to build a SET application using SETREF and I don't want to discourage you from doing so, I would expect commercial SET toolkits to offer a lot more than the base SET protocol engine and sample apps that come with SETREF: e.g., commercial-quality infrastructure items (like a crypto engine, a cert-management system, a cert/key database, etc.) and support for the application and business logic of the cardholder, merchant, payment gateway, and CA components above and beyond that provided by the SET methods per se. Also, keep in mind that one of the primary purposes of SETREF was to help explicate the specification by providing sample code that other developers could examine, so in developing SETREF, we favored qualities such as readability and clarity rather than, say, performance or robustness in the face of errors. One might expect commercial implementations to favor the latter at the expense of the former.

Afterword

• • •

THE CD-ROM, ERRATA, AND THE WEBSITE

My argument is that there need not be a "doer behind the deed," but that the doer is variably constucted in and through the deed.

—Judith Butler, *Gender Trouble*

T he CD-ROM that accompanies this book is mostly technical but also includes explanations of SET in general.

CD-ROM CONTENTS

• •

1. SETREF Libraries v 1.0

As part of the developement of SET, the payment card companies had Terisa Systems construct a "standard" SET application that could be used in the interoperability trials.

That application is known as the reference implementation or "SETREF."

The C source code provided by the payment card companies' standards effort to the development community is enclosed, thanks to the courtesy of MasterCard and VISA. The README files are a very important place to start when trying to understand the limitations and benefits of this source. Don't attempt any compilations without reading them first. Since SET is theoretically cryptographically independent, there are no cryptographic modules included with SETREF. To be able to fully compile the code, those modules must be obtained by the user for use with SETREF.

SETREF is a great place to start when attempting to code SET applications, but it is only a framework. As pointed out in Chapter 7, SETREF is example code; not user-friendly code. Additional work is necessary to make the example user-worthy. But SETREF is a great way for the novice to see how a SET application is constructed.

2. GTE Demo

GTE contributed a neat demo of the overall SET system that they use at computer shows to condense things to fit within the 45 second attention span of the average show attendee. The CD has both Mac and PC versions present. I like this demo because it shows the SET concepts in a clear, nonthreatening way, suitable for most vice-presidents.

3. Working S/Pay Demo System

RSA Data Security, Inc. has graciously contributed to this effort a working SET Web-based environment that generates and passes the actual encrypted SET messages between Cardholder, Merchant, and Acquirer. Due to the servers and clients that are set up in memory, the Demo runs on a Pentium-class PC that has 32 megabytes of RAM.

Complete documentation for the demo is in Word format and is enclosed inside the S/Pay on the CD-ROM. The text program files should be viewable on either a Mac or PC. Before trying anything with the demo, please read the documentation thoroughly, starting with the Quickstart.pdf file, which is viewable with the Acrobat Reader program. This Quickstart file deals with setup issues and is mandatory reading for the demo to function properly.[*]

4. Self-certification checklist

Tenth Mountain has been selected by the SET consortium to test applications for compliance with SET specifications. As part of this effort, they have produced a checklist document that outlines specific steps an application must pass to be SET 1.0 compliant. These documents are supplied on the CD as a series of Acrobat Reader 3.0 files. They allow a vendor to evaluate if their product is internally compliant with the standards necessary to implement SET. Through these checklists, a vendor will be able to evaluate any product areas that need improving before SET compliance can be authorized.

Users will find the checklist interesting as it delineates some of the internal fortitude a programs needs to be SET-compliant.

---

[*] There is also a file (QUICKST.PDF) in AdobeAcrobat format that describes how to set up the demo system without the normal cryptographic modules in place. This is also required reading before messing about with the demo. If you don't already have an Acrobat viewer program, it may be downloaded from www. adobe.com.

5. trval.c listing

A text listing of the C program "trval.c" cited in Chapter 7 is included. This should cut down errors due to a transcription of the program.

6. asn1.txt listing

This is a text-listing of the latest ASN.1, as in Appendix A but searchable by a word processor's "Find" command. I've found this form of ASN.1 useful as a searchable index of SET PDU structures.

7. Aram's Shareware BER/DER Viewer

Aram Perez has consented to let me distribute the ASN.1 DER/BER viewer that he wrote for Windows with this book. It will display an ASN.1 BER/DER encoded file as a "tree" under Windows 95/NT. This utility is rather useful in examining ASN.1 encoded files, and I encourage you to send Aram his shareware fee if you use it.

ERRATA AND THE WEBSITE

The problem with writing about leading-edge technology is that it changes. I've tried to keep up, but I'm sure that entropy will win out in the end (it always does). Therefore, to communicate any errata in the text and to describe revisions to the SET protocol that occur after the publication date, I have set up a support Web page at *<http://pages.prodigy.net/larryloeb/setpage.htm>* for this book. This web page has the latest links and informational updates that couldn't make it into this edition, and I urge you to consult it. It will help you keep abreast of things that are happening in the SET field. It is also a simple way for you to contact me with your suggestions and comments, which will be appreciated.

I'll see you on the bitstream!

Appendix

$\bullet\ \bullet\ \bullet$

The SET Protocol in ASN.1 Notation

```
-- History
--    31 May 1997 Version 1.0

SetMessage
  { joint-iso-itu-t(2) internationalRA(23) set(42) module(6) 0 }
      DEFINITIONS IMPLICIT TAGS ::= BEGIN


--
-- This module defines types for use in the SET protocol certificate and
-- payment flow messages.
--

-- EXPORTS All;

IMPORTS

   ALGORITHM-IDENTIFIER, AlgorithmIdentifier {}, Name, SETString {}
      FROM SetAttribute

   SIGNED {}
      FROM SetCertificate

   EXTENSION, Extensions, ub-cityName, ub-postalCode, ub-stateProvince
      FROM SetCertificateExtensions

   CardCInitReq, CardCInitRes, CertInqReq, CertInqRes, CertReq, CertRes,
   Me-AqCInitReq, Me-AqCInitRes, RegFormReq, RegFormRes
      FROM SetCertMsgs

   AuthReq, AuthRes, AuthRevReq, AuthRevRes, BatchAdminReq,
```

```
    BatchAdminRes, CapReq, CapRes, CapRevReq, CapRevRes, CredReq,
    CredRes, CredRevReq, CredRevRes, InqReq, InqRes, PCertReq,
    PCertRes, PInitReq, PInitRes, PReq, PRes
        FROM SetPayMsgs

    CA, ContentEncryptionAlgorithms, Digest, DigestAlgorithms, Digests, EE, S {}
        FROM SetPKCS7Plus

    ub-phone
        FROM SetMarketData;


MessageWrapper ::= SEQUENCE {
    messageHeader  MessageHeader,
    message        [0] EXPLICIT MESSAGE.&Type (Message),
    mwExtensions   [1] MsgExtensions {{MWExtensionsIOS}} OPTIONAL
}

-- An information object set is defined for each extensible PDU
--
-- Note: each of these information object sets uses the extension
-- marker (...) to allow vendors to add supported extensions to
-- their local copy of the ASN.1. Extensions added by vendors
-- should appear after the extension marker.

MWExtensionsIOS EXTENSION ::= { ... }

MessageHeader ::= SEQUENCE {
    version     INTEGER { setVer1(1) } (setVer1),
    revision    INTEGER (0) DEFAULT 0,   -- This is version 1.0
    date        Date,
    messageIDs  [0] MessageIDs  OPTIONAL,
    rrpid       [1] RRPID  OPTIONAL,
    swIdent     SWIdent
}

MessageIDs ::= SEQUENCE {
    lid-C  [0] LocalID  OPTIONAL,
    lid-M  [1] LocalID  OPTIONAL,
    xID    [2] XID  OPTIONAL
}

MESSAGE ::= TYPE-IDENTIFIER            -- ISO/IEC 8824-2:1995(E), Annex A

Message ::= CHOICE {

    purchaseInitRequest         [ 0] EXPLICIT PInitReq,
    purchaseInitResponse        [ 1] EXPLICIT PInitRes,

    purchaseRequest             [ 2] EXPLICIT PReq,
    purchaseResponse            [ 3] EXPLICIT PRes,

    inquiryRequest              [ 4] EXPLICIT InqReq,
    inquiryResponse             [ 5] EXPLICIT InqRes,

    authorizationRequest        [ 6] EXPLICIT AuthReq,
```

```
    authorizationResponse            [ 7] EXPLICIT AuthRes,

    authReversalRequest              [ 8] EXPLICIT AuthRevReq,
    authReversalResponse             [ 9] EXPLICIT AuthRevRes,

    captureRequest                   [10] EXPLICIT CapReq,
    captureResponse                  [11] EXPLICIT CapRes,

    captureReversalRequest           [12] EXPLICIT CapRevReq,
    captureReversalResponse          [13] EXPLICIT CapRevRes,

    creditRequest                    [14] EXPLICIT CredReq,
    creditResponse                   [15] EXPLICIT CredRes,

    creditReversalRequest            [16] EXPLICIT CredRevReq,
    creditReversalResponse           [17] EXPLICIT CredRevRes,

    pCertificateRequest              [18] EXPLICIT PCertReq,
    pCertificateResponse             [19] EXPLICIT PCertRes,

    batchAdministrationRequest       [20] EXPLICIT BatchAdminReq,
    batchAdministrationResponse      [21] EXPLICIT BatchAdminRes,

    cardholderCInitRequest           [22] EXPLICIT CardCInitReq,
    cardholderCInitResponse          [23] EXPLICIT CardCInitRes,

    meAqCInitRequest                 [24] EXPLICIT Me-AqCInitReq,
    meAqCInitResponse                [25] EXPLICIT Me-AqCInitRes,

    registrationFormRequest          [26] EXPLICIT RegFormReq,
    registrationFormResponse         [27] EXPLICIT RegFormRes,

    certificateRequest               [28] EXPLICIT CertReq,
    certificateResponse              [29] EXPLICIT CertRes,

    certificateInquiryRequest        [30] EXPLICIT CertInqReq,
    certificateInquiryResponse       [31] EXPLICIT CertInqRes,

    error                           [999] EXPLICIT Error
}

-- Note: the parameter InfoObjectSet in the following definitions
-- allows a distinct information object set to be specified for
-- each PDU that can be extended thus permitting the organization
-- defining the extension to indicate where it intends for the
-- extension to appear.

MsgExtensions {EXTENSION:InfoObjectSet} ::=
    SEQUENCE OF MsgExtension {{InfoObjectSet}}

MsgExtension {EXTENSION:InfoObjectSet} ::= SEQUENCE {
    extnID      EXTENSION.&id({InfoObjectSet}),
    critical    EXTENSION.&critical({InfoObjectSet}{@extnID})
                DEFAULT FALSE,
    extnValue   [0] EXPLICIT EXTENSION.&ExtenType ({InfoObjectSet}{@extnID})
}
```

```
Error ::= CHOICE {
   signedError     [0] EXPLICIT SignedError,
   unsignedError   [1] EXPLICIT ErrorTBS
}

SignedError ::= S {EE, ErrorTBS}

ErrorTBS ::= SEQUENCE {
   errorCode   ErrorCode,
   errorNonce  Nonce,
   errorOID    [0] OBJECT IDENTIFIER  OPTIONAL,
   errorThumb  [1] EXPLICIT CertThumb  OPTIONAL,
   errorMsg    [2] EXPLICIT ErrorMsg
 }

ErrorMsg ::= CHOICE {                              -- Either the
   messageHeader [0] EXPLICIT MessageHeader,       -- MessageHeader or a
   badWrapper    [1] OCTET STRING (SIZE(1..20000)) -- copy of the message
}

ErrorCode ::= ENUMERATED {
   unspecifiedFailure      (1),
   messageNotSupported     (2),
   decodingFailure         (3),
   invalidCertificate      (4),
   expiredCertificate      (5),
   revokedCertificate      (6),
   missingCertificate      (7),
   signatureFailure        (8),
   badMessageHeader        (9),
   wrapperMsgMismatch      (10),
   versionTooOld           (11),
   versionTooNew           (12),
   unrecognizedExtension   (13),
   messageTooBig           (14),
   signatureRequired       (15),
   messageTooOld           (16),
   messageTooNew           (17),
   thumbsMismatch          (18),
   unknownRRPID            (19),
   unknownXID              (20),
   unknownLID              (21),
   challengeMismatch       (22)
 }

-- Brand CRL Identifiers

BrandCRLIdentifier ::= SIGNED {
   EncodedBrandCRLID
} ( CONSTRAINED BY { -- Verify Or Sign UnsignedBrandCRLIdentifier -- } )

EncodedBrandCRLID ::= TYPE-IDENTIFIER.&Type (UnsignedBrandCRLIdentifier)

UnsignedBrandCRLIdentifier ::= SEQUENCE {
   version           INTEGER { bVer1(0) } (bVer1),
   sequenceNum       INTEGER (0..MAX),
```

```
   brandID           BrandID,
   notBefore         GeneralizedTime,
   notAfter          GeneralizedTime,
   crlIdentifierSeq  [0] CRLIdentifierSeq  OPTIONAL,
   bCRLExtensions    [1] Extensions   OPTIONAL
}

-- Notification to Brand CA that a CRL has been updated

CRLNotification ::= S{CA, CRLNotificationTBS}

CRLNotificationTBS ::= SEQUENCE {
   date          Date,        -- Date of notification
   crlThumbprint  Digest
}

CRLNotificationRes ::= S{CA, CRLNotificationResTBS}

CRLNotificationResTBS ::= SEQUENCE {
   date          Date,        -- Copied from CRLNotification
   crlThumbprint  Digest
}

-- Distribution of BrandCRLIdentifier to CAs and payment gateways

BCIDistribution ::= S{CA, BCIDistributionTBS}

BCIDistributionTBS ::= SEQUENCE {
   date  Date,
   bci   [0] BrandCRLIdentifier
}

BrandID ::= SETString { ub-BrandID }

CRLIdentifierSeq ::= SEQUENCE OF CRLIdentifier

CRLIdentifier ::= SEQUENCE {
   issuerName  Name,              -- CRL issuer Distinguished Name
   crlNumber   INTEGER (0..MAX)   -- cRLNumber extension sequence number
}

-- Common definitions

BackKeyData ::= SEQUENCE {
   backAlgID  ALGORITHM-IDENTIFIER.&id({ContentEncryptionAlgorithms}),
   backKey    BackKey
}

BackKey ::= OCTET STRING (SIZE(1..24))                    -- Secret

BIN ::= NumericString (SIZE(6))         -- Bank identification number

CardExpiry ::= NumericString (SIZE(6)) -- YYYYMM expiration date of card

CertThumb ::= SEQUENCE {
   digestAlgorithm  AlgorithmIdentifier {{DigestAlgorithms}},
```

```
    thumbprint      Digest
}

Challenge ::= OCTET STRING (SIZE(20))    -- Signature freshness challenge

CountryCode ::= INTEGER (1..999)    -- ISO-3166 country code

Currency ::= INTEGER (1..999)        -- ISO-4217 currency code

Date ::= GeneralizedTime

DateTime ::= SEQUENCE {
    date    Date,
    timeInd  BOOLEAN DEFAULT FALSE
}

Distance ::= SEQUENCE {
    scale  DistanceScale,
    dist   INTEGER (0..MAX)
}

DistanceScale ::= ENUMERATED {
    miles        (0),
    kilometers  (1)
}

Language ::= VisibleString (SIZE(1..ub-RFC1766-language))

LocalID ::= OCTET STRING (SIZE(1..20))

Location ::= SEQUENCE {
    countryCode     CountryCode,
    city            [0] EXPLICIT SETString { ub-cityName }  OPTIONAL,
    stateProvince   [1] EXPLICIT SETString { ub-stateProvince }  OPTIONAL,
    postalCode      [2] EXPLICIT SETString { ub-postalCode }  OPTIONAL,
    locationID      [3] EXPLICIT SETString { ub-locationID }  OPTIONAL
}

MerchantID ::= SETString { ub-MerchantID }

Nonce ::= OCTET STRING (SIZE(20))

PAN ::= NumericString (SIZE(1..19))

PANData ::= SEQUENCE {
    pan         PAN,
    cardExpiry  CardExpiry,
    panSecret   Secret,
    exNonce     Nonce
}

PANData0 ::= SEQUENCE {
    pan         PAN,
    cardExpiry  CardExpiry,
    cardSecret  Secret,
    exNonce     Nonce
```

```
}

PANToken ::= SEQUENCE {
   pan          PAN,
   cardExpiry   CardExpiry,
   exNonce      Nonce
}

PaySysID ::= VisibleString (SIZE(1..ub-paySysID))

Phone ::= SETString { ub-phone }

RRPID ::= OCTET STRING(SIZE(20)) -- Request response pair identification

Secret ::= OCTET STRING (SIZE(20))

SWIdent ::= VisibleString (SIZE(1..ub-SWIdent))    -- Software identification

Thumbs ::= SEQUENCE {
   digestAlgorithm   AlgorithmIdentifier {{DigestAlgorithms}},
   certThumbs        [0] EXPLICIT Digests  OPTIONAL,
   crlThumbs         [1] EXPLICIT Digests  OPTIONAL,
   brandCRLIdThumbs  [2] EXPLICIT Digests  OPTIONAL
}

TransIDs ::= SEQUENCE {
   lid-C      LocalID,
   lid-M      [0] LocalID  OPTIONAL,
   xid        XID,
   pReqDate   Date,
   paySysID   [1] PaySysID  OPTIONAL,
   language   Language          -- Cardholder requested session language
}

URL ::= VisibleString (SIZE(1..ub-URL))       -- Universal Resource Locator

XID ::= OCTET STRING (SIZE(20))

-- Upper bounds of SETString{} types

ub-BrandID           INTEGER ::=  40
ub-MerchantID        INTEGER ::=  30
ub-SWIdent           INTEGER ::= 256
ub-acqBusinessID     INTEGER ::=  32
ub-locationID        INTEGER ::=  10
ub-paySysID          INTEGER ::=  64
ub-RFC1766-language  INTEGER ::=  35
ub-URL               INTEGER ::= 512

END


SetCertMsgs
  { joint-iso-itu-t(2) internationalRA(23) set(42) module(6) 1}
      DEFINITIONS IMPLICIT TAGS ::= BEGIN
```

```
--
-- Types used in the SET Certificate Management Protocol messages.
--

-- EXPORTS All;

IMPORTS

   SETString {}, SignatureAlgorithms
      FROM SetAttribute

   SubjectPublicKeyInfo{}
      FROM SetCertificate

   BackKeyData, BIN, BrandCRLIdentifier, BrandID,
   CertThumb,Challenge, Currency, Date, Language, LocalID, MerchantID,
   Nonce, PAN, PANData0, RRPID, Thumbs, ub-acqBusinessID, URL
      FROM SetMessage

   CA, EE, Enc {}, EncK {}, EncX {}, EXH {}, KeyEncryptionAlgorithms, L {},
   S {}, SO {}
      FROM SetPKCS7Plus;


-- Certificate Management Payload Components

AcctInfo ::= CHOICE {
   panData0  [0] EXPLICIT PANData0,
   acctData  [1] EXPLICIT AcctData
}

AcctData ::= SEQUENCE {
   acctIdentification  AcctIdentification,
   exNonce             Nonce
}

AcctIdentification ::= VisibleString (SIZE(ub-acctIdentification))

IDData ::= CHOICE {                        -- Merchants and Acquirers only
   merchantAcquirerID  [0] MerchantAcquirerID,
   acquirerID          [1] AcquirerID
}

MerchantAcquirerID ::= SEQUENCE {
   merchantBIN  BIN,
   merchantID   MerchantID     -- By prior agreement of Merchant/Acquirer
}

AcquirerID ::= SEQUENCE {
   acquirerBIN        BIN,
   acquirerBusinessID  AcquirerBusinessID  OPTIONAL
}

AcquirerBusinessID ::= NumericString (SIZE(1..ub-acqBusinessID))

RequestType ::= ENUMERATED {  -- Indicates requestor and type of request
```

```
   cardInitialSig    (1),
-- cardInitialEnc     (2),                                      Reserved
-- cardInitialBoth    (3),                                      Reserved
   merInitialSig      (4),
   merInitialEnc      (5),
   merInitialBoth     (6),
   pgwyInitialSig     (7),
   pgwyInitialEnc     (8),
   pgwyInitialBoth    (9),
   cardRenewalSig    (10),
-- cardRenewalEnc    (11),                                      Reserved
-- cardRenewalBoth   (12),                                      Reserved
   merRenewalSig     (13),
   merRenewalEnc     (14),
   merRenewalBoth    (15),
   pgwyRenewalSig    (16),
   pgwyRenewalEnc    (17),
   pgwyRenewalBoth   (18)
}

RegFormOrReferral ::= CHOICE {
   regFormData    [0] RegFormData,
   referralData   [1] ReferralData
}

RegFormData ::= SEQUENCE {
   regTemplate  RegTemplate  OPTIONAL,
   policy       PolicyText
}

RegTemplate ::= SEQUENCE {
   regFormID     INTEGER (0..MAX),    -- CA assigned identifier
   brandLogoURL  [0] URL OPTIONAL,
   cardLogoURL   [1] URL OPTIONAL,
   regFieldSeq   RegFieldSeq OPTIONAL
}

RegFieldSeq ::= SEQUENCE SIZE(1..ub-FieldList) OF RegField

RegField ::= SEQUENCE {
   fieldId        [0] OBJECT IDENTIFIER  OPTIONAL,
   fieldName          FieldName,
   fieldDesc      [1] EXPLICIT SETString { ub-FieldDesc }  OPTIONAL,
   fieldLen           INTEGER (1..ub-FieldValue) DEFAULT ub-FieldValue,
   fieldRequired  [2] BOOLEAN DEFAULT FALSE,
   fieldInvisible [3] BOOLEAN DEFAULT FALSE
}

ReferralData ::= SEQUENCE {
   reason            Reason  OPTIONAL,  -- Displayed on requestor's system
   referralURLSeq  ReferralURLSeq  OPTIONAL
} ( WITH COMPONENTS { ..., reason PRESENT } |
    WITH COMPONENTS { ..., referralURLSeq PRESENT } )

Reason ::= SETString { ub-Reason }
```

```
ReferralURLSeq ::= SEQUENCE OF ReferralURL    -- Ordered by preference

ReferralURL ::= URL

PolicyText ::= SETString { ub-PolicyText }

-- Certificate Initialization Pair - Cardholder

CardCInitReq ::= SEQUENCE {
   rrpid      RRPID,
   lid-EE     LocalID,
   chall-EE   Challenge,
   brandID    BrandID,
   thumbs     [0] EXPLICIT Thumbs  OPTIONAL
}

CardCInitRes ::= S { CA, CardCInitResTBS }

CardCInitResTBS ::= SEQUENCE {
   rrpid              RRPID,
   lid-EE             LocalID,
   chall-EE           Challenge,
   lid-CA             LocalID  OPTIONAL,
   caeThumb           [0] EXPLICIT CertThumb,
   brandCRLIdentifier [1] EXPLICIT BrandCRLIdentifier  OPTIONAL,
   thumbs             [2] EXPLICIT Thumbs  OPTIONAL
}

-- Certificate Initialization Pair - Merchant or Payment Gateway

Me-AqCInitReq ::= SEQUENCE {
   rrpid        RRPID,
   lid-EE       LocalID,
   chall-EE     Challenge,
   requestType  RequestType,
   idData       IDData,
   brandID      BrandID,
   language     Language,
   thumbs       [0] EXPLICIT Thumbs  OPTIONAL
}

Me-AqCInitRes ::= S { CA, Me-AqCInitResTBS }

Me-AqCInitResTBS ::= SEQUENCE {
   rrpid              RRPID,
   lid-EE             LocalID,
   chall-EE           Challenge,
   lid-CA             [0] LocalID  OPTIONAL,
   chall-CA           Challenge,
   requestType        RequestType,
   regFormOrReferral  RegFormOrReferral,
   acctDataField      [1] RegField  OPTIONAL,
   caeThumb           [2] EXPLICIT CertThumb,
   brandCRLIdentifier [3] EXPLICIT BrandCRLIdentifier  OPTIONAL,
   thumbs             [4] EXPLICIT Thumbs  OPTIONAL
}
```

```
-- Registration Form Pair - Cardholder Only

RegFormReq ::= EXH { CA, RegFormReqData, PANOnly }

-- Intermediate results of EXH
RegFormReqTBE ::= L { RegFormReqData, PANOnly }

RegFormReqData ::= SEQUENCE {
   rrpid         RRPID,
   lid-EE        LocalID,
   chall-EE2     Challenge,
   lid-CA        [0] LocalID  OPTIONAL,
   requestType   RequestType,
   language      Language,
   thumbs        [1] EXPLICIT Thumbs  OPTIONAL
}

PANOnly ::= SEQUENCE {
   pan       PAN,
   exNonce   Nonce
}

RegFormRes ::= S { CA, RegFormResTBS }

RegFormResTBS ::= SEQUENCE {
   rrpid              RRPID,
   lid-EE             LocalID,
   chall-EE2          Challenge,
   lid-CA             [0] LocalID  OPTIONAL,
   chall-CA           Challenge,
   caeThumb           [1] EXPLICIT CertThumb  OPTIONAL,
   requestType        RequestType,
   formOrReferal      RegFormOrReferral,
   brandCRLIdentifier [2] EXPLICIT BrandCRLIdentifier  OPTIONAL,
   thumbs             [3] EXPLICIT Thumbs  OPTIONAL
}

-- Certificate Request Pair

CertReq ::= CHOICE {
   encx [0] EXPLICIT EncX { EE, CA, CertReqData, AcctInfo },
   enc  [1] EXPLICIT Enc { EE, CA, CertReqData }
}

-- Intermediate results of Enc and EncX
CertReqTBE ::= S { EE, CertReqData }

CertReqTBEX ::= SEQUENCE {
   certReqData  CertReqData,
   s            SO { EE, CertReqTBS }
}

CertReqTBS ::= SEQUENCE {
   certReqData CertReqData,
   acctInfo    AcctInfo
}
```

```
CertReqData ::= SEQUENCE {
    rrpid           RRPID,
    lid-EE          LocalID,
    chall-EE3       Challenge,
    lid-CA          [0] LocalID  OPTIONAL,
    chall-CA        [1] Challenge  OPTIONAL,
    requestType     RequestType,
    requestDate     Date,
    idData          [2] EXPLICIT IDData  OPTIONAL,
    regFormID       INTEGER (0..MAX),    -- CA assigned identifier
    regForm         [3] RegForm  OPTIONAL,
    caBackKeyData   [4] EXPLICIT BackKeyData  OPTIONAL,
    publicKeySorE   PublicKeySorE,
    eeThumb         [5] EXPLICIT CertThumb  OPTIONAL,
    thumbs          [6] EXPLICIT Thumbs  OPTIONAL
}

RegForm ::= SEQUENCE SIZE(1..ub-FieldList) OF RegFormItems

RegFormItems ::= SEQUENCE {
    fieldName   FieldName,
    fieldValue  FieldValue
}

FieldName ::= SETString { ub-FieldName }

FieldValue ::= CHOICE {
    setString    SETString { ub-FieldValue },
    octetString  OCTET STRING (SIZE(1..ub-FieldValue))
}

PublicKeySorE ::= SEQUENCE {
    publicKeyS [0] EXPLICIT SubjectPublicKeyInfo{{SignatureAlgorithms}}
                                                              OPTIONAL,
    publicKeyE [1] EXPLICIT SubjectPublicKeyInfo{{KeyEncryptionAlgorithms}}
                                                              OPTIONAL
} --
    -- At least one component shall be present. A user may request a
    -- signature certificate, an encryption certificate, or both.
    --
    ( WITH COMPONENTS { ..., publicKeyS PRESENT } |
      WITH COMPONENTS { ..., publicKeyE PRESENT } )

CertRes ::= CHOICE {
    certResTBS    [0] EXPLICIT S { CA, CertResData },
    certResTBSK   [1] EXPLICIT EncK { CAKey, CA, CertResData }
}

-- Intermediate results of EncK
CertResTBE ::= S { CA, CertResData }

CertResData ::= SEQUENCE {
    rrpid             RRPID,
    lid-EE            LocalID,
    chall-EE3         Challenge,
    lid-CA            LocalID,
```

```
   certStatus          CertStatus,
   certThumbs          [0] EXPLICIT Thumbs  OPTIONAL,
   brandCRLIdentifier  [1] EXPLICIT BrandCRLIdentifier  OPTIONAL,
   thumbs              [2] EXPLICIT Thumbs  OPTIONAL
}

CertStatus ::= SEQUENCE {
   certStatusCode  CertStatusCode,
   nonceCCA        [0] Nonce  OPTIONAL,
   eeMessage           SETString { ub-eeMessage }  OPTIONAL,
   caMsg           [1] CAMsg  OPTIONAL,
   failedItemSeq   [2] FailedItemSeq  OPTIONAL
}

FailedItemSeq ::= SEQUENCE SIZE(1..ub-FieldList) OF FailedItem

FailedItem ::= SEQUENCE {
   itemNumber  INTEGER (1..50),
   itemReason  SETString { ub-Reason }
}

CertStatusCode ::= ENUMERATED {          -- In-process status of CertReq
   requestComplete          (1),
   invalidLanguage          (2),
   invalidBIN               (3),
   sigValidationFail        (4),
   decryptionError          (5),
   requestInProgress        (6),
   rejectedByIssuer         (7),
   requestPended            (8),
   rejectedByAquirer        (9),
   regFormAnswerMalformed   (10),
   rejectedByCA             (11),
   unableToEncryptResponse  (12)
}

CAMsg ::= SEQUENCE {
   cardLogoURL    [0] URL  OPTIONAL,
   brandLogoURL   [1] URL  OPTIONAL,
   cardCurrency   [2] Currency  OPTIONAL,
   cardholderMsg  [3] EXPLICIT
                      SETString { ub-cardholderMsg }  OPTIONAL
}

CAKey ::= BackKeyData

-- Certificate Inquiry Pair

CertInqReq ::= S { EE, CertInqReqTBS }

CertInqReqTBS ::= SEQUENCE {
   rrpid      RRPID,
   lid-EE     LocalID,
   chall-EE3  Challenge,
   lid-CA     LocalID
}
```

```
CertInqRes ::= CertRes

-- Upper bounds of SETString{} types

ub-acctIdentification   INTEGER ::=    74
ub-cardholderMsg        INTEGER ::=   128
ub-eeMessage            INTEGER ::=   128
ub-FieldDesc            INTEGER ::=   200
ub-FieldList            INTEGER ::=    50
ub-FieldName            INTEGER ::=   128
ub-FieldValue           INTEGER ::=   128
ub-PolicyText           INTEGER ::= 20000
ub-Reason               INTEGER ::=   512


END


SetPayMsgs
  { joint-iso-itu-t(2) internationalRA(23) set(42) module(6) 2 }
      DEFINITIONS IMPLICIT TAGS ::= BEGIN

--
-- This module defines types for SET protocol payment messages.
--

-- EXPORTS All;

IMPORTS

   SETString {}
      FROM SetAttribute

   EXTENSION
      FROM SetCertificateExtensions

   BackKeyData, BIN, BrandCRLIdentifier, BrandID,
   CertThumb, Challenge, Currency, Date, Language, LocalID,
   Location, MerchantID, MsgExtensions {}, Nonce, PANData, PANToken,
   Phone, RRPID, Secret, SWIdent, Thumbs, TransIDs, URL, XID
      FROM SetMessage

   C, DD {},
   Enc {}, EncB {}, EncBX {}, EncK{}, EncX {}, EX {},
   EXH {}, HMAC {}, L {}, M, P, P1, P2, S {}, SO {}
      FROM SetPKCS7Plus

   CommercialCardData, MarketAutoCap, MarketHotelCap, MarketTransportCap,
   ub-reference
      FROM SetMarketData;

-- Purchase Initialization Pair

PInitReq ::= SEQUENCE {                    -- Purchase Initialization Request
   rrpid            RRPID,
   language         Language,
```

```
   localID-C        LocalID,
   localID-M        [0] LocalID  OPTIONAL,
   chall-C          Challenge,
   brandID          BrandID,
   bin              BIN,
   thumbs           [1] EXPLICIT Thumbs  OPTIONAL,
   piRqExtensions   [2] MsgExtensions {{PIRqExtensionsIOS}}  OPTIONAL
}

PIRqExtensionsIOS EXTENSION ::= { ... }

PInitRes ::= S { M, PInitResData }

PInitResData ::= SEQUENCE {
   transIDs            TransIDs,
   rrpid               RRPID,
   chall-C             Challenge,
   chall-M             Challenge,
   brandCRLIdentifier  [0] EXPLICIT BrandCRLIdentifier  OPTIONAL,
   peThumb             [1] EXPLICIT CertThumb,
   thumbs              [2] EXPLICIT Thumbs  OPTIONAL,
   piRsExtensions      [3] MsgExtensions {{PIRsExtensionsIOS}}  OPTIONAL
}

PIRsExtensionsIOS EXTENSION ::= { ... }

-- Purchase Pair

PReq ::= CHOICE {
   pReqDualSigned  [0] EXPLICIT PReqDualSigned,
   pReqUnsigned    [1] EXPLICIT PReqUnsigned
}

-- Signed components used by a cardholder with a certificate

PReqDualSigned ::= SEQUENCE {
   piDualSigned  PIDualSigned,
   oiDualSigned  OIDualSigned
}

PIDualSigned ::= SEQUENCE {
   piSignature  PISignature,
   exPIData     EX { P, PI-OILink, PANData }
}

-- Intermediate results of EX
PIDualSignedTBE ::= L { PI-OILink, PANData }

PI-OILink ::= L { PIHead, OIData }

OIDualSigned ::= L { OIData, PIData }

PISignature ::= SO { C, PI-TBS }

PI-TBS ::= SEQUENCE {
   hPIData   HPIData,
```

```
   hOIData   HOIData
}

HPIData ::= DD { PIData }                        -- PKCS#7 DigestedData

HOIData ::= DD { OIData }                        -- PKCS#7 DigestedData

PI ::= CHOICE {
   piUnsigned    [0] EXPLICIT PIUnsigned,
   piDualSigned  [1] EXPLICIT PIDualSigned,
   authToken     [2] EXPLICIT AuthToken
}

PIData ::= SEQUENCE {
   piHead    PIHead,
   panData   PANData
}

PIHead ::= SEQUENCE {
   transIDs          TransIDs,
   inputs            Inputs,
   merchantID        MerchantID,
   installRecurData  [0] InstallRecurData  OPTIONAL,
   transStain        TransStain,
   swIdent           SWIdent,
   acqBackKeyData    [1] EXPLICIT BackKeyData  OPTIONAL,
   piExtensions      [2] MsgExtensions {{PIExtensionsIOS}} OPTIONAL
}

PIExtensionsIOS EXTENSION ::= { ... }

Inputs ::= SEQUENCE {
   hod       HOD,
   purchAmt  CurrencyAmount
}

TransStain ::= HMAC { XID, Secret }

OIData ::= SEQUENCE {                            -- Order Information Data
   transIDs      TransIDs,
   rrpid         RRPID,
   chall-C       Challenge,
   hod           HOD,
   odSalt        Nonce,
   chall-M       Challenge  OPTIONAL,
   brandID       BrandID,
   bin           BIN,
   odExtOIDs     [0] OIDList  OPTIONAL,
   oiExtensions  [1] MsgExtensions {{OIExtensionsIOS}} OPTIONAL
}

OIExtensionsIOS EXTENSION ::= { ... }

OIDList ::= SEQUENCE OF OBJECT IDENTIFIER

HOD ::= DD { HODInput }
```

```
HODInput ::= SEQUENCE {
   od                 OD,
   purchAmt           CurrencyAmount,
   odSalt             Nonce,
   installRecurData   [0] InstallRecurData  OPTIONAL,
   odExtensions       [1] MsgExtensions {{ODExtensionsIOS}} OPTIONAL
}

ODExtensionsIOS EXTENSION ::= { ... }

OD ::= OCTET STRING                              -- Order description

-- Unsigned components used by a cardholder without a certificate

PReqUnsigned ::= SEQUENCE {   -- Sent by cardholders without certificates
   piUnsigned  PIUnsigned,
   oiUnsigned  OIUnsigned
}

OIUnsigned ::= L { OIData, PIDataUnsigned }

PIDataUnsigned ::= SEQUENCE {
   piHead    PIHead,
   panToken  PANToken
}

PIUnsigned ::= EXH { P, PI-OILink, PANToken }

-- Intermediate results of EXH
PIUnsignedTBE ::= L { PI-OILink, PANToken }

PRes ::= S { M, PResData }

PResData ::= SEQUENCE {
   transIDs            TransIDs,
   rrpid               RRPID,
   chall-C             Challenge,
   brandCRLIdentifier  [0] EXPLICIT BrandCRLIdentifier  OPTIONAL,
   pResPayloadSeq      PResPayloadSeq
}

PResPayloadSeq ::= SEQUENCE SIZE(1..MAX) OF PResPayload

PResPayload ::= SEQUENCE {
   completionCode  CompletionCode,
   results         Results  OPTIONAL,
   pRsExtensions   [0] MsgExtensions {{PRsExtensionsIOS}} OPTIONAL
}

PRsExtensionsIOS EXTENSION ::= { ... }

CompletionCode ::= ENUMERATED {
   meaninglessRatio        (0),   -- PurchAmt = 0; ratio cannot be computed
   orderRejected           (1),   -- Merchant cannot process order
   orderReceived           (2),   -- No processing to report
   orderNotReceived        (3),   -- InqReq received without PReq
```

```
      authorizationPerformed  (4),   -- See AuthStatus for details
      capturePerformed        (5),   -- See CapStatus for details
      creditPerformed         (6)    -- See CreditStatus for details
}

Results ::= SEQUENCE {
   acqCardMsg     [0] EXPLICIT AcqCardMsg  OPTIONAL,
   authStatus     [1] AuthStatus  OPTIONAL,
   capStatus      [2] CapStatus  OPTIONAL,
   credStatusSeq  [3] CreditStatusSeq  OPTIONAL
}

AuthStatus ::= SEQUENCE {
   authDate   Date,
   authCode   AuthCode,
   authRatio  FloatingPoint,
   currConv   [0] CurrConv  OPTIONAL
}

CapStatus ::= SEQUENCE {
   capDate   Date,
   capCode   CapCode,
   capRatio  FloatingPoint
}

CreditStatusSeq ::= SEQUENCE SIZE(1..MAX) OF CreditStatus

CreditStatus ::= SEQUENCE {
   creditDate   Date,
   creditCode   CapRevOrCredCode,
   creditRatio  FloatingPoint
}

-- Purchase Inquiry Pair

InqReq ::= CHOICE {
   inqReqSigned    [0] EXPLICIT InqReqSigned,
   inqReqUnsigned  [1] EXPLICIT InqReqData
}

InqReqSigned ::= S { C, InqReqData }

InqReqData ::= SEQUENCE {              -- Signed by cardholder, if signed
   transIDs         TransIDs,
   rrpid            RRPID,
   chall-C2         Challenge,
   inqRqExtensions  [0] MsgExtensions {{InqRqExtensionsIOS}}  OPTIONAL
}

InqRqExtensionsIOS EXTENSION ::= { ... }

InqRes ::= PRes

-- Authorization Pair

AuthReq ::= EncB { M, P, AuthReqData, PI }
```

```
-- Intermediate results of EncB
AuthReqTBE ::= S { M, AuthReqTBS }

AuthReqTBS ::= L { AuthReqData, PI }

AuthReqData ::= SEQUENCE {
   authReqItem  AuthReqItem,
   mThumbs      [0] EXPLICIT Thumbs  OPTIONAL,
   captureNow   BOOLEAN DEFAULT FALSE,
   saleDetail   [1] SaleDetail  OPTIONAL
} ( WITH COMPONENTS {..., captureNow (TRUE) } |
    WITH COMPONENTS {..., captureNow (FALSE), saleDetail ABSENT } )

AuthReqItem ::= SEQUENCE {
   authTags        AuthTags,
   checkDigests    [0] CheckDigests  OPTIONAL,
   authReqPayload  AuthReqPayload
}

AuthTags ::= SEQUENCE {
   authRRTags  RRTags,
   transIDs    TransIDs,
   authRetNum  AuthRetNum  OPTIONAL
}

CheckDigests ::= SEQUENCE {
   hOIData  HOIData,
   hod2     HOD
}

AuthReqPayload ::= SEQUENCE {
   subsequentAuthInd    BOOLEAN DEFAULT FALSE,
   authReqAmt           CurrencyAmount,          -- May differ from PurchAmt
   avsData              [0] AVSData  OPTIONAL,
   specialProcessing    [1] SpecialProcessing  OPTIONAL,
   cardSuspect          [2] CardSuspect  OPTIONAL,
   requestCardTypeInd   BOOLEAN DEFAULT FALSE,
   installRecurData     [3] InstallRecurData  OPTIONAL,
   marketSpecAuthData   [4] EXPLICIT MarketSpecAuthData  OPTIONAL,
   merchData            MerchData,
   aRqExtensions        [5] MsgExtensions {{ARqExtensionsIOS}} OPTIONAL
}

ARqExtensionsIOS EXTENSION ::= { ... }

AVSData ::= SEQUENCE {
   streetAddress  SETString { ub-AVSData } OPTIONAL,
   location       Location
}

SpecialProcessing ::= ENUMERATED {
   directMarketing    (0),
   preferredCustomer  (1)
}

CardSuspect ::= ENUMERATED {    -- Indicates merchant suspects cardholder
```

```
   --
   -- Specific values indicate why the merchant is suspicious
   --
   unspecifiedReason  (0)  -- Either the merchant does not differentiate
                           -- reasons for suspicion, or the specific
                           -- reason does not appear in the list
}

MerchData ::= SEQUENCE {
   merchCatCode  MerchCatCode  OPTIONAL,
   merchGroup    MerchGroup  OPTIONAL
}

MerchCatCode ::= NumericString (SIZE(ub-merType))  -- ANSI X9.10
        -- Merchant Category Code (MCCs) are assigned by acquirer to
        -- describe the merchant's product, service or type of business

MerchGroup ::= ENUMERATED {
   commercialTravel  (1),
   lodging           (2),
   automobileRental  (3),
   restaurant        (4),
   medical           (5),
   mailOrPhoneOrder  (6),
   riskyPurchase     (7),
   other             (8)
}

AuthRes ::= CHOICE {
   encB   [0] EXPLICIT EncB { P, M, AuthResData, AuthResBaggage },
   encBX  [1] EXPLICIT EncBX { P, M, AuthResData, AuthResBaggage, PANToken }
}

-- Intermediate results of EncB and EncBX
AuthResTBE ::= S { P, AuthResTBS }

AuthResTBEX ::= SEQUENCE {
   authResTBS  AuthResTBS,
   s           SO { P, AuthResTBSX }
}

AuthResTBS ::= L { AuthResData, AuthResBaggage}

AuthResTBSX ::= SEQUENCE {
   authResTBS  AuthResTBS,
   panToken    PANToken
}

AuthResData ::= SEQUENCE {
   authTags             AuthTags,
   brandCRLIdentifier   [0] EXPLICIT BrandCRLIdentifier  OPTIONAL,
   peThumb              [1] EXPLICIT CertThumb  OPTIONAL,
   authResPayload       AuthResPayload
}

AuthResBaggage ::= SEQUENCE {
```

```
      capToken    [0] EXPLICIT CapToken  OPTIONAL,
      acqCardMsg  [1] EXPLICIT AcqCardMsg  OPTIONAL,
      authToken   [2] EXPLICIT AuthToken  OPTIONAL
}

AcqBackKey ::= BackKeyData

AcqCardMsg ::= EncK { AcqBackKey, P, AcqCardCodeMsg }

-- Intermediate result of EncK
AcqCardCodeMsgTBE ::= S { P, AcqCardCodeMsg }

AcqCardCodeMsg ::= SEQUENCE {
   acqCardCode      AcqCardCode,
   acqCardMsgData   AcqCardMsgData
}

AcqCardCode ::= ENUMERATED {
   messageOfDay        (0),
   accountInfo         (1),
   callCustomerService (2)
}

AcqCardMsgData ::= SEQUENCE {
   acqCardText   [0] EXPLICIT SETString { ub-acqCardText }  OPTIONAL,
   acqCardURL    [1] URL  OPTIONAL,
   acqCardPhone  [2] EXPLICIT SETString { ub-acqCardPhone }  OPTIONAL
}

AuthResPayload ::= SEQUENCE {
   authHeader      AuthHeader,
   capResPayload   CapResPayload  OPTIONAL,
   aRsExtensions   [0] MsgExtensions {{ARsExtensionsIOS}} OPTIONAL
}

ARsExtensionsIOS EXTENSION ::= { ... }

AuthHeader ::= SEQUENCE {
   authAmt         CurrencyAmount,
   authCode        AuthCode,
   responseData    ResponseData,
   batchStatus     [0] BatchStatus  OPTIONAL,
   currConv        CurrConv  OPTIONAL          -- Merchant to cardholder
}

AuthCode ::= ENUMERATED {
   approved            ( 0),
   unspecifiedFailure  ( 1),
   declined            ( 2),
   noReply             ( 3),
   callIssuer          ( 4),
   amountError         ( 5),
   expiredCard         ( 6),
   invalidTransaction  ( 7),
   systemError         ( 8),
   piPreviouslyUsed    ( 9),
```

```
    recurringTooSoon       (10),
    recurringExpired       (11),
    piAuthMismatch         (12),
    installRecurMismatch   (13),
    captureNotSupported    (14),
    signatureRequired      (15),
    cardMerchBrandMismatch (16)
}

ResponseData ::= SEQUENCE {
    authValCodes  [0] AuthValCodes  OPTIONAL,
    respReason    [1] RespReason  OPTIONAL,
    cardType          CardType  OPTIONAL,
    avsResult     [2] AVSResult  OPTIONAL,
    logRefID          LogRefID  OPTIONAL
}

AuthValCodes ::= SEQUENCE {
    approvalCode    [0] ApprovalCode  OPTIONAL,
    authCharInd     [1] AuthCharInd  OPTIONAL,
    validationCode  [2] ValidationCode  OPTIONAL,
    marketSpec          MarketSpecDataID  OPTIONAL
}

RespReason ::= ENUMERATED {
    issuer                      (0),
    standInTimeOut              (1),
    standInFloorLimit           (2),
    standInSuppressInquiries    (3),
    standInIssuerUnavailable    (4),
    standInIssuerRequest        (5)
}

CardType ::= ENUMERATED {
    unavailable             ( 0),
    classic                 ( 1),
    gold                    ( 2),
    platinum                ( 3),
    premier                 ( 4),
    debit                   ( 5),
    pinBasedDebit           ( 6),
    atm                     ( 7),
    electronicOnly          ( 8),
    unspecifiedConsumer     ( 9),
    corporateTravel         (10),
    purchasing              (11),
    business                (12),
    unspecifiedCommercial   (13),
    privateLabel            (14),
    proprietary             (15)
}

AVSResult ::= ENUMERATED {
    resultUnavailable   (0),
    noMatch             (1),
    addressMatchOnly    (2),
```

```
      postalCodeMatchOnly  (3),
      fullMatch            (4)
}

LogRefID ::= NumericString (SIZE(1..ub-logRefID))

ApprovalCode ::= VisibleString (SIZE(ub-approvalCode))

AuthCharInd ::= ENUMERATED {
      directMarketing      (0),
      recurringPayment     (1),
      addressVerification  (2),
      preferredCustomer    (3),
      incrementalAuth      (4)
}

ValidationCode ::= VisibleString (SIZE(ub-validationCode))

-- Auth Reversal Pair

AuthRevReq ::= EncB { M, P, AuthRevReqData, AuthRevReqBaggage }

-- Intermediate results of EncB
AuthRevReqTBE ::= S { M, AuthRevReqTBS }

AuthRevReqTBS ::= L { AuthRevReqData, AuthRevReqBaggage }

AuthRevReqData ::= SEQUENCE {
      authRevTags       AuthRevTags,
      mThumbs           [0] EXPLICIT Thumbs  OPTIONAL,
      authReqData       [1] AuthReqData  OPTIONAL,
      authResPayload    [2] AuthResPayload  OPTIONAL,
      authNewAmt        CurrencyAmount,
      aRvRqExtensions   [3] MsgExtensions {{ARvRqExtensionsIOS}} OPTIONAL
}

ARvRqExtensionsIOS EXTENSION ::= { ... }

AuthRevReqBaggage ::= SEQUENCE {
      pi        PI,
      capToken  CapToken  OPTIONAL
}

AuthRevTags ::= SEQUENCE {
      authRevRRTags  AuthRevRRTags,
      authRetNum     AuthRetNum  OPTIONAL
}

AuthRevRRTags ::= RRTags

AuthRetNum ::= INTEGER (0..MAX)

AuthRevRes ::= CHOICE {
      encB [0] EXPLICIT EncB { P, M, AuthRevResData, AuthRevResBaggage },
      enc  [1] EXPLICIT Enc { P, M, AuthRevResData }
}
```

```
-- Intermediate results of Enc and EncB
AuthRevResTBE ::= S { P, AuthRevResData }

AuthRevResTBEB ::= S { P, AuthRevResTBS }

AuthRevResTBS ::= L { AuthRevResData, AuthRevResBaggage }

AuthRevResBaggage ::= SEQUENCE {
   capTokenNew   CapToken  OPTIONAL,
   authTokenNew  AuthToken  OPTIONAL
}

AuthRevResData ::= SEQUENCE {
   authRevCode        AuthRevCode,
   authRevTags        AuthRevTags,
   brandCRLIdentifier [0] EXPLICIT BrandCRLIdentifier  OPTIONAL,
   peThumb            [1] EXPLICIT CertThumb  OPTIONAL,
   authNewAmt         CurrencyAmount,                    -- May be zero
   authResDataNew     AuthResDataNew,
   aRvRsExtensions    [2] MsgExtensions {{ARvRsExtensionsIOS}} OPTIONAL
}

ARvRsExtensionsIOS EXTENSION ::= { ... }

AuthRevCode ::= ENUMERATED {
   approved            ( 0),
   unspecifiedFailure  ( 1),
   noReply             ( 2),
   amountError         ( 3),
   expiredCard         ( 4),
   invalidTransaction  ( 5),
   systemError         ( 6),
   missingCapToken     ( 7),
   invalidCapToken     ( 8),
   invalidAmount       ( 9)
}

AuthResDataNew ::= SEQUENCE {
   transIDs          TransIDs,
   authResPayloadNew AuthResPayload  OPTIONAL    -- Contains new data
}

-- Capture Pair

CapReq ::= CHOICE {
   encB  [0] EXPLICIT EncB { M, P, CapReqData, CapTokenSeq },
   encBX [1] EXPLICIT EncBX { M, P, CapReqData, CapTokenSeq, PANToken }
}

-- Intermediate results of EncB and EncBX
CapReqTBE ::= S { M, CapReqTBS }

CapReqTBEX ::= SEQUENCE {
   capReqTBS CapReqTBS,
   s         SO { M, CapReqTBSX }
}
```

```
CapReqTBS ::= L { CapReqData, CapTokenSeq }

CapReqTBSX ::= SEQUENCE {
   capReqTBS   CapReqTBS,
   panToken    PANToken
}

CapReqData ::= SEQUENCE {
   capRRTags        CapRRTags,
   mThumbs          [0] EXPLICIT Thumbs  OPTIONAL,
   capItemSeq       CapItemSeq,
   cRqExtensions    [1] MsgExtensions {{CRqExtensionsIOS}} OPTIONAL
}

CRqExtensionsIOS EXTENSION ::= { ... }

CapRRTags ::= RRTags

CapItemSeq ::= SEQUENCE SIZE(1..MAX) OF CapItem

CapItem ::= SEQUENCE {
   transIDs    TransIDs,
   authRRPID   RRPID,
   capPayload  CapPayload
}

CapPayload ::= SEQUENCE {
   capDate          Date,
   capReqAmt        CurrencyAmount,
   authReqItem      [0] AuthReqItem  OPTIONAL,
   authResPayload   [1] AuthResPayload  OPTIONAL,
   saleDetail       [2] SaleDetail  OPTIONAL,
   cPayExtensions   [3] MsgExtensions {{CPayExtensionsIOS}} OPTIONAL
}

CPayExtensionsIOS EXTENSION ::= { ... }

CapRes ::= Enc { P, M, CapResData }

-- Intermediate results of Enc
CapResTBE ::= S { P, CapResData }

CapResData ::= SEQUENCE {
   capRRTags           CapRRTags,
   brandCRLIdentifier  [0] EXPLICIT BrandCRLIdentifier  OPTIONAL,
   peThumb             [1] EXPLICIT CertThumb  OPTIONAL,
   batchStatusSeq      [2] BatchStatusSeq  OPTIONAL,
   capResItemSeq       CapResItemSeq,
   cRsExtensions       [3] MsgExtensions {{CRsExtensionsIOS}} OPTIONAL
}

CRsExtensionsIOS EXTENSION ::= { ... }

CapResItemSeq ::= SEQUENCE SIZE(1..MAX) OF CapResItem

CapResItem ::= SEQUENCE {
```

```
    transIDs        TransIDs,
    authRRPID       RRPID,
    capResPayload   CapResPayload
}

CapResPayload ::= SEQUENCE {
    capCode              CapCode,
    capAmt               CurrencyAmount,
    batchID              [0] BatchID  OPTIONAL,
    batchSequenceNum     [1] BatchSequenceNum  OPTIONAL,
    cRsPayExtensions     [2] MsgExtensions {{CRsPayExtensionsIOS}} OPTIONAL
}

CRsPayExtensionsIOS EXTENSION ::= { ... }

CapCode ::= ENUMERATED {
    success              (0),
    unspecifiedFailure   (1),
    duplicateRequest     (2),
    authExpired          (3),
    authDataMissing      (4),
    invalidAuthData      (5),
    capTokenMissing      (6),
    invalidCapToken      (7),
    batchUnknown         (8),
    batchClosed          (9),
    unknownXID           (10),
    unknownLID           (11)
}

-- Capture Reversal Or Credit

CapRevOrCredReqData ::= SEQUENCE {
    capRevOrCredRRTags       RRTags,
    mThumbs                  [0] EXPLICIT Thumbs  OPTIONAL,
    capRevOrCredReqItemSeq   CapRevOrCredReqItemSeq,
    cRvRqExtensions          [1] MsgExtensions {{CRvRqExtensionsIOS}} OPTIONAL
}

CRvRqExtensionsIOS EXTENSION ::= { ... }

CapRevOrCredReqItemSeq ::= SEQUENCE SIZE(1..MAX) OF CapRevOrCredReqItem

CapRevOrCredReqItem ::= SEQUENCE {
    transIDs                 TransIDs,
    authRRPID                RRPID,
    capPayload               CapPayload,
    newBatchID               [0] BatchID  OPTIONAL,
    capRevOrCredReqDate      Date,
    capRevOrCredReqAmt       [1] CurrencyAmount  OPTIONAL,
    newAccountInd            BOOLEAN DEFAULT FALSE,
    cRvRqItemExtensions      [2] MsgExtensions {{CRvRqItemExtensionsIOS}} OPTIONAL
}

CRvRqItemExtensionsIOS EXTENSION ::= { ... }
```

```
CapRevOrCredResData ::= SEQUENCE {
   capRevOrCredRRTags      RRTags,
   brandCRLIdentifier      [0] EXPLICIT BrandCRLIdentifier  OPTIONAL,
   peThumb                 [1] EXPLICIT CertThumb  OPTIONAL,
   batchStatusSeq          [2] BatchStatusSeq  OPTIONAL,
   capRevOrCredResItemSeq  CapRevOrCredResItemSeq,
   cRvRsExtensions         [3] MsgExtensions {{CRvRsExtensionsIOS}} OPTIONAL
}

CRvRsExtensionsIOS EXTENSION ::= { ... }

CapRevOrCredResItemSeq ::= SEQUENCE SIZE(1..MAX) OF CapRevOrCredResItem

CapRevOrCredResItem ::= SEQUENCE {
   transIDs                TransIDs,
   authRRPID               RRPID,
   capRevOrCredResPayload  CapRevOrCredResPayload
}

CapRevOrCredResPayload ::= SEQUENCE {
   capRevOrCredCode        CapRevOrCredCode,
   capRevOrCredActualAmt   CurrencyAmount,
   batchID                 [0] BatchID  OPTIONAL,
   batchSequenceNum        [1] BatchSequenceNum  OPTIONAL,
   cRvRsPayExtensions      [2] MsgExtensions {{CRvRsPayExtensionsIOS}} OPTIONAL
}

CRvRsPayExtensionsIOS EXTENSION ::= { ... }

CapRevOrCredCode ::= ENUMERATED {
   success             (0),
   unspecifiedFailure  (1),
   duplicateRequest    (2),
   originalProcessed   (3),
   originalNotFound    (4),
   capPurged           (5),
   capDataMismatch     (6),
   missingCapData      (7),
   missingCapToken     (8),
   invalidCapToken     (9),
   batchUnknown        (10),
   batchClosed         (11)
}

-- Capture Reversal Pair

CapRevReq ::= CHOICE {
   encB   [0] EXPLICIT EncB { M, P, CapRevData, CapTokenSeq },
   encBX  [1] EXPLICIT EncBX { M, P, CapRevData, CapTokenSeq, PANToken }
}

-- Intermediate results of EncB and EncBX
CapRevReqTBE ::= S { M, CapRevReqTBS }

CapRevReqTBEX ::= SEQUENCE {
   capRevReqTBS  CapRevReqTBS,
```

```
   s              SO { M, CapRevReqTBSX }
}

CapRevReqTBS ::= L { CapRevData, CapTokenSeq }

CapRevReqTBSX ::= SEQUENCE {
   capRevReqTBS  CapRevReqTBS,
   panToken      PANToken
}

CapRevData ::= [0] EXPLICIT CapRevOrCredReqData

CapRevRes ::= Enc { P, M, CapRevResData }

-- Intermediate results of Enc
CapRevResTBE ::= S { P, CapRevResData }

CapRevResData ::= [0] EXPLICIT CapRevOrCredResData

-- Credit Pair

CredReq ::= CHOICE {
   encB   [0] EXPLICIT EncB { M, P, CredReqData, CapTokenSeq },
   encBX  [1] EXPLICIT EncBX { M, P, CredReqData, CapTokenSeq, PANToken }
}

-- Intermediate results of EncB and EncBX
CredReqTBE ::= S { M, CredReqTBS }

CredReqTBEX ::= SEQUENCE {
   credReqTBS  CredReqTBS,
   s           SO { M, CredReqTBSX }
}

CredReqTBS ::= L { CredReqData, CapTokenSeq }

CredReqTBSX ::= SEQUENCE {
   credReqTBS  CredReqTBS,
   panToken    PANToken
}

CredReqData ::= [1] EXPLICIT CapRevOrCredReqData

CredRes ::= Enc { P, M, CredResData }

-- Intermediate results of Enc
CredResTBE ::= S { P, CredResData }

CredResData ::= [1] EXPLICIT CapRevOrCredResData

-- Credit Reversal Pair

CredRevReq ::= CHOICE {
   encB   [0] EXPLICIT EncB { M, P, CredRevReqData, CapTokenSeq },
   encBX  [1] EXPLICIT EncBX { M, P, CredRevReqData, CapTokenSeq, PANToken }
}
```

```
-- Intermediate results of EncB and EncBX
CredRevReqTBE ::= S { M, CredRevReqTBS }

CredRevReqTBEX ::= SEQUENCE {
   credRevReqTBS  CredRevReqTBS,
   s              SO { M, CredRevReqTBSX }
}

CredRevReqTBS ::= L { CredRevReqData, CapTokenSeq }

CredRevReqTBSX ::= SEQUENCE {
   credRevReqTBS  CredRevReqTBS,
   panToken       PANToken
}

CredRevReqData ::= [2] EXPLICIT CapRevOrCredReqData

CredRevRes ::= Enc { P, M, CredRevResData }

-- Intermediate results of Enc
CredRevResTBE ::= S { P, CredRevResData }

CredRevResData ::= [2] EXPLICIT CapRevOrCredResData

-- Payment Gateway Certificate Request Pair

PCertReq ::= S { M, PCertReqData }

PCertReqData ::= SEQUENCE {
   pCertRRTags     RRTags,
   mThumbs         [0] EXPLICIT Thumbs  OPTIONAL,
   brandAndBINSeq  BrandAndBINSeq,
   pcRqExtensions  [1] MsgExtensions {{PCRqExtensionsIOS}}  OPTIONAL
}

PCRqExtensionsIOS EXTENSION ::= { ... }

BrandAndBINSeq ::= SEQUENCE SIZE(1..MAX) OF BrandAndBIN

BrandAndBIN ::= SEQUENCE {
   brandID  BrandID,
   bin      BIN  OPTIONAL
}

PCertRes ::= S { P, PCertResTBS }

PCertResTBS ::= SEQUENCE {
   pCertRRTags            RRTags,
   pCertResItemSeq        PCertResItemSeq,
   brandCRLIdentifierSeq  [0] BrandCRLIdentifierSeq  OPTIONAL,
   pcRsExtensions         [1] MsgExtensions {{PCRsExtensionsIOS}}  OPTIONAL
}

PCRsExtensionsIOS EXTENSION ::= { ... }

PCertResItemSeq ::= SEQUENCE OF PCertResItem
```

```
PCertResItem ::= SEQUENCE {
   pCertCode   PCertCode,
   certThumb   [0] EXPLICIT CertThumb   OPTIONAL
}

PCertCode ::= ENUMERATED {
   success               (0),
   unspecifiedFailure    (1),
   brandNotSupported     (2),
   unknownBIN            (3)
}

BrandCRLIdentifierSeq ::= SEQUENCE SIZE(1..MAX) OF [0] EXPLICIT
BrandCRLIdentifier

-- Batch Administration Pair

BatchAdminReq ::= Enc { M, P, BatchAdminReqData }

-- Intermediate results of Enc
BatchAdminReqTBE ::= S { M, BatchAdminReqData }

BatchAdminReqData ::= SEQUENCE {
   batchAdminRRTags        RRTags,
   batchID                 [0] BatchID  OPTIONAL,
   brandAndBINSeq          [1] BrandAndBINSeq  OPTIONAL,
   batchOperation          [2] BatchOperation  OPTIONAL,
   returnBatchSummaryInd   BOOLEAN DEFAULT FALSE,
   returnTransactionDetail [3] ReturnTransactionDetail  OPTIONAL,
   batchStatus             [4] BatchStatus  OPTIONAL,
   transDetails            [5] TransDetails  OPTIONAL,
   baRqExtensions          [6] MsgExtensions {{BARqExtensionsIOS}} OPTIONAL
}

BARqExtensionsIOS EXTENSION ::= { ... }

BatchOperation ::= ENUMERATED {
   open   (0),
   purge  (1),
   close  (2)
}

ReturnTransactionDetail ::= SEQUENCE {
   startingPoint  INTEGER (MIN..MAX),
   maximumItems   INTEGER (1..MAX),
   errorsOnlyInd  BOOLEAN DEFAULT FALSE,
   brandID        [0] EXPLICIT BrandID  OPTIONAL
}

TransDetails ::= SEQUENCE {
   nextStartingPoint     INTEGER (MIN..MAX),
   transactionDetailSeq  TransactionDetailSeq
}

BatchAdminRes ::= Enc { P, M, BatchAdminResData }
```

```
-- Intermediate results of Enc
BatchAdminResTBE ::= S { P, BatchAdminResData }

BatchAdminResData ::= SEQUENCE {
    batchAdminTags         RRTags,
    batchID                BatchID,
    baStatus               BAStatus  OPTIONAL,
    batchStatus            [0] BatchStatus  OPTIONAL,
    transmissionStatus     [1] TransmissionStatus  OPTIONAL,
    settlementInfo         [2] SettlementInfo  OPTIONAL,
    transDetails           [3] TransDetails  OPTIONAL,
    baRsExtensions         [4] MsgExtensions {{BARsExtensionsIOS}} OPTIONAL
}

BARsExtensionsIOS EXTENSION ::= { ... }

TransmissionStatus ::= ENUMERATED {
    pending                (0),
    inProgress             (1),
    batchRejectedByAcquirer (2),
    completedSuccessfully  (3),
    completedWithItemErrors (4)
}

SettlementInfo ::= SEQUENCE {
    settlementAmount       CurrencyAmount,
    settlementType         AmountType,
    settlementAccount      SETString { ub-SettlementAccount },
    settlementDepositDate  Date
}

BAStatus ::= ENUMERATED {
    success                ( 0),
    unspecifiedFailure     ( 1),
    brandNotSupported      ( 2),
    unknownBIN             ( 3),
    batchIDunavailable     ( 4),
    batchAlreadyOpen       ( 5),
    unknownBatchID         ( 6),
    brandBatchMismatch     ( 7),
    totalsOutOfBalance     ( 8),
    unknownStartingPoint   ( 9),
    stopItemDetail         (10),
    unknownBatchOperation  (11)
}

ClosedWhen ::= SEQUENCE {
    closeStatus    CloseStatus,
    closeDateTime  Date
}

CloseStatus ::= ENUMERATED {
    closedbyMerchant  (0),
    closedbyAcquirer  (1)
}
```

```
BatchStatusSeq ::= SEQUENCE OF BatchStatus

BatchStatus ::= SEQUENCE {
   openDateTime      Date,
   closedWhen        [0] ClosedWhen  OPTIONAL,
   batchDetails      BatchDetails,
   batchExtensions   [1] MsgExtensions {{BSExtensionsIOS}} OPTIONAL
}

BSExtensionsIOS EXTENSION ::= { ... }

BatchDetails ::= SEQUENCE {
   batchTotals           BatchTotals,
   brandBatchDetailsSeq  BrandBatchDetailsSeq  OPTIONAL
}

BrandBatchDetailsSeq ::= SEQUENCE SIZE(1..MAX) OF BrandBatchDetails

BrandBatchDetails ::= SEQUENCE {
   brandID      BrandID,
   batchTotals  BatchTotals
}

BatchTotals ::= SEQUENCE {
   transactionCountCredit     INTEGER (0..MAX),
   transactionTotalAmtCredit  CurrencyAmount,
   transactionCountDebit      INTEGER (0..MAX),
   transactionTotalAmtDebit   CurrencyAmount,
   batchTotalExtensions       [0] MsgExtensions {{BTExtensionsIOS}} OPTIONAL
}

BTExtensionsIOS EXTENSION ::= { ... }

TransactionDetailSeq ::= SEQUENCE OF TransactionDetail

TransactionDetail ::= SEQUENCE {
   transIDs            TransIDs,
   authRRPID           RRPID,
   brandID             BrandID,
   batchSequenceNum    BatchSequenceNum,
   reimbursementID     ReimbursementID  OPTIONAL,
   transactionAmt      CurrencyAmount,
   transactionAmtType  AmountType,
   transactionStatus   [0] TransactionStatus  OPTIONAL,
   transExtensions     [1] MsgExtensions {{TransExtensionsIOS}} OPTIONAL
}

TransExtensionsIOS EXTENSION ::= { ... }

AmountType ::= ENUMERATED {
   credit  (0),
   debit   (1)
}

TransactionStatus ::= ENUMERATED {
   success             (0),
```

```
   unspecifiedFailure  (1)
}

ReimbursementID ::= ENUMERATED {
   unspecified     (0),
   standard        (1),
   keyEntered      (2),
   electronic      (3),
   additionalData  (4),
   enhancedData    (5),
   marketSpecific  (6)
}

-- Payment Message Components

AuthToken  ::= EncX { P1, P2, AuthTokenData, PANToken }

-- Intermediate results of EncX
AuthTokenTBE ::= SEQUENCE {
   authTokenData  AuthTokenData,
   s              SO { P1, AuthTokenTBS }
}

AuthTokenTBS ::= SEQUENCE {
   authTokenData  AuthTokenData,
   panToken       PANToken
}

AuthTokenData ::= SEQUENCE {
   transIDs           TransIDs,
   purchAmt           CurrencyAmount,
   merchantID         MerchantID,
   acqBackKeyData     BackKeyData  OPTIONAL,
   installRecurData   [0] InstallRecurData  OPTIONAL,
   recurringCount     [1] INTEGER (1..MAX)  OPTIONAL,
   prevAuthDateTime   Date,
   totalAuthAmount    [2] CurrencyAmount  OPTIONAL,
   authTokenOpaque    [3] EXPLICIT TokenOpaque OPTIONAL
}

BatchID ::= INTEGER (0..MAX)

BatchSequenceNum ::= INTEGER (1..MAX)

CapToken ::= CHOICE {
   encX  [0] EXPLICIT EncX { P1, P2, CapTokenData, PANToken },
   enc   [1] EXPLICIT Enc { P1, P2, CapTokenData },
   null  [2] EXPLICIT NULL
}

-- Intermediate results of Enc and EncX
CapTokenTBE ::= S { P1, CapTokenData }

CapTokenTBEX ::= SEQUENCE {
   capTokenData  CapTokenData,
   s             SO { P1, CapTokenTBS }
```

```
}

CapTokenTBS ::= SEQUENCE {
   capTokenData  CapTokenData,
   panToken      PANToken
}

CapTokenData ::= SEQUENCE {
   authRRPID    RRPID,
   authAmt      CurrencyAmount,
   tokenOpaque  TokenOpaque
}

CapTokenSeq ::= SEQUENCE SIZE(1..MAX) OF CapToken

CurrencyAmount ::= SEQUENCE {
   currency  Currency, -- Currency code as defined in ISO-4217
   amount    INTEGER (0..MAX),
   amtExp10  INTEGER (MIN..MAX)
                       -- Base ten exponent, such that the value in local
                       -- currency is "amount * (10 ** amtExp10)"
                       -- The exponent shall be the same value as defined
                       -- for the minor unit of currency in ISO-4217.
}

CurrConv ::= SEQUENCE {
   currConvRate  FloatingPoint,
   cardCurr      Currency
}

FloatingPoint ::= REAL (WITH COMPONENTS {..., base (2)})

MarketAutoAuth ::= SEQUENCE {
   duration  Duration
}

MarketHotelAuth ::= SEQUENCE {
   duration  Duration,
   prestige  Prestige  OPTIONAL
}

Duration ::= INTEGER (1..99)                         -- Number of days

Prestige ::= ENUMERATED {
   unknown  (0),
   level-1  (1),  -- Transaction floor limits for each level are
   level-2  (2),  -- defined by brand policy and may vary between
   level-3  (3)   -- national markets.
}

MarketSpecAuthData ::= CHOICE {
   auto-rental  [0] MarketAutoAuth,
   hotel        [1] MarketHotelAuth,
   transport    [2] MarketTransportAuth
}
```

```
MarketSpecCapData ::= CHOICE {
   auto-rental  [0] MarketAutoCap,
   hotel        [1] MarketHotelCap,
   transport    [2] MarketTransportCap
}

MarketSpecSaleData ::= SEQUENCE {
   marketSpecDataID   MarketSpecDataID OPTIONAL,
   marketSpecCapData  MarketSpecCapData OPTIONAL
}

MarketTransportAuth ::= NULL

MarketSpecDataID ::= ENUMERATED {
  failedEdit  (0),
  auto        (1),
  hotel       (2),
  transport   (3)
}

MerOrderNum ::= VisibleString (SIZE(1..ub-merOrderNum))

MerTermIDs ::= SEQUENCE {
   merchantID  MerchantID,
   terminalID  VisibleString (SIZE(1..ub-terminalID)) OPTIONAL,
   agentNum    INTEGER (0..MAX)  OPTIONAL,
   chainNum    [0] INTEGER (0..MAX)  OPTIONAL,
   storeNum    [1] INTEGER (0..MAX)  OPTIONAL
}

RRTags ::= SEQUENCE {
   rrpid        RRPID,
   merTermIDs   MerTermIDs,
   currentDate  Date
}

SaleDetail ::= SEQUENCE {
   batchID                 [ 0] BatchID  OPTIONAL,
   batchSequenceNum        [ 1] BatchSequenceNum  OPTIONAL,
   payRecurInd             [ 2] PayRecurInd  OPTIONAL,
   merOrderNum             [ 3] MerOrderNum  OPTIONAL,
   authCharInd             [ 4] AuthCharInd  OPTIONAL,
   marketSpecSaleData      [ 5] MarketSpecSaleData  OPTIONAL,
   commercialCardData      [ 6] CommercialCardData  OPTIONAL,
   orderSummary            [ 7] EXPLICIT SETString { ub-summary }  OPTIONAL,
   customerReferenceNumber [ 8] EXPLICIT SETString { ub-reference }  OPTIONAL,
   customerServicePhone    [ 9] EXPLICIT Phone  OPTIONAL,
   okToPrintPhoneInd       [10] BOOLEAN DEFAULT TRUE,
   saleExtensions          [11] MsgExtensions {{SaleExtensionsIOS}}  OPTIONAL
}

SaleExtensionsIOS EXTENSION ::= { ... }

PayRecurInd ::= ENUMERATED {
   unknown            (0),
   singleTransaction  (1),
```

```
   recurringTransaction  (2),
   installmentPayment    (3),
   otherMailOrder        (4)
}

InstallRecurData ::= SEQUENCE {
   installRecurInd  InstallRecurInd,
   irExtensions     [0] MsgExtensions {{IRExtensionsIOS}} OPTIONAL
}

IRExtensionsIOS EXTENSION ::= { ... }

InstallRecurInd ::= CHOICE {
   installTotalTrans [0] INTEGER (2..MAX),
   recurring         [1] Recurring
}

Recurring ::= SEQUENCE {
   recurringFrequency  INTEGER (1..ub-recurringFrequency),
   recurringExpiry     Date
}

TokenOpaque ::= TYPE-IDENTIFIER.&Type        -- Gateway-defined data

-- Upper bound of SETString{} type

ub-acqCardText        INTEGER ::= 128
ub-acqCardPhone       INTEGER ::=  50
ub-approvalCode       INTEGER ::=   6
ub-AVSData            INTEGER ::= 128
ub-logRefID           INTEGER ::=  32
ub-merOrderNum        INTEGER ::=  25
ub-merType            INTEGER ::=   4
ub-recurringFrequency INTEGER ::= 366
ub-SettlementAccount  INTEGER ::=  50
ub-summary            INTEGER ::=  35
ub-terminalID         INTEGER ::=  48
ub-validationCode     INTEGER ::=   4

END



SetCertificate
  { joint-iso-itu-t(2) internationalRA(23) set(42) module(6) 3 }
     DEFINITIONS EXPLICIT TAGS ::= BEGIN

--
-- This module defines types for CRL and X.509v3 certificate support.
--

-- EXPORTS All;

IMPORTS

   ALGORITHM-IDENTIFIER, AlgorithmIdentifier {}, Name,
```

```
    SignatureAlgorithms, SupportedAlgorithms
        FROM SetAttribute

    Extensions
        FROM SetCertificateExtensions;


UnsignedCertificate ::= SEQUENCE {
    version                 [0] CertificateVersion,
    serialNumber            CertificateSerialNumber,
    signature               AlgorithmIdentifier {{SignatureAlgorithms}},
    issuer                  Name,
    validity                Validity,
    subject                 Name,
    subjectPublicKeyInfo    SubjectPublicKeyInfo{{SupportedAlgorithms}},
    issuerUniqueID          [1] IMPLICIT UniqueIdentifier OPTIONAL,
    subjectUniqueID         [2] IMPLICIT UniqueIdentifier OPTIONAL,
    extensions              [3] Extensions          -- Required for SET usage
}

CertificateVersion ::= INTEGER { ver3(2) } ( ver3 )

CertificateSerialNumber ::= INTEGER

-- Compute the encrypted hash of this value if issuing a certificate,
-- or recompute the issuer's signature on this value if validating a
-- certificate.
--
EncodedCertificate ::= TYPE-IDENTIFIER.&Type (UnsignedCertificate)

Certificate::=   SIGNED {
    EncodedCertificate
} ( CONSTRAINED BY { -- Verify Or Sign Certificate -- } )

SIGNED { ToBeSigned } ::= SEQUENCE {
    toBeSigned  ToBeSigned,
    algorithm   AlgorithmIdentifier {{SignatureAlgorithms}},
    signature   BIT STRING
}

Validity ::= SEQUENCE {
    notBefore  UTCTime,      -- Not valid before this date
    notAfter   UTCTime       -- Not valid after this date
}

UniqueIdentifier ::= BIT STRING          -- Not used in the SET protocol

SubjectPublicKeyInfo {ALGORITHM-IDENTIFIER:Algorithms} ::= SEQUENCE {
    algorithm         AlgorithmIdentifier {{Algorithms}},
    subjectPublicKey  BIT STRING
}

END
```

```
SetCertificateExtensions
  { joint-iso-itu-t(2) internationalRA(23) set(42) module(6) 4 }
      DEFINITIONS IMPLICIT TAGS ::= BEGIN

--
-- Defines X.509 Version 3 certificate extensions.
--

-- EXPORTS All;

IMPORTS

    Name, SETString {}, SupportedAlgorithms
        FROM SetAttribute

    CertificateSerialNumber, SubjectPublicKeyInfo
        FROM SetCertificate

    BIN, CountryCode, Language, MerchantID, URL
        FROM SetMessage

    DD {}, DetachedDigest
        FROM SetPKCS7Plus;


-- X.509v3 Certificate Extensions

EXTENSION ::= CLASS {
    &id         OBJECT IDENTIFIER UNIQUE,
    &critical   BOOLEAN DEFAULT FALSE,
    &ExtenType
}
WITH SYNTAX {
    SYNTAX          &ExtenType
    [ CRITICAL      &critical ]
    IDENTIFIED BY  &id
}

Extensions ::= SEQUENCE OF Extension

ExtensionSet EXTENSION ::= {                    -- Information Object Set
    --
    -- Standard X.509v3 extensions
    --
    authorityKeyIdentifier |  -- not critical
    keyUsage               |  -- critical
    privateKeyUsagePeriod  |  -- not critical
    certificatePolicies    |  -- critical
    subjectAltName         |  -- not critical
    issuerAltName          |  -- not critical
    basicConstraints       |  -- critical
    cRLNumber              |  -- not critical
    --
    -- SET Private extensions
    --
    hashedRootKey          |  -- critical
```

```
   certificateType          |  -- critical
   merchantData             |  -- not critical
   cardCertRequired         |  -- not critical
   tunneling                |  -- not critical
   setExtensions,              -- not critical
   ...
}

Extension ::= SEQUENCE {
   extnID      EXTENSION.&id({ExtensionSet}),
   critical    EXTENSION.&critical({ExtensionSet}{@extnID}) DEFAULT FALSE,
   extnValue   OCTET STRING -- DER representation of &ExtenType extension
                            -- object for the object identified by extnID
}

-- Key and policy information extensions --

authorityKeyIdentifier EXTENSION ::= {
   SYNTAX          AuthorityKeyIdentifier
   IDENTIFIED BY id-ce-authorityKeyIdentifier
}

AuthorityKeyIdentifier ::= SEQUENCE {
   keyIdentifier               [0] KeyIdentifier  OPTIONAL,
   authorityCertIssuer         [1] GeneralNames  OPTIONAL,
   authorityCertSerialNumber   [2] CertificateSerialNumber  OPTIONAL
} ( WITH COMPONENTS {  keyIdentifier ABSENT,
       authorityCertIssuer PRESENT, authorityCertSerialNumber PRESENT } )

KeyIdentifier ::= OCTET STRING

keyUsage EXTENSION ::= {
   SYNTAX        KeyUsage
   CRITICAL      TRUE
   IDENTIFIED BY id-ce-keyUsage
}

KeyUsage ::= BIT STRING {
   digitalSignature  (0),
   nonRepudiation    (1),
   keyEncipherment   (2),
   dataEncipherment  (3),
   keyAgreement      (4),
   keyCertSign       (5),            -- For use in CA-certificates only
   cRLSign           (6)            -- For use in CA-certificates only
}

privateKeyUsagePeriod EXTENSION ::= {
   SYNTAX        PrivateKeyUsagePeriod
   IDENTIFIED BY id-ce-privateKeyUsagePeriod
}

PrivateKeyUsagePeriod ::= SEQUENCE {
   notBefore [0] GeneralizedTime  OPTIONAL,
   notAfter  [1] GeneralizedTime  OPTIONAL
} ( WITH COMPONENTS { ..., notBefore PRESENT } |
```

```
   WITH COMPONENTS { ..., notAfter  PRESENT } )

certificatePolicies EXTENSION ::= {
   SYNTAX        CertificatePoliciesSyntax
   CRITICAL      TRUE
   IDENTIFIED BY id-ce-certificatePolicies
}

CertificatePoliciesSyntax ::= SEQUENCE SIZE(1..MAX) OF PolicyInformation

PolicyInformation ::= SEQUENCE {
   policyIdentifier  CertPolicyId,
   policyQualifiers  SEQUENCE SIZE(1..MAX) OF
                                        PolicyQualifierInfo  OPTIONAL
}

CertPolicyId ::= OBJECT IDENTIFIER

PolicyQualifierInfo ::= SEQUENCE {
   policyQualifierId  CERT-POLICY-QUALIFIER.&id
                                     ({SupportedPolicyQualifiers}),
   qualifier          CERT-POLICY-QUALIFIER.&Qualifier
                      ({SupportedPolicyQualifiers}{@policyQualifierId})
                                                          OPTIONAL
}

SupportedPolicyQualifiers CERT-POLICY-QUALIFIER ::= {
   setPolicyQualifier,
   ...
}

CERT-POLICY-QUALIFIER ::= CLASS {
   &id          OBJECT IDENTIFIER UNIQUE,
   &Qualifier  OPTIONAL
}
WITH SYNTAX {
   POLICY-QUALIFIER-ID  &id
   [ QUALIFIER-TYPE      &Qualifier ]
}

setPolicyQualifier CERT-POLICY-QUALIFIER ::= {
   POLICY-QUALIFIER-ID  id-set-setQualifier
   QUALIFIER-TYPE       SetPolicyQualifier
}

SetPolicyQualifier ::= SEQUENCE {
   rootQualifier      SETQualifier,
   additionalPolicies  AdditionalPolicies  OPTIONAL
}

AdditionalPolicies ::= SEQUENCE SIZE(1..3) OF AdditionalPolicy

AdditionalPolicy ::= SEQUENCE {
   policyOID        CertPolicyId  OPTIONAL,
   policyQualifier  SETQualifier  OPTIONAL,
   policyAddedBy    CertificateTypeSyntax
```

```
}

SETQualifier ::= SEQUENCE {
   policyDigest    DetachedDigest  OPTIONAL,
   terseStatement  SETString {ub-terseStatement}  OPTIONAL,
   policyURL       [0] URL  OPTIONAL,
   policyEmail     [1] URL  OPTIONAL
}

-- Certificate subject and certificate issuer attributes extensions --

subjectAltName EXTENSION ::= {
   SYNTAX          GeneralNames
   IDENTIFIED BY id-ce-subjectAltName
}

GeneralNames ::= SEQUENCE SIZE(1..MAX) OF GeneralName

GeneralName ::= CHOICE {
   directoryName               [4] EXPLICIT Name,
   uniformResourceIdentifier   [6] IA5String,
   registeredID                [8] OBJECT IDENTIFIER
   -- Other choices defined in X.509 not used by SET
}

issuerAltName EXTENSION ::= {
   SYNTAX          GeneralNames
   IDENTIFIED BY id-ce-issuerAltName
}

-- Certification path constraints extensions --

basicConstraints EXTENSION ::= {
   SYNTAX          BasicConstraintsSyntax
   CRITICAL        TRUE
   IDENTIFIED BY id-ce-basicConstraints
}

BasicConstraintsSyntax ::= SEQUENCE {
   cA                 BOOLEAN  DEFAULT FALSE,
   pathLenConstraint  INTEGER (0..MAX)  OPTIONAL
}

-- Basic CRL extensions --

cRLNumber EXTENSION ::= {                         -- For use in CRLs only
   SYNTAX          CRLNumber
   IDENTIFIED BY id-ce-cRLNumber
}

CRLNumber ::= INTEGER (0..MAX)

-- Set protocol private extensions --

hashedRootKey EXTENSION ::= {               -- Only in root certificates
   SYNTAX          HashedRootKeySyntax
```

```
    CRITICAL        TRUE
    IDENTIFIED BY id-set-hashedRootKey
}

HashedRootKeySyntax ::= RootKeyThumb

RootKeyThumb ::= SEQUENCE {
    rootKeyThumbprint  DD { SubjectPublicKeyInfo{{SupportedAlgorithms}} }
}

certificateType EXTENSION ::= {
    SYNTAX          CertificateTypeSyntax
    CRITICAL        TRUE
    IDENTIFIED BY id-set-certificateType
}

CertificateTypeSyntax ::= BIT STRING {
    card  (0),
    mer   (1),
    pgwy  (2),
    cca   (3),
    mca   (4),
    pca   (5),
    gca   (6),
    bca   (7),
    rca   (8),
    acq   (9)
}

merchantData EXTENSION ::= {
    SYNTAX          MerchantDataSyntax
    IDENTIFIED BY id-set-merchantData
}

MerchantDataSyntax ::= SEQUENCE {
    merID           MerchantID,
    merAcquirerBIN  BIN,
    merNameSeq      MerNameSeq,
    merCountry      CountryCode,
    merAuthFlag     BOOLEAN DEFAULT TRUE
}

MerNameSeq ::= SEQUENCE SIZE(1..32) OF MerNames

MerNames::= SEQUENCE {
    language      [0] Language OPTIONAL,
    name          [1] EXPLICIT SETString { ub-merName },
    city          [2] EXPLICIT SETString { ub-cityName },
    stateProvince [3] EXPLICIT SETString { ub-stateProvince }  OPTIONAL,
    postalCode    [4] EXPLICIT SETString { ub-postalCode }  OPTIONAL,
    countryName   [5] EXPLICIT SETString { ub-countryName }
}

cardCertRequired EXTENSION ::= {
    SYNTAX          BOOLEAN
    IDENTIFIED BY id-set-cardCertRequired
```

```
}

tunneling EXTENSION ::= {
   SYNTAX          TunnelingSyntax
   IDENTIFIED BY id-set-tunneling
}

TunnelingSyntax ::= SEQUENCE {
   tunneling    BOOLEAN DEFAULT TRUE,
   tunnelAlgIDs  TunnelAlg
}

TunnelAlg ::= SEQUENCE OF OBJECT IDENTIFIER

setExtensions EXTENSION ::= {
   SYNTAX          SETExtensionsSyntax
   IDENTIFIED BY id-set-setExtensions
}

SETExtensionsSyntax ::= SEQUENCE OF OBJECT IDENTIFIER

-- Upper bounds of SETString{} types

ub-countryName      INTEGER ::=   50
ub-cityName         INTEGER ::=   50
ub-merName          INTEGER ::=   25
ub-postalCode       INTEGER ::=   14
ub-stateProvince    INTEGER ::=   50
ub-terseStatement   INTEGER ::= 2048

-- Object identifiers

id-ce                          OBJECT IDENTIFIER ::= { 2 5 29 }
id-ce-keyUsage                 OBJECT IDENTIFIER ::= { id-ce 15 }
id-ce-privateKeyUsagePeriod    OBJECT IDENTIFIER ::= { id-ce 16 }
id-ce-subjectAltName           OBJECT IDENTIFIER ::= { id-ce 17 }
id-ce-issuerAltName            OBJECT IDENTIFIER ::= { id-ce 18 }
id-ce-basicConstraints         OBJECT IDENTIFIER ::= { id-ce 19 }
id-ce-cRLNumber                OBJECT IDENTIFIER ::= { id-ce 20 }
id-ce-certificatePolicies      OBJECT IDENTIFIER ::= { id-ce 32 }
id-ce-authorityKeyIdentifier   OBJECT IDENTIFIER ::= { id-ce 35 }

id-set OBJECT IDENTIFIER ::=
    { joint-iso-itu-t(2) internationalRA(23) set(42) }

-- Object identifiers assigned under id-set arc

OID ::= OBJECT IDENTIFIER

id-set-contentType                     OID ::= { id-set 0 }
id-set-msgExt                          OID ::= { id-set 1 }
id-set-field                           OID ::= { id-set 2 }
id-set-attribute                       OID ::= { id-set 3 }
id-set-algorithm                       OID ::= { id-set 4 }
id-set-policy                          OID ::= { id-set 5 }
id-set-module                          OID ::= { id-set 6 }
```

```
id-set-certExt                          OID ::= { id-set 7 }
id-set-brand                            OID ::= { id-set 8 }
id-set-vendor                           OID ::= { id-set 9 }
id-set-national                         OID ::= { id-set 10 }

   -- Content type
id-set-content-PANData                  OID ::= { id-set-contentType 0 }
id-set-content-PANToken                 OID ::= { id-set-contentType 1 }
id-set-content-PANOnly                  OID ::= { id-set-contentType 2 }
id-set-content-OIData                   OID ::= { id-set-contentType 3 }
id-set-content-PI                       OID ::= { id-set-contentType 4 }
id-set-content-PIData                   OID ::= { id-set-contentType 5 }
id-set-content-PIDataUnsigned           OID ::= { id-set-contentType 6 }
id-set-content-HODInput                 OID ::= { id-set-contentType 7 }
id-set-content-AuthResBaggage           OID ::= { id-set-contentType 8 }
id-set-content-AuthRevReqBaggage        OID ::= { id-set-contentType 9 }
id-set-content-AuthRevResBaggage        OID ::= { id-set-contentType 10 }
id-set-content-CapTokenSeq              OID ::= { id-set-contentType 11 }
id-set-content-PInitResData             OID ::= { id-set-contentType 12 }
id-set-content-PI-TBS                   OID ::= { id-set-contentType 13 }
id-set-content-PResData                 OID ::= { id-set-contentType 14 }
id-set-content-InqReqData               OID ::= { id-set-contentType 15 }
id-set-content-AuthReqTBS               OID ::= { id-set-contentType 16 }
id-set-content-AuthResTBS               OID ::= { id-set-contentType 17 }
id-set-content-AuthResTBSX              OID ::= { id-set-contentType 18 }
id-set-content-AuthTokenTBS             OID ::= { id-set-contentType 19 }
id-set-content-CapTokenData             OID ::= { id-set-contentType 20 }
id-set-content-CapTokenTBS              OID ::= { id-set-contentType 21 }
id-set-content-AcqCardCodeMsg           OID ::= { id-set-contentType 22 }
id-set-content-AuthRevReqTBS            OID ::= { id-set-contentType 23 }
id-set-content-AuthRevResData           OID ::= { id-set-contentType 24 }
id-set-content-AuthRevResTBS            OID ::= { id-set-contentType 25 }
id-set-content-CapReqTBS                OID ::= { id-set-contentType 26 }
id-set-content-CapReqTBSX               OID ::= { id-set-contentType 27 }
id-set-content-CapResData               OID ::= { id-set-contentType 28 }
id-set-content-CapRevReqTBS             OID ::= { id-set-contentType 29 }
id-set-content-CapRevReqTBSX            OID ::= { id-set-contentType 30 }
id-set-content-CapRevResData            OID ::= { id-set-contentType 31 }
id-set-content-CredReqTBS               OID ::= { id-set-contentType 32 }
id-set-content-CredReqTBSX              OID ::= { id-set-contentType 33 }
id-set-content-CredResData              OID ::= { id-set-contentType 34 }
id-set-content-CredRevReqTBS            OID ::= { id-set-contentType 35 }
id-set-content-CredRevReqTBSX           OID ::= { id-set-contentType 36 }
id-set-content-CredRevResData           OID ::= { id-set-contentType 37 }
id-set-content-PCertReqData             OID ::= { id-set-contentType 38 }
id-set-content-PCertResTBS              OID ::= { id-set-contentType 39 }
id-set-content-BatchAdminReqData        OID ::= { id-set-contentType 40 }
id-set-content-BatchAdminResData        OID ::= { id-set-contentType 41 }
id-set-content-CardCInitResTBS          OID ::= { id-set-contentType 42 }
id-set-content-Me-AqCInitResTBS         OID ::= { id-set-contentType 43 }
id-set-content-RegFormResTBS            OID ::= { id-set-contentType 44 }
id-set-content-CertReqData              OID ::= { id-set-contentType 45 }
id-set-content-CertReqTBS               OID ::= { id-set-contentType 46 }
id-set-content-CertResData              OID ::= { id-set-contentType 47 }
id-set-content-CertInqReqTBS            OID ::= { id-set-contentType 48 }
id-set-content-ErrorTBS                 OID ::= { id-set-contentType 49 }
```

```
id-set-content-PIDualSignedTBE          OID ::= { id-set-contentType 50 }
id-set-content-PIUnsignedTBE            OID ::= { id-set-contentType 51 }
id-set-content-AuthReqTBE               OID ::= { id-set-contentType 52 }
id-set-content-AuthResTBE               OID ::= { id-set-contentType 53 }
id-set-content-AuthResTBEX              OID ::= { id-set-contentType 54 }
id-set-content-AuthTokenTBE             OID ::= { id-set-contentType 55 }
id-set-content-CapTokenTBE              OID ::= { id-set-contentType 56 }
id-set-content-CapTokenTBEX             OID ::= { id-set-contentType 57 }
id-set-content-AcqCardCodeMsgTBE        OID ::= { id-set-contentType 58 }
id-set-content-AuthRevReqTBE            OID ::= { id-set-contentType 59 }
id-set-content-AuthRevResTBE            OID ::= { id-set-contentType 60 }
id-set-content-AuthRevResTBEB           OID ::= { id-set-contentType 61 }
id-set-content-CapReqTBE                OID ::= { id-set-contentType 62 }
id-set-content-CapReqTBEX               OID ::= { id-set-contentType 63 }
id-set-content-CapResTBE                OID ::= { id-set-contentType 64 }
id-set-content-CapRevReqTBE             OID ::= { id-set-contentType 65 }
id-set-content-CapRevReqTBEX            OID ::= { id-set-contentType 66 }
id-set-content-CapRevResTBE             OID ::= { id-set-contentType 67 }
id-set-content-CredReqTBE               OID ::= { id-set-contentType 68 }
id-set-content-CredReqTBEX              OID ::= { id-set-contentType 69 }
id-set-content-CredResTBE               OID ::= { id-set-contentType 70 }
id-set-content-CredRevReqTBE            OID ::= { id-set-contentType 71 }
id-set-content-CredRevReqTBEX           OID ::= { id-set-contentType 72 }
id-set-content-CredRevResTBE            OID ::= { id-set-contentType 73 }
id-set-content-BatchAdminReqTBE         OID ::= { id-set-contentType 74 }
id-set-content-BatchAdminResTBE         OID ::= { id-set-contentType 75 }
id-set-content-RegFormReqTBE            OID ::= { id-set-contentType 76 }
id-set-content-CertReqTBE               OID ::= { id-set-contentType 77 }
id-set-content-CertReqTBEX              OID ::= { id-set-contentType 78 }
id-set-content-CertResTBE               OID ::= { id-set-contentType 79 }
id-set-content-CRLNotificationTBS       OID ::= { id-set-contentType 80 }
id-set-content-CRLNotificationResTBS    OID ::= { id-set-contentType 81 }
id-set-content-BCIDistributionTBS       OID ::= { id-set-contentType 82 }

-- Message extensions
-- None currently defined

-- Fields
id-set-fullName                         OID ::= { id-set-field 0 }
id-set-givenName                        OID ::= { id-set-field 1 }
id-set-familyName                       OID ::= { id-set-field 2 }
id-set-birthFamilyName                  OID ::= { id-set-field 3 }
id-set-placeName                        OID ::= { id-set-field 4 }
id-set-identificationNumber             OID ::= { id-set-field 5 }
id-set-month                            OID ::= { id-set-field 6 }
id-set-date                             OID ::= { id-set-field 7 }
id-set-address                          OID ::= { id-set-field 8 }
id-set-telephone                        OID ::= { id-set-field 9 }
id-set-amount                           OID ::= { id-set-field 10 }
id-set-accountNumber                    OID ::= { id-set-field 11 }
id-set-passPhrase                       OID ::= { id-set-field 12 }

   -- Attributes
id-set-attribute-cert                   OID ::= { id-set-attribute 0 }

id-set-rootKeyThumb                     OID ::= { id-set-attribute-cert 0 }
```

```
id-set-additionalPolicy                       OID ::= { id-set-attribute-cert 1 }

-- Algorithms
-- None currently defined

-- Policy
id-set-policy-root                            OID ::= { id-set-policy 0 }

-- SET private certificate extensions
id-set-hashedRootKey                          OID ::= { id-set-certExt 0 }
id-set-certificateType                        OID ::= { id-set-certExt 1 }
id-set-merchantData                           OID ::= { id-set-certExt 2 }
id-set-cardCertRequired                       OID ::= { id-set-certExt 3 }
id-set-tunneling                              OID ::= { id-set-certExt 4 }
id-set-setExtensions                          OID ::= { id-set-certExt 5 }
id-set-setQualifier                           OID ::= { id-set-certExt 6 }

-- Brands
id-set-IATA-ATA          OID ::= { id-set-brand 1 }
                         -- contact: rfcrum@air-travel-card.com
id-set-Diners            OID ::= { id-set-brand 30 }
                         -- contact: william.burnett@citicorp.com
id-set-AmericanExpress   OID ::= { id-set-brand 34 }
                         -- contact: david.armes@aexp.com
id-set-JCB               OID ::= { id-set-brand 35 }
                         -- contact: ohashi@cp.jcb.co.jp
id-set-Visa              OID ::= { id-set-brand 4 }
                         -- contact: tlewis@visa.com
id-set-MasterCard        OID ::= { id-set-brand 5 }
                         -- contact: paul-hollis@mastercard.com
id-set-Novus             OID ::= { id-set-brand 6011 }
                         -- contact: gallman@novusnet.com


-- Vendors
id-set-GlobeSet          OID ::= { id-set-vendor 0 }
                         -- contact: terence@globeset.com
id-set-IBM               OID ::= { id-set-vendor 1 }
                         -- contact: mepeters@raleigh.ibm.com
id-set-Cybercash         OID ::= { id-set-vendor 2 }
                         -- contact: dee@cybercash.com
id-set-Terisa            OID ::= { id-set-vendor 3 }
                         -- contact: briank@terisa.com
id-set-RSADSI            OID ::= { id-set-vendor 4 }
                         -- contact: baldwin@rsa.com
id-set-VeriFone          OID ::= { id-set-vendor 5 }
                         -- contact: trong@vfi.com
id-set-Trintech          OID ::= { id-set-vendor 6 }
                         -- contact: doneill@trintech.com
id-set-BankGate          OID ::= { id-set-vendor 7 }
                         -- contact: johnv@bankgate.com
id-set-GTE               OID ::= { id-set-vendor 8 }
                         -- contact: jeanne.gorman@gsc.gte.com
id-set-CompuSource       OID ::= { id-set-vendor 9 }
                         -- contact: simonr@compusource.co.za
id-set-Griffin           OID ::= { id-set-vendor 10 }
                         -- contact: asn1@mindspring.com
```

```
id-set-Certicom          OID ::= { id-set-vendor 11 }
                         -- contact: sshannon@certicom.ca
id-set-OSS               OID ::= { id-set-vendor 12 }
                         -- contact: baos@oss.com
id-set-TenthMountain     OID ::= { id-set-vendor 13 }
                         -- contact: dapkus@tenthmountain.com
id-set-Antares           OID ::= { id-set-vendor 14 }
                         -- contact: bzcd0@toraag.com
id-set-ECC               OID ::= { id-set-vendor 15 }
                         -- contact: beattie@ecconsultants.com
id-set-Maithean          OID ::= { id-set-vendor 16 }
                         -- contact: sullivan@maithean.com
id-set-Netscape          OID ::= { id-set-vendor 17 }
                         -- contact: rich@netscape.com
id-set-VeriSign          OID ::= { id-set-vendor 18 }
                         -- contact: simpson@verisign.com
id-set-BlueMoney         OID ::= { id-set-vendor 19 }
                         -- contact: jeremy@bluemoney.com
id-set-Lacerte           OID ::= { id-set-vendor 20 }
                         -- contact: lacerte@lacerte.com
id-set-Fujitsu           OID ::= { id-set-vendor 21 }
                         -- contact: sfuruta@inet.mmp.fujitsu.co.jp
id-set-eLab              OID ::= { id-set-vendor 22 }
                         -- contact: rah@shipwright.com
id-set-Entrust           OID ::= { id-set-vendor 23 }
                         -- contact: mortimer@entrust.com
id-set-VIAnet            OID ::= { id-set-vendor 24 }
                         -- contact: via.net@mail.eunet.pt
id-set-III               OID ::= { id-set-vendor 25 }
                         -- contact: wu@iii.org.tw
id-set-OpenMarket        OID ::= { id-set-vendor 26 }
                         -- contact: treese@OpenMarket.com
id-set-Lexem             OID ::= { id-set-vendor 27 }
                         -- contact: lje@lexem.fr
id-set-Intertrader       OID ::= { id-set-vendor 28 }
                         -- contact: rachel@intertrader.com
id-set-Persimmon         OID ::= { id-set-vendor 29 }
                         -- contact: carol.smith@persimmon.com
id-set-NABLE             OID ::= { id-set-vendor 30 }
                         -- contact: tony@nabletech.com
id-set-espace-net        OID ::= { id-set-vendor 31 }
                         -- contact: fm@well.com
id-set-Hitachi           OID ::= { id-set-vendor 32 }
                         -- contact: horimai@iabs.hitachi.co.jp
id-set-Microsoft         OID ::= { id-set-vendor 33 }
                         -- contact: rickj@microsoft.com
id-set-NEC               OID ::= { id-set-vendor 34 }
                         -- contact: nakata@mms.mt.nec.co.jp
id-set-Mitsubishi        OID ::= { id-set-vendor 35 }
                         -- contact: yoshitake@iss.isl.melco.co.jp
id-set-NCR               OID ::= { id-set-vendor 36 }
                         -- contact: Julian.Inza@spain.ncr.com
id-set-e-COMM            OID ::= { id-set-vendor 37 }
                         -- contact: 101643.426@compuserve.com
id-set-Gemplus           OID ::= { id-set-vendor 38 }
                         -- contact: florent.neu@ccmail.edt.fr
```

```
-- National markets: The value following id-set-national corresponds
-- to ISO-3166 numeric codes
id-set-Japan               OID ::= { id-set-national 392 }

END



SetCRL
  { joint-iso-itu-t(2) internationalRA(23) set(42) module(6) 5 }
      DEFINITIONS EXPLICIT TAGS ::= BEGIN

--
-- This module defines types for Certificate Revocation List support.
--

-- EXPORTS All;

IMPORTS

   AlgorithmIdentifier{}, Name, SignatureAlgorithms
      FROM SetAttribute

   CertificateSerialNumber, SIGNED {}
      FROM SetCertificate

   Extensions
      FROM SetCertificateExtensions;


UnsignedCertificateRevocationList ::= SEQUENCE {
   version               INTEGER { crlVer2(1) } ( crlVer2 ),
   signature             AlgorithmIdentifier {{SignatureAlgorithms}},
   issuer                Name,
   thisUpdate            UTCTime,
   nextUpdate            UTCTime,
   revokedCertificates   CRLEntryList  OPTIONAL,
   crlExtensions         [0] Extensions  OPTIONAL
}

CRLEntryList ::= SEQUENCE OF CRLEntry

CRLEntry ::= SEQUENCE{
   userCertificate       CertificateSerialNumber,
   revocationDate        UTCTime,
   crlEntryExtensions    Extensions  OPTIONAL
}

EncodedCRL ::= TYPE-IDENTIFIER.&Type (UnsignedCertificateRevocationList)

CRL ::= SIGNED {
   EncodedCRL
} (CONSTRAINED BY { -- Validate Or Issue CRL -- })


END
```

```
SetPKCS7Plus
   { joint-iso-itu-t(2) internationalRA(23) set(42) module(6) 6 }
      DEFINITIONS EXPLICIT TAGS ::= BEGIN


--
-- This module defines types for manipulating RSA PKCS #7 Cryptographic
-- Messages, as well as SET-specific messages which contain these types.
-- Note that SET uses definitions for PKCS-7 version 1.6.
--

-- EXPORTS All;

IMPORTS

   ALGORITHM-IDENTIFIER, AlgorithmIdentifier {}, ATTRIBUTE,
   Attribute {}, Name
      FROM SetAttribute

   Certificate, CertificateSerialNumber
      FROM SetCertificate

   CRL
      FROM SetCRL

   CardExpiry, PAN
      FROM SetMessage;


CRLSequence ::= SEQUENCE OF CRL

IssuerAndSerialNumber ::= SEQUENCE {   -- Uniquely identifies certificate
   issuer        Name,
   serialNumber  CertificateSerialNumber
}

CONTENTS ::= TYPE-IDENTIFIER

Contents CONTENTS ::= {
   { SignedData IDENTIFIED BY signedData },
   ...
}

ContentInfo ::= SEQUENCE {
   contentType  ContentType,
   content      [0] EXPLICIT CONTENTS.&Type({Contents}
                                              {@contentType})  OPTIONAL
}

ContentType ::= CONTENTS.&id({Contents})

SignedData ::= SEQUENCE {                                    -- PKCS#7
   sdVersion          INTEGER { sdVer2(2) } (sdVer2),
   digestAlgorithms   DigestAlgorithmIdentifiers,
   contentInfo        ContentInfo,
   certificates       [2] IMPLICIT Certificates  OPTIONAL,
   crls               [3] IMPLICIT CRLSequence  OPTIONAL,
```

```
      signerInfos        SignerInfos
}

SignerInfos ::= SEQUENCE OF SignerInfo
    (WITH COMPONENTS { ..., authenticatedAttributes   PRESENT,
                    unauthenticatedAttributes ABSENT })

SignerInfo ::= SEQUENCE {
    siVersion                  INTEGER { siVer2(2) } (siVer2),
    issuerAndSerialNumber      IssuerAndSerialNumber,
    digestAlgorithm            AlgorithmIdentifier {{DigestAlgorithms}},
    authenticatedAttributes    [2] EXPLICIT
                                   AttributeSeq {{Authenticated}}  OPTIONAL,
    digestEncryptionAlgorithm  AlgorithmIdentifier
{{DigestEncryptionAlgorithms}},
    encryptedDigest            EncryptedDigest,
    unauthenticatedAttributes  [3] EXPLICIT AttributeSeq {{...}}  OPTIONAL
}

Authenticated ATTRIBUTE ::={
    { WITH SYNTAX ContentType   ID contentType   } |
    { WITH SYNTAX MessageDigest ID messageDigest } ,
    ...
}

MessageDigest ::= Digest

Digests ::= SEQUENCE OF Digest

Digest ::= OCTET STRING (SIZE(1..20))

Certificates ::= SEQUENCE OF Certificate

DigestAlgorithmIdentifiers ::=
    SEQUENCE OF AlgorithmIdentifier { {DigestAlgorithms} }

DigestAlgorithms ALGORITHM-IDENTIFIER ::= {
    { NULL IDENTIFIED BY id-sha1 },
    ...
}

DigestEncryptionAlgorithms ALGORITHM-IDENTIFIER ::= {
    { NULL IDENTIFIED BY id-rsaEncryption },
    ...
}

EncryptedData ::= SEQUENCE {
    version            INTEGER { enVer0(0) } (enVer0),
    encryptedContentInfo  EncryptedContentInfo
}

EnvelopedData ::= SEQUENCE {
    edVersion          INTEGER { edVer1(1) } (edVer1),
    recipientInfos     RecipientInfos,
    encryptedContentInfo  EncryptedContentInfo
}
```

```
RecipientInfos ::= SEQUENCE OF RecipientInfo

EncryptedContentInfo ::= SEQUENCE {
   contentType        ContentType,
   contentEncryptionAlgorithm
                   AlgorithmIdentifier {{ContentEncryptionAlgorithms}},
   encryptedContent   [0] IMPLICIT EncryptedContent   OPTIONAL
}

EncryptedContent ::= OCTET STRING

ContentEncryptionAlgorithms ALGORITHM-IDENTIFIER ::= {
   { CBC8Parameter IDENTIFIED BY id-desCDMF } |
   { CBC8Parameter IDENTIFIED BY id-desCBC  },
   ...
}

CBC8Parameter ::= OCTET STRING (SIZE(8))

RecipientInfo ::= SEQUENCE {
   riVersion              INTEGER { riVer0(0) } (riVer0),
   issuerAndSerialNumber  IssuerAndSerialNumber,
   keyEncryptionAlgorithm AlgorithmIdentifier {{KeyEncryptionAlgorithms}},
   encryptedKey           EncryptedKey
}

KeyEncryptionAlgorithms ALGORITHM-IDENTIFIER ::= {
   { NULL IDENTIFIED BY rsaOAEPEncryptionSET },
   ...
}

-- When using the algorithm rsaOAEPEncryptionSET, the OAEP block is encrypted
-- using the recipient's public key and the result carried in EncryptedKey.
EncryptedKey ::= OCTET STRING (SIZE(1..128))

DigestedData ::= SEQUENCE {
   ddVersion        INTEGER { ddVer0(0) } (ddVer0),
   digestAlgorithm  AlgorithmIdentifier {{DigestAlgorithms}},
   contentInfo      ContentInfo,
   digest           Digest
}

EncryptedDigest ::= OCTET STRING

AttributeSeq { ATTRIBUTE:InfoObjectSet } ::=
                             SEQUENCE OF Attribute { {InfoObjectSet} }

-- Cryptographic Parameterized Types --

L { T1, T2 } ::= SEQUENCE {                    -- Linkage from t1 to t2
   t1  T1,
   t2  DD { T2 }                               -- PKCS#7 DigestedData
}

DD { ToBeHashed } ::= DetachedDigest
   (CONSTRAINED BY { -- digest of the DER representation, including --
```

```
                              -- the tag and length octets, of -- ToBeHashed })
DetachedDigest ::= DigestedData                             -- No parameter
   (WITH COMPONENTS {..., contentInfo (WITH COMPONENTS
                     {..., content ABSENT}) })


H { ToBeHashed } ::= OCTET STRING (SIZE(1..20)) (CONSTRAINED BY {
        -- HASH is an n-byte value, which is the results --
        -- of the application of a valid digest procedure      --
        -- applied to -- ToBeHashed })

HMAC { ToBeHashed, Key } ::= Digest
   (CONSTRAINED BY { -- HMAC keyed digest of -- ToBeHashed,
                                        -- using -- Key })

HMACPanData ::= SEQUENCE {                 -- For HMAC, unique cardholder data
   pan          PAN,
   cardExpiry   CardExpiry
}

S { SIGNER, ToBeSigned } ::= SignedData
   (CONSTRAINED BY { SIGNER, -- signs -- ToBeSigned })
   (WITH COMPONENTS { ..., contentInfo
       (WITH COMPONENTS {
                 ..., content PRESENT }) } ^
    WITH COMPONENTS { ..., signerInfos (SIZE(1..2)) })

SO { SIGNER, ToBeSigned } ::= SignedData              -- Detached content
   (CONSTRAINED BY { SIGNER, -- signs -- ToBeSigned })
   (WITH COMPONENTS { ..., contentInfo
       (WITH COMPONENTS{
                 ..., content ABSENT }) } ^
    WITH COMPONENTS { ..., signerInfos (SIZE(1..2)) })


-- Set Encapsulation Types


-- Simple Encapsulation with Signature --

Enc { SIGNER, RECIPIENT, T } ::= E {
   RECIPIENT,
   S { SIGNER, T }
}


-- Simple Encapsulation with Signature and a Provided Key --

EncK { KeyData, SIGNER, T } ::= EK {
   KeyData,
   S { SIGNER, T }
}


-- Extra Encapsulation with Signature --
```

```
EncX { SIGNER, RECIPIENT, T, Parameter } ::= E {
   RECIPIENT,
   SEQUENCE {
       t  T,
       s  SO { SIGNER, SEQUENCE { t  T, p  Parameter } }
     }
} (CONSTRAINED BY { Parameter -- data, which shall contain a fresh --
                    -- nonce 'n', is included in the OAEP block.  -- } )


-- Simple Encapsulation with Signature and Baggage --

EncB { SIGNER, RECIPIENT, T, Baggage } ::= SEQUENCE {
   enc      Enc { SIGNER, RECIPIENT, L { T, Baggage } },
   baggage  Baggage
}


-- Extra Encapsulation with Signature and Baggage --

EncBX { SIGNER, RECIPIENT, T, Baggage, Parameter } ::= SEQUENCE {
   encX     EncX { SIGNER, RECIPIENT, L { T, Baggage }, Parameter },
   baggage  Baggage
}


-- Other Cryptographic Messages --

E { RECIPIENT, ToBeEnveloped } ::= EnvelopedData
   (CONSTRAINED BY { ToBeEnveloped, -- is encrypted, and the --
                     -- session key is encrypted using the --
                     -- public key of -- RECIPIENT } )
   (WITH COMPONENTS {..., encryptedContentInfo
               (WITH COMPONENTS { ..., encryptedContent PRESENT }) } ^
    WITH COMPONENTS { ..., recipientInfos (SIZE(1)) })

EH { RECIPIENT, ToBeEnveloped } ::= E {
   RECIPIENT,
   ToBeEnveloped
} (CONSTRAINED BY { -- H(ToBeEnveloped) included in the OAEP block -- })

EX { RECIPIENT, ToBeEnveloped, Parameter } ::= E {
   RECIPIENT,
   L { ToBeEnveloped, Parameter }
}(CONSTRAINED BY { Parameter -- data is included in the OAEP block -- })

EXH { RECIPIENT, ToBeEnveloped, Parameter } ::= EX {
   RECIPIENT,
   ToBeEnveloped,
   Parameter
} (CONSTRAINED BY { -- H(ToBeEnveloped) included in the OAEP block -- })

EK { KeyData, ToBeEnveloped } ::= EncryptedData
   (CONSTRAINED BY { ToBeEnveloped, -- encrypted with -- KeyData } )
   (WITH COMPONENTS { ..., encryptedContentInfo
               (WITH COMPONENTS { ..., encryptedContent PRESENT}) })
```

```
ENTITY-IDENTIFIER ::= TYPE-IDENTIFIER                -- Generic placeholder

C  ::= ENTITY-IDENTIFIER  -- Cardholder
M  ::= ENTITY-IDENTIFIER  -- Merchant
P  ::= ENTITY-IDENTIFIER  -- Payment Gateway
EE ::= ENTITY-IDENTIFIER  -- End Entity
CA ::= ENTITY-IDENTIFIER  -- Certifying Authority
P1 ::= ENTITY-IDENTIFIER  -- Gateway One
P2 ::= ENTITY-IDENTIFIER  -- Gateway Two

-- Object Identifiers --

secsig OBJECT IDENTIFIER ::= {
   iso(1) identified-organization(3) oiw(14) secsig(3) }

pkcs-1 OBJECT IDENTIFIER ::= {
   iso(1) member-body(2) us(840) rsadsi(113549) pkcs(1) 1 }

rsaOAEPEncryptionSET OBJECT IDENTIFIER ::= { pkcs-1 6 }

id-rsaEncryption OBJECT IDENTIFIER ::= { pkcs-1 1 }

id-sha1-with-rsa-signature  OBJECT IDENTIFIER ::= { pkcs-1 5 }

id-sha1  OBJECT IDENTIFIER ::= { secsig 2 26 }

id-desCBC  OBJECT IDENTIFIER ::= { secsig 2 7 }

id-desCDMF  OBJECT IDENTIFIER ::= {
   iso(1) member-body(2) us(840) rsadsi(113549) encryptionAlgorithm(3) 10}

pkcs-7 OBJECT IDENTIFIER ::= {
   iso(1) member-body(2) us(840) rsadsi(113549) pkcs(1) 7 }

data OBJECT IDENTIFIER ::= { pkcs-7 1 }
signedData OBJECT IDENTIFIER ::= { pkcs-7 2 }
envelopedData OBJECT IDENTIFIER ::= { pkcs-7 3 }
digestedData OBJECT IDENTIFIER ::= { pkcs-7 5 }

pkcs-9 OBJECT IDENTIFIER ::= {
   iso(1) member-body(2) us(840) rsadsi(113549) pkcs(1) 9 }

contentType OBJECT IDENTIFIER ::= { pkcs-9 3 }

messageDigest OBJECT IDENTIFIER ::= { pkcs-9 4 }

END



SetAttribute
  { joint-iso-itu-t(2) internationalRA(23) set(42) module(6) 7 }
      DEFINITIONS EXPLICIT TAGS ::= BEGIN

--
-- This module defines types from ISO/IEC 9594-2:1995(E), Annex B, known
```

```
-- as the Information Framework. A minimal number of types have been
-- copied in order to constrain certificate names in SET. Specific SET
-- implementations may wish to copy additional X.501 types as necessary
-- to facilitate directory manipulation. National language support is
-- achieved through the DirectoryString type, copied from the X-500
-- series SelectedAttributeTypes module, and restricted for use in SET.
--

-- EXPORTS All;

IMPORTS

    id-sha1-with-rsa-signature, KeyEncryptionAlgorithms
        FROM SetPKCS7Plus;

-- attributes

commonName ATTRIBUTE ::= {
   WITH SYNTAX  DirectoryString { ub-common-name }
   ID id-at-commonName
}

countryName ATTRIBUTE ::= {
   WITH SYNTAX  PrintableString( SIZE(2) )
   ID id-at-countryName
}

organizationName ATTRIBUTE ::= {
   WITH SYNTAX  DirectoryString { ub-organization-name }
   ID id-at-organizationName
}

organizationalUnitName ATTRIBUTE ::= {
   WITH SYNTAX  DirectoryString { ub-organizational-unit-name }
   ID id-at-organizationalUnitName
}

-- attribute data types

Attribute { ATTRIBUTE:InfoObjectSet } ::= SEQUENCE {
   type    ATTRIBUTE.&id({InfoObjectSet}),
   values  SET SIZE(1) OF ATTRIBUTE.&Type({InfoObjectSet}{@type})
}

AttributeTypeAndValue ::= SEQUENCE {
   type    ATTRIBUTE.&id({SupportedAttributes}),
   value   ATTRIBUTE.&Type({SupportedAttributes}{@type})
}

SupportedAttributes ATTRIBUTE ::= {
   countryName            |
   organizationName       |
   organizationalUnitName |
   commonName
}
```

```
ALGORITHM-IDENTIFIER ::= TYPE-IDENTIFIER

AlgorithmIdentifier { ALGORITHM-IDENTIFIER:InfoObjectSet } ::= SEQUENCE {
    algorithm   ALGORITHM-IDENTIFIER.&id({InfoObjectSet}),
    parameters  ALGORITHM-IDENTIFIER.&Type({InfoObjectSet}
                                                   {@algorithm}) OPTIONAL
}

SupportedAlgorithms ALGORITHM-IDENTIFIER ::= {
    ...,
    KeyEncryptionAlgorithms |
    SignatureAlgorithms
  }

SignatureAlgorithms ALGORITHM-IDENTIFIER ::= {
    sha1-with-rsa-signature,
    ...
}

sha1-with-rsa-signature ALGORITHM-IDENTIFIER ::= {
    NULL IDENTIFIED BY id-sha1-with-rsa-signature }

-- naming data types

Name ::= CHOICE { -- only one possibility for now --
                  distinguishedName RDNSequence }

RDNSequence ::= SEQUENCE SIZE (1..5) OF RelativeDistinguishedName

RelativeDistinguishedName ::= SET SIZE(1) OF AttributeTypeAndValue

ATTRIBUTE ::= CLASS {
    &derivation             ATTRIBUTE OPTIONAL,
    &Type                   OPTIONAL,     -- &Type or &derivation required
    &equality-match         MATCHING-RULE OPTIONAL,
    &ordering-match         MATCHING-RULE OPTIONAL,
    &substrings-match       MATCHING-RULE OPTIONAL,
    &single-valued          BOOLEAN DEFAULT FALSE,
    &collective             BOOLEAN DEFAULT FALSE,
-- operational extensions
    &no-user-modification   BOOLEAN DEFAULT FALSE,
    &usage                  AttributeUsage DEFAULT userApplications,
    &id                     OBJECT IDENTIFIER UNIQUE
}
WITH SYNTAX {
-- [ SUBTYPE OF               &derivation ]           --
-- [ -- WITH SYNTAX           &Type -- ] --
-- [ EQUALITY MATCHING RULE   &equality-match ]       --
-- [ ORDERING MATCHING RULE   &ordering-match ]       --
-- [ SUBSTRINGS MATCHING RULE &substrings-match ]     --
-- [ SINGLE VALUE             &single-valued ]        --
-- [ COLLECTIVE               &collective ]           --
-- [ NO USER MODIFICATION     &no-user-modification ] --
    ID                      &id
}
```

```
AttributeUsage ::= ENUMERATED {
   userApplications      (0),
   directoryOperation    (1),
   distributedOperation  (2),
   dSAOperation          (3)
}

-- MATCHING-RULE information object class specification

MATCHING-RULE ::= CLASS {
   &AssertionType  OPTIONAL,
   &id             OBJECT IDENTIFIER UNIQUE
}
WITH SYNTAX {
   [ SYNTAX  &AssertionType ]
   ID        &id
}

DirectoryString { INTEGER:maxSIZE } ::= CHOICE {
   printableString  PrintableString (SIZE(1..maxSIZE)),
   bmpString        BMPString (SIZE(1..maxSIZE))
}

SETString { INTEGER:maxSIZE } ::= CHOICE {
    visibleString  VisibleString (SIZE(1..maxSIZE)),
    bmpString      BMPString (SIZE(1..maxSIZE))
  }

-- Upper bounds of type Name components

ub-common-name              INTEGER ::=  64
ub-organization-name        INTEGER ::=  64
ub-organizational-unit-name INTEGER ::=  64

ds    OBJECT IDENTIFIER ::= { joint-iso-itu-t(2) ds(5) }

id-at                          OBJECT IDENTIFIER ::= { ds 4 }
id-at-commonName               OBJECT IDENTIFIER ::= { id-at 3 }
id-at-countryName              OBJECT IDENTIFIER ::= { id-at 6 }
id-at-organizationName         OBJECT IDENTIFIER ::= { id-at 10 }
id-at-organizationalUnitName   OBJECT IDENTIFIER ::= { id-at 11 }

END




SetMarketData
  { joint-iso-itu-t(2) internationalRA(23) set(42) module(6) 8 }
     DEFINITIONS IMPLICIT TAGS ::= BEGIN

-- EXPORTS All;

IMPORTS

   Date, DateTime, Distance, Location, Phone
     FROM SetMessage
```

```
    CurrencyAmount, FloatingPoint, ub-merType
       FROM SetPayMsgs

    SETString
       FROM SetAttribute;

CommercialCardData ::= SEQUENCE {
    chargeInfo         [0] ChargeInfo  OPTIONAL,
    merchantLocation   [1] Location  OPTIONAL,
    shipFrom           [2] Location  OPTIONAL,
    shipTo             [3] Location  OPTIONAL,
    itemSeq            [4] ItemSeq  OPTIONAL
}

ChargeInfo ::= SEQUENCE {
    totalFreightShippingAmount  [ 0] CurrencyAmount  OPTIONAL,
    totalDutyTariffAmount       [ 1] CurrencyAmount  OPTIONAL,
    dutyTariffReference         [ 2] EXPLICIT SETString { ub-reference }
OPTIONAL,
    totalNationalTaxAmount      [ 3] CurrencyAmount  OPTIONAL,
    totalLocalTaxAmount         [ 4] CurrencyAmount  OPTIONAL,
    totalOtherTaxAmount         [ 5] CurrencyAmount  OPTIONAL,
    totalTaxAmount              [ 6] CurrencyAmount  OPTIONAL,
    merchantTaxID               [ 7] EXPLICIT SETString { ub-taxID } OPTIONAL,
    merchantDutyTariffRef       [ 8] EXPLICIT SETString { ub-reference }
OPTIONAL,
    customerDutyTariffRef       [ 9] EXPLICIT SETString { ub-reference }
OPTIONAL,
    summaryCommodityCode        [10] EXPLICIT SETString { ub-commCode }
OPTIONAL,
    merchantType                [11] EXPLICIT SETString { ub-merType }  OPTIONAL
}

ItemSeq ::= SEQUENCE SIZE(1..ub-items) OF Item

Item ::= SEQUENCE {
    quantity           INTEGER (1..MAX) DEFAULT 1,
    unitOfMeasureCode  [ 0] EXPLICIT SETString { ub-unitMeasure }  OPTIONAL,
    descriptor         SETString { ub-description  },
    commodityCode      [ 1] EXPLICIT SETString { ub-commCode }  OPTIONAL,
    productCode        [ 2] EXPLICIT SETString { ub-productCode }  OPTIONAL,
    unitCost           [ 3] CurrencyAmount  OPTIONAL,
    netCost            [ 4] CurrencyAmount  OPTIONAL,
    discountInd        BOOLEAN DEFAULT FALSE,
    discountAmount     [ 5] CurrencyAmount  OPTIONAL,
    nationalTaxAmount  [ 6] CurrencyAmount  OPTIONAL,
    nationalTaxRate    [ 7] FloatingPoint  OPTIONAL,
    nationalTaxType    [ 8] EXPLICIT SETString { ub-taxType }  OPTIONAL,
    localTaxAmount     [ 9] CurrencyAmount  OPTIONAL,
    otherTaxAmount     [10] CurrencyAmount  OPTIONAL,
    itemTotalCost      CurrencyAmount
}

MarketAutoCap ::= SEQUENCE {
    renterName             [0] EXPLICIT SETString { ub-renterName }  OPTIONAL,
    rentalLocation         [1] Location  OPTIONAL,
```

```
    rentalDateTime           DateTime,
    autoNoShow               [2] AutoNoShow  OPTIONAL,
    rentalAgreementNumber    [3] EXPLICIT SETString { ub-rentalNum }  OPTIONAL,
    referenceNumber          [4] EXPLICIT SETString { ub-rentalRefNum }  OPTIONAL,
    insuranceType            [5] EXPLICIT SETString { ub-insuranceType }
OPTIONAL,
    autoRateInfo             [6] AutoRateInfo  OPTIONAL,
    returnLocation           [7] Location  OPTIONAL,
    returnDateTime           DateTime,
    autoCharges              AutoCharges
}

AutoNoShow ::= ENUMERATED {
    normalVehicle   (0),
    specialVehicle  (1)
}

AutoRateInfo ::= SEQUENCE {
    autoApplicableRate    AutoApplicableRate,
    lateReturnHourlyRate  [0] CurrencyAmount  OPTIONAL,
    distanceRate          [1] CurrencyAmount  OPTIONAL,
    freeDistance          [2] Distance  OPTIONAL,
    vehicleClassCode      [3] EXPLICIT SETString { ub-vehicleClass }  OPTIONAL,
    corporateID           [4] EXPLICIT SETString { ub-corpID }  OPTIONAL
}

AutoApplicableRate ::= CHOICE {
    dailyRentalRate   [0] CurrencyAmount,
    weeklyRentalRate  [1] CurrencyAmount
}

AutoCharges ::= SEQUENCE {
    regularDistanceCharges  CurrencyAmount,
    lateReturnCharges       [ 0] CurrencyAmount  OPTIONAL,
    totalDistance           [ 1] Distance  OPTIONAL,
    extraDistanceCharges    [ 2] CurrencyAmount  OPTIONAL,
    insuranceCharges        [ 3] CurrencyAmount  OPTIONAL,
    fuelCharges             [ 4] CurrencyAmount  OPTIONAL,
    autoTowingCharges       [ 5] CurrencyAmount  OPTIONAL,
    oneWayDropOffCharges    [ 6] CurrencyAmount  OPTIONAL,
    telephoneCharges        [ 7] CurrencyAmount  OPTIONAL,
    violationsCharges       [ 8] CurrencyAmount  OPTIONAL,
    deliveryCharges         [ 9] CurrencyAmount  OPTIONAL,
    parkingCharges          [10] CurrencyAmount  OPTIONAL,
    otherCharges            [11] CurrencyAmount  OPTIONAL,
    totalTaxAmount          [12] CurrencyAmount  OPTIONAL,
    auditAdjustment         [13] CurrencyAmount  OPTIONAL
}

MarketHotelCap ::= SEQUENCE {
    arrivalDate      Date,
    hotelNoShow      [0] HotelNoShow  OPTIONAL,
    departureDate    Date,
    durationOfStay   [1] INTEGER (0..99)  OPTIONAL,
    folioNumber      [2] EXPLICIT SETString { ub-hotelFolio }  OPTIONAL,
    propertyPhone    [3] Phone  OPTIONAL,
```

```
   customerServicePhone   [4] Phone  OPTIONAL,
   programCode            [5] EXPLICIT SETString { ub-programCode }  OPTIONAL,
   hotelRateInfo          [6] HotelRateInfo  OPTIONAL,
   hotelCharges           HotelCharges
}

HotelNoShow ::= ENUMERATED {
   guaranteedLateArrival  (0)
}

HotelRateInfo ::= SEQUENCE {
   dailyRoomRate  CurrencyAmount,
   dailyTaxRate   CurrencyAmount  OPTIONAL
}

HotelCharges ::= SEQUENCE {
   roomCharges            CurrencyAmount,
   roomTax                [ 0] CurrencyAmount  OPTIONAL,
   prepaidExpenses        [ 1] CurrencyAmount  OPTIONAL,
   foodBeverageCharges    [ 2] CurrencyAmount  OPTIONAL,
   roomServiceCharges     [ 3] CurrencyAmount  OPTIONAL,
   miniBarCharges         [ 4] CurrencyAmount  OPTIONAL,
   laundryCharges         [ 5] CurrencyAmount  OPTIONAL,
   telephoneCharges       [ 6] CurrencyAmount  OPTIONAL,
   businessCenterCharges  [ 7] CurrencyAmount  OPTIONAL,
   parkingCharges         [ 8] CurrencyAmount  OPTIONAL,
   movieCharges           [ 9] CurrencyAmount  OPTIONAL,
   healthClubCharges      [10] CurrencyAmount  OPTIONAL,
   giftShopPurchases      [11] CurrencyAmount  OPTIONAL,
   folioCashAdvances      [12] CurrencyAmount  OPTIONAL,
   otherCharges           [13] CurrencyAmount  OPTIONAL,
   totalTaxAmount         [14] CurrencyAmount  OPTIONAL,
   auditAdjustment        [15] CurrencyAmount  OPTIONAL
}

MarketTransportCap ::= SEQUENCE {
   passengerName      SETString { ub-passName },
   departureDate      Date,
   origCityAirport    SETString { ub-airportCode },
   tripLegSeq         [0] TripLegSeq  OPTIONAL,
   ticketNumber       [1] EXPLICIT SETString { ub-ticketNum }  OPTIONAL,
   travelAgencyCode   [2] EXPLICIT SETString { ub-taCode }  OPTIONAL,
   travelAgencyName   [3] EXPLICIT SETString { ub-taName }  OPTIONAL,
   restrictions       [4] Restrictions  OPTIONAL
}

TripLegSeq ::= SEQUENCE SIZE(1..16) OF TripLeg

TripLeg ::= SEQUENCE {
   dateOfTravel     Date,
   carrierCode      SETString { ub-carrierCode },
   serviceClass     SETString { ub-serviceClass },
   stopOverCode     StopOverCode,
   destCityAirport  SETString { ub-airportCode },
   fareBasisCode    [0] SETString { ub-fareBasis }  OPTIONAL,
   departureTax     [1] CurrencyAmount  OPTIONAL
```

```
}

StopOverCode ::= ENUMERATED {
   noStopOverPermitted  (0),
   stopOverPermitted    (1)
}

Restrictions ::= ENUMERATED {
   unspecifiedRestriction  (0)
}

ub-airportCode     INTEGER ::=    3
ub-carrierCode     INTEGER ::=    2
ub-commCode        INTEGER ::=   15
ub-corpID          INTEGER ::=   12
ub-description     INTEGER ::=   35
ub-fareBasis       INTEGER ::=    6
ub-hotelFolio      INTEGER ::=   25
ub-insuranceType   INTEGER ::=    1
ub-items           INTEGER ::=  999
ub-passName        INTEGER ::=   20
ub-phone           INTEGER ::=   20
ub-productCode     INTEGER ::=   12
ub-programCode     INTEGER ::=    2
ub-reference       INTEGER ::=   28
ub-rentalNum       INTEGER ::=   25
ub-rentalRefNum    INTEGER ::=    8
ub-renterName      INTEGER ::=   40
ub-serviceClass    INTEGER ::=    1
ub-taCode          INTEGER ::=    8
ub-taName          INTEGER ::=   25
ub-taxID           INTEGER ::=   10
ub-taxType         INTEGER ::=    4
ub-ticketNum       INTEGER ::=   13
ub-vehicleClass    INTEGER ::=    2
ub-unitMeasure     INTEGER ::=   12

END



SetPKCS10
  { joint-iso-itu-t(2) internationalRA(23) set(42) module(6) 9 }
      DEFINITIONS IMPLICIT TAGS ::= BEGIN

-- EXPORTS All;

IMPORTS

   Attribute {}, ATTRIBUTE, Name, SupportedAlgorithms
      FROM SetAttribute

   SIGNED {}, SubjectPublicKeyInfo {}
      FROM SetCertificate

   AdditionalPolicy, CertificateTypeSyntax, GeneralNames, id-ce-keyUsage,
```

```
    id-ce-privateKeyUsagePeriod, id-ce-subjectAltName,
    id-set-additionalPolicy, id-set-certificateType, id-set-tunneling,
    KeyUsage, PrivateKeyUsagePeriod, TunnelingSyntax
        FROM SetCertificateExtensions;

AttributeSet   { ATTRIBUTE:InfoObjectSet } ::=
                            SET OF Attribute { {InfoObjectSet} }

EncodedCertificationRequestInfo ::=
                    TYPE-IDENTIFIER.&Type (CertificationRequestInfo)

CertificationRequest ::= SIGNED {
    EncodedCertificationRequestInfo
} ( CONSTRAINED BY { -- Verify Or Sign CertificationRequest -- } )

CertificationRequestInfo ::= SEQUENCE {
    version                 INTEGER { criVer1(0) } (criVer1),
    subject                 Name,
    subjectPublicKeyInfo    SubjectPublicKeyInfo {{SupportedAlgorithms}},
    attributes              [0] IMPLICIT AttributeSet {{SupportedCRIAttributes}}
}

SupportedCRIAttributes ATTRIBUTE ::= {
    --
    -- Attributes corresponding to standard X.509v3 extensions
    --
    { WITH SYNTAX KeyUsage               ID id-ce-keyUsage             } |
    { WITH SYNTAX PrivateKeyUsagePeriod  ID id-ce-privateKeyUsagePeriod } |
    { WITH SYNTAX GeneralNames           ID id-ce-subjectAltName       } |
    --
    -- Attributes corresponding to SET private extensions
    --
    { WITH SYNTAX CertificateTypeSyntax  ID id-set-certificateType     } |
    { WITH SYNTAX TunnelingSyntax        ID id-set-tunneling           } |
    --
    -- Attributes corresponding to certificate policy
    --
    { WITH SYNTAX AdditionalPolicy       ID id-set-additionalPolicy    },
    ...
}

END
```

INDEX